Marxism, Modernity, and Postcolonial Studies

At a time when even much of the political left seems to believe
that transnational capitalism is here to stay, *Marxism, Modernity,
and Postcolonial Studies* refuses to accept the inevitability of the
so-called "New World Order." By giving substantial attention to
topics such as globalization, racism, and modernity, it provides
a specifically Marxist intervention into postcolonial and cultural
studies. An international team of contributors locate a common
ground of issues engaging Marxist and postcolonial critics alike.
Arguing that Marxism is not the inflexible, monolithic irrelevance some critics assume it to be, this collection aims to open
avenues of debate – especially on the crucial concept of "modernity" – which have been closed off by the widespread neglect
of Marxist analysis in postcolonial studies. Politically focused,
at times polemical, and always provocative, this book is a major
contribution to contemporary debates on literary theory, cultural
studies, and the definition of postcolonial studies.

CRYSTAL BARTOLOVICH is Associate Professor of English and
Textual Studies at Syracuse University. Her publications include
essays in *Masses, Classes and the Public Sphere* (2000), *A companion
to Postcolonial Studies* (2000), *Cannibalism and the Colonial World*
(Cambridge, 1998), and the *minnesota review*.

NEIL LAZARUS is Professor of English and Comparative Literary
Studies at Warwick University. He is the author of *Resistance in
Postcolonial African Fiction* (1990) and *Nationalism and Cultural
Practice in the Postcolonial World* (Cambridge, 1999). He has
also published articles in journals such as *Research in African
Literatures, Differences, Diaspora, Rethinking Marxism, Textual
Practice*, and *New Formations*. He has contributed to volumes
such as *Postcolonial Discourses: An Anthology* (2001), *Frantz Fanon:
Critical Perspectives* (1999), and *Cultural Readings of Imperialism:
Edward Said and the Gravity of History* (1997).

Cultural Margins

General editor
Timothy Brennan ᴶᴵ
*Department of Cultural Studies and Comparative Literature and English,
University of Minnesota*

The series Cultural Margins originated in response to the rapidly increasing interest in postcolonial and minority discourses among literary and humanist scholars in the US, Europe, and elsewhere. The aim
of the series is to present books which investigate the complex cultural
zone within and through which dominant and minority societies in-
teract and negotiate their differences. Studies in the series range from
examinations of the debilitating effects of cultural marginalisation,
to analyses of the forms of power found at the margins of culture, to
books which map the varied and complex components involved in the
relations of domination and subversion. This is an international series,
addressing questions crucial to the deconstruction and reconstruction
of cultural identity in the late twentieth-century world.

MARXISM, MODERNITY, AND POSTCOLONIAL STUDIES

Edited by

Crystal Bartolovich and Neil Lazarus

CAMBRIDGE
UNIVERSITY PRESS

CAMBRIDGE UNIVERSITY PRESS
Cambridge, New York, Melbourne, Madrid, Cape Town, Singapore, São Paulo

Cambridge University Press
The Edinburgh Building, Cambridge CB2 2RU, UK

Published in the United States of America by Cambridge University Press, New York

www.cambridge.org
Information on this title: www.cambridge.org/9780521813679

First published 2002

A catalogue record for this publication is available from the British Library

ISBN-13 978-0-521-81367-9 hardback
ISBN-10 0-521-81367-0 hardback

ISBN-13 978-0-521-89059-5 paperback
ISBN-10 0-521-89059-4 paperback

Transferred to digital printing 2005

For Michael Sprinker

Contents

Contents

Introduction: Marxism, modernity, and postcolonial studies

Crystal Bartolovich

This book has its origins in a panel on "Marxism and Postcoloniality" organized by the editors for a "Rethinking Marxism" conference at Amherst several years ago. The large turnout for, and lively discussion during, that session – even as a blizzard swirled around the building housing the meeting rooms – convinced us that we should try to recapture the intellectual excitement of that day by continuing the conversation in print. Some of the contributors to this volume were participants in that conference; others were invited to add their thoughts later. All, however, share with the editors the convictions that Marxism and "postcolonial studies" have something to say to each other – and that there might be more productive ways of dealing with their differences than have been exhibited hitherto. There has, in fact, been little direct, serious dialogue *between* Marxists and postcolonial theorists. The neglect (even ignorance) of Marxism in postcolonial studies has often been countered by the reflexive dismissal of the entire field of postcolonial studies by Marxist writers. In this longstanding dispute, a good deal of oversimplification, caricature, and trivialization has crept into the discourse on both sides, with the charges each group hurls against the other being by now well known: Marxism is said to be indelibly Eurocentric, complicit with the dominative master-narratives of modernity (including that of colonialism itself) and, in its approach to texts, vulgarly reductionistic and totalizing; postcolonial studies, in turn, is viewed as complicit with imperialism in its contemporary guise as globalization, oriented exclusively to metropolitan academic adventurism, and, in its approach to texts, irredeemably dematerializing and unhistorical. In contrast to these polarizing and exclusionary positions, this volume advocates a strong and visible *Marxist* postcolonial studies.

Marxism, modernity, and postcolonial studies

Insisting on a specifically Marxist understanding of problems raised by the question of "postcoloniality" takes on an added urgency given the spectacular success of postcolonial studies within the metropolitan academy since its inception nearly twenty years ago. For these are years in which Marxism itself has had to combat a growing consensus in the intellectual culture at large – on the political left as well as the right – that capitalism is an untranscendable horizon: as the academic credibility and prestige of postcolonial studies has risen steeply, Marxism has been confronted with widespread capitalist triumphalism in the wake of the events of 1989, when we were all, as Eduardo Galeano put it, "invited to the world burial of socialism" (1991: 250). Meanwhile, advertisements for academic positions in postcolonial studies and/or "ethnic" or "global" studies – mostly in English departments, but also in the disciplines of history, anthropology, art, and others – have been proliferating. Several dedicated academic journals – among them *Public Culture, Postcolonial Studies, Diaspora, Third Text,* and *Interventions* – have begun publication, and countless other journals have devoted special issues to "postcolonial theory" or "the postcolonial condition." In addition to the hundreds of books and thousands of articles that might be said to be *in* the field of postcolonial studies today or indeed to make it up – from Edward Said's *Orientalism* and the works of Homi Bhabha, Gayatri Spivak, V. Y. Mudimbe, Arjun Appadurai, and Trinh Minh-ha to the mass of specialist work on particular authors, periods, situations, events, and concepts – there has recently emerged a burgeoning production of texts that take the field itself as their object: witness the publication – merely over the course of the past decade – of books by Boehmer (1995), Childs and Williams (1997), Gandhi (1998), Loomba (1998a), Moore-Gilbert (1997), Quayson (2000), and Young (1990).[1] Perhaps it is not surprising that Marxists have eyed this burgeoning production – which is for the most part so ambivalent toward, so unsystematic in its treatment of, the realities of "actually existing capitalism" – with suspicion. Even within postcolonial studies, there has been an acknowledgment that

neo-colonial imbalances in the contemporary world order ... have in fact not been engaged with enough by postcolonial critics who grapple with the shades of the colonial past much more than with the difficulties of the postcolonial present. If postcolonial studies is to survive in any meaningful way, it needs to absorb itself far more deeply with the contemporary world, and with the local circumstances within which colonial institutions and ideas are being moulded into the disparate cultural and socioeconomic practices which define our contemporary "globality."

(*Loomba 1998a: 256–57*)

Crystal Bartolovich

Agreeing with this, the contributors to this volume further assert that Marxism is the theoretical perspective best suited to accomplishing the concerted and effective critique of the violence of the contemporary world order as well as of the ravages of the colonial past that Loomba calls for here.

However, our conviction as to the privileged role of Marxism in this critique is unlikely to be welcomed unequivocally within the field of postcolonial studies. For unquestionably (as a metropolitan disciplinary formation, at least) this field has been deeply and constitutively informed by theoretical protocols and procedures – Foucauldian discourse analysis, deconstruction, Lacanianism – which are not merely indifferent, but, in their dominant forms, actively and explicitly hostile, to Marxism. As Stuart Hall has conceded recently, in response to Arif Dirlik, among others: "two halves of the current debate about 'late modernity' – the postcolonial and the analysis of the new developments in global capitalism – have indeed largely proceeded in relative isolation from one another" (Hall 1996a: 257–58). Hall attributes the failure by postcolonial theorists to attend to these "developments in global capitalism" – and, more generally, we would add, to any of the larger questions of political economy – to the fact that

the discourses of the "post" have emerged, and been (often silently) articulated against the practical, political, historical and theoretical effects of the collapse of a certain kind of economistic, teleological and, in the end, reductionistic Marxism. What has resulted from the abandonment of this deterministic economism has been, not alternative ways of thinking questions about the economic relations and their effects . . . but instead a massive, gigantic and eloquent disavowal. (258)

About the "disavowal" of Marxism within much of postcolonial studies, Hall is surely correct, though what he might have given more emphasis to – as this volume does – is how *heterogeneous* Marxism has actually always been. Not only has the "reductionistic" version of Marxism Hall conjures up had critics *within* Marxism all along, but Marxists have been working in a number of ways from the start on the very issues and concerns – such as imperialism, nationalism, racism, subalternity, and so on – which have become central to postcolonial studies, though you would be hard pressed to find much acknowledgment of this in the work of many of the scholars active in the field. Among our primary agendas in this volume, accordingly, is the reactivation of this *disavowed* Marxist heritage in the theorization of the (post-)colonial world. At the same time we attempt to bring to the forefront some of the specifically Marxist interests and tendencies

3

located in the work of critics (among whom Gayatri Chakravorty Spivak is probably the most prominent) who have situated themselves, or have been situated, in postcolonial studies from early on. We seek to confront head on the ambivalence toward, or rejection of, Marxism characteristic of "post-"discourses in general, and indicate the particular ways the Marxist tradition has itself dealt with the theoretical and practical dilemmas that "post-"theorists have raised.

Some critical commentary on the Editorial of a recent issue of the journal *Postcolonial Studies* (3.3) can suggest the stakes of our project, and its variance with dominant trends in contemporary postcolonial studies. In this Editorial, the regular journal editors supplement a guest-edited special issue – on the theme of fashion – by reproducing photographs of objects from an exhibition entitled "1000 Extra/ordinary Objects," which was curated in Florence under Benetton's auspices to celebrate the tenth anniversary of the Benetton magazine, COLORS. They take as their point of departure Benetton's own press release, which presents the exhibition as "an anthropological report on our world, which goes beyond the boundaries between ordinary and extraordinary, designer objects and those in everyday use, reality and representation, and between haute couture and the commonplace" (qtd. Cairns et al. 2000: 247). Discussing this press release, the editors point out that it is a mere rationalization: the claim to "anthropology" masks the truth that the exhibit is a giant advertisement for Benetton. "This is commerce," the editors write, "even if sophisticated, state of the art commerce, which achieves its ends through seduction" (247). This "critique" seems unexceptionable, if banal. But having delivered themselves of it, the editors then move immediately to disavow it, fleeing from their own critical position instead of developing it, as if embarrassed that it had ever occurred to them. First they declare that their own initial assessment of the exhibit is "seriously incomplete"; and then they move to decry "left critique" more generally:

> too leaden-footed a left critique falls into economism by treating the radical aesthetic disjuncture of advertising as epiphenomenal, as a simple but clever ruse to hide the cash register devices of the Benetton group. What is not registered by this focus on cash, however, is the productive, seductive effect of their promotional materials' shock effect. What is not registered, in other words, is our own seduction by their techniques of representation. Perhaps part of the reason for our ambivalence lies in our inability to pin these two sides of the Benetton story down. (247)

The editors speak here of "ambivalence," but the further their discussion of the exhibit proceeds, the less ambivalent their position becomes. Indeed, they progressively make it clear that they have nothing but scorn for *any* attempt to "follow the money," not simply those which are "economistic." Because they genuinely appear to believe that "Benetton's extraordinary market reach, its seeming penetration of every corner of the globe" is an effect of the "profound semiotic indeterminacy and mobility" of its images, the economic, for them, becomes *entirely* superfluous (248). Toward the end of the Editorial, then, they confidently propose a "semiotic" attack on Benetton (as if this were novel or radical). Putting the old Foucauldian reading of Borges's "Chinese encyclopedia" through its tired paces yet again (is there, at this point in time, any trope in all of critical theory more thoroughly trodden than this one?) they come up with a "tactic" which involves emphasizing the "convoluted folds and ludic openings in the seamless datum of Benetton's semiotic world" (251)! They appear to assume that this confrontation with categorical contingency will cause the world according to Benetton to totter if not necessarily to fall.

We might all agree, perhaps, that a "leaden-footed" pursuit of the path of political economy is best avoided (indeed, the contributors to this volume would insist that it *has been* avoided in Marxist theory now for many, many years). But surely this ought not to lead to a wholesale flight from political economy – so characteristic of postcolonial studies in general today – as demonstrated here by the editors of *Postcolonial Studies.* Does it really never occur to the editors of that journal to explore Benetton's labor practices, the sources of its income, or the economic colonization of everyday life demonstrated by the exhibit, and to imagine that these material forces might have something to do with Benetton's "semiotic" success? Certainly, the essays in *this* volume reject the facile supposition that to mention "cash" is already to have fallen into "economism." There are *mediations*, to be sure, but there are (irreducibly) *relations* between "the economic" and "the cultural," nevertheless, which are simultaneously multiplied and rendered more elusive as capital permeates more and more aspects of our existence. Only by a direct address of *all* the tactics (not merely the narrowly semiotic ones) of the Benettons of the world can these relations be understood, and attacked, effectively.

Recognizing this, Henri Lefebvre famously observed that Marxism is "a critical knowledge of everyday life," a definition in which the crucial term for him was not only the "everyday," ineluctably allied with his name ever since, but also the "critical," without which the quotidian would refuse to give up its secrets. A Marxist analysis of the everyday "is not satisfied with merely uncovering and criticizing this real, practical life in the minutiae of social life," or focusing solely on the issues of subjectivity, cultural fragmentation, and dispersion of power typical of much postcolonial analysis (as the editors of *Postcolonial Studies* attest). Rather, Lefebvre urged, it ought, "by a process of rational integration . . . to pass from the individual to the social" – and, ultimately, to materialize itself in collective action toward social justice (Lefebvre 1992: 148). Like other theorists of the "ordinary" from Raymond Williams and Walter Benjamin to C. L. R. James, Stuart Hall, and Frantz Fanon, Lefebvre insisted on taking seeming trivialities seriously, believing that anyone devoted to resisting capitalist domination could not afford to ignore its permeation into the nooks and crannies of all aspects of our lives. And while Lefebvre did not direct his attention to the (post-)colonial condition, certainly for Fanon, James, and Hall, among others, the insidiousness of *colonial* regimes consisted, similarly, in their ability to capture subjects in the everyday, in language and culture. What distinguishes a specifically Marxist critique, however, from a more general anticolonialism, is the insistence that cultural analysis of the everyday (and the extraordinary alike) is inseparable from questions of political economy, in and outside the metropole; and that the critique of colonialism, and of the social order that has followed formal decolonization, is inextricable from the critique of capitalism.

As a brief rejoinder to the *Postcolonial Studies* analysis of Benetton, we would like to draw attention to a certain theme in the popular business culture of the 1990s which unabashedly celebrates capital's ongoing expansionism by deploying imperial tropes – and demands precisely the sort of analysis *Postcolonial Studies* would have us avoid. Consider, for example, the magazine spread which set portraits of "history's most ambitious leaders" (Lenin among them) next to a luminous bottle of Coca-Cola, with the caption: "Only one launched a campaign that conquered the world."[2] Or ponder the publicity letter advertising the publication of the 1996 *World Development Report: From Plan to Market*, which focused on Eastern Europe and the "challenges" and "expanding opportunities" it provides for "policymakers . . . scholars . . . and global investors." This letter *opens* with a citation from the famous "all that is solid melts into air" passage from the *Manifesto*, and goes on to note simply: "that's how Marx and Engels described the arrival of capitalism in the nineteenth century, and it's no less true of the economies in transition at the close of the twentieth." There is no suggestion that the *Manifesto* (which is never named) is a text which advocates "an association [of workers], in which the free development of each is the condition for the free development of all" (1988: 61). To the contrary, the *Report* evidently has an entirely different sort of "freedom" in mind: it "drives home the utter necessity of liberalizing economies through trade and openness to new markets, stabilizing them through reduced inflation and fiscal discipline." In other words, its vision is one of "free markets" and the subjugation of all peoples to the neoliberal policies that benefit metropolitan investors (as well as scholars and policy makers, apparently), with an eye to securing profits in territory that was formerly off-limits. By quoting Marx to the opposite of his purpose, the advertisement for the *Report* transforms the *Manifesto* into a document which comes not to bury capitalism, but to *praise* it.

To ignore the economic in an analysis of such gestures can only entail capitulation to them. The advertising agency which sponsored the "world conquest" spread goes so far as to suggest that its efforts have resulted in a *proper* revolution, whereas all earlier attempts failed because they did not choose "the right weapon." Interestingly, it does not even trouble to differentiate itself from "history's most ambitious leaders." Nor does it appear to find it troubling to think of advertising as a "weapon" – and, thus, to imply that its own projected conquest of the world is as much a matter of force as was, say, Napoleon's or Hitler's. The advertisement also enacts with stunning confidence the shift from a world in which struggles for power are depicted as involving human actors to one in which even politics has been usurped by the commodity form itself: a bottle of Coke, not that company's CEO, is credited with "success." And "success," furthermore, is explicitly *defined* as the mass subjection of consumers to the commodity which "speaks" in advertising. Likewise, the *World Development Report* advertisement takes capitalism's rule for granted, and views its (formal) movement into the former Soviet Union as monumental if inevitable. Indeed, the specter of counter-revolution haunts its rhetoric, though it is more circumspect than the Coca Cola advertisement: "consider that between 1917 and 1950, countries containing one-third of the world's population seceded from the market economy and instituted central planning... Today's transition back to a market economy is an event of equal significance." The historical narrative suggests that people once thought about (and even attempted to live) *alternatives* to capitalism, but that this is no longer the case. Marx has been conjured up to preside diagnostically over this "transition," presumably because, like a deactivated virus, he can no longer do any harm.

However, one might ask why, then, Marx needs to be adduced at all? While the advertisements we have just described offer direct articulations of the triumphalism that amounted to something rather like a spirit of the age during the 1990s, it can be argued that in conjuring up Marxism explicitly, such advertisements also speak to a continued need to "manage" the *possibility* of socialism, even after its supposed liquidation as a threat to actually existing capitalism. And the need to manage, of course, implies a continued power – implies, indeed, that the "specter" cited in the *Manifesto* has not yet been laid to rest – even at the very moment when the map of the world is being actively remolded in accordance with what Samir Amin (1997: 95) has called "the logic of unilateral capital." "Everyday" appeals to an ostensibly discredited Marx(ism) paradoxically indicate its persistent afterlife – as well as the value of an ongoing Marxist critique of capitalist expansionism.

Among the factors that render a supposedly moribund Marx(ism) so embarrassing to the currently dominant order – and thus mandate its continued management – is Marxism's insistence that it is *capitalism* which stalks about the world "dripping from head to toe, from every pore, with blood and dirt" (Marx 1990: 926). It is, thus, *capitalism* that is "dirt" – matter out of place in Mary Douglas's influential formulation – in any project to attain a just society. To expose this face of capital, the essays in this volume brush history against the grain to reveal its shadowy side: they direct our attention to what has been displaced and cast aside in the march of "civilization" and "modernization." Brennan and Larsen, for instance, both locate a *disavowed* "Marx" at the gateway of the "theory" machine that dominates trendier scholarship in the humanities and social sciences today; Nimtz and Jani recover and assert the lost and ignored aspects of Marx's texts that indicate a more nuanced approach to imperialism and the movement of history than is often acknowledged; Lazarus, Scott, and Ganguly address themselves to concepts (such as "the West" and "race") which still await adequate theorization in postcolonial studies, while resuscitating others (such as "imperialism" or "authenticity") that have been prematurely junked; Parry and San Juan direct our attention to the (marginalized) contributions to Marxism generated in the movements against imperialism in Africa; Arrighi and Cleary show how the histories of East Asia and Ireland, respectively, disrupt or falsify dominant assumptions about the development of capitalism and the coherence of "Europe"; and Gopal proposes that an adequate theorization of the figure of "woman," especially in non-metropolitan contexts, carries the capacity to unsettle not only the received understandings of modernity, but also the prevailing counter-understandings developed in postcolonial studies.

By focusing their attention on abandoned and undervalued aspects of history, these essays follow the methodological path Walter Benjamin explored so assiduously throughout his work, but especially in his *Arcades Project*: "rags and refuse – these I will not inventory but allow, in the only way possible, to come into their own: by making use of them" (1999: 460). The essays collected here as a whole show a particular concern for investigating what has been rendered archaic, rejected, or forgotten in mainstream postcolonial studies: the most important – from a Marxist perspective – being the primacy of the critique of capitalism itself.

This project is intended as a counter-force *within* postcolonial theory, where it has, in general, become perfectly acceptable – even conventional – to make no mention of Marxism, even when the situations described seem to call out for it (from Paul Gilroy's highly visible neglect of the spatial implications of Marxist world systems theory in *The Black Atlantic* [1993] to the host of specialist work taking a non-Marxist worldview for granted, such as Eleni Coundouriotis's *Claiming History* [1999], an otherwise insightful study of African fiction which evades altogether the Marxist inflections of liberation movements). When the subject of Marxism *is* brought up, it is typically with hostility. In the writings of some postcolonial scholars, for example, Marxism is held *primarily* accountable for the difficulties that certain decolonized states have experienced in the "postcolonial" era (Miller 1990: 31–67; Quayson 2000: 14–16). To see the problem with such analyses, one need only consult C. L. R. James's (1977) patient and careful assessment of Nkrumah, which seeks – without in any way excusing or explaining away manifest failures and mistakes – to situate the critique where it properly belongs: in the profound dilemmas all post-independence states faced by virtue both of their intrication in a set of global relations they did not control and their inheritance of internal difficulties which were to a large degree a legacy of colonialism itself (cf. Davidson 1992; 1978: 283–382). What is centrally at issue in these differences between Marxist and postcolonialist perspectives, in short, is the former's emphasis on the continuity and even extension of capitalism's rule in the "postcolonial" world, even though this perspective has been abandoned across much of the *left*, which, as Slavoj Žižek has put it in a recent critique of multiculturalism, "silently accepts that capitalism is here to stay ... [such that] the very mention of capitalism as world system tends to give rise to the accusation of 'essentialism,' 'fundamentalism' and other crimes" (1997: 46). Working against such assumptions and charges, the contributors to this volume not only emphasize the importance of examining all parts of the world in irreducible, mutually implicating relation to each other from early modernity, but of understanding *capitalism* (not "Eurocentrism" or "cultural imperialism") as underwriting those relations in their historically specific form of "uneven and combined development" (see San Juan's essay for elaboration). They further insist that precisely because of these material interrelations, Marx and Marxism *belong* (and have always belonged) to the whole world, not merely to Europe, or still less, to that mythical entity "the West." Whether we look to the Marx of liberation struggles against imperialism in the postwar period (as do several contributors to this volume, including Parry and San Juan), the "creole culture of anti-imperialism" between the wars (explored here by Brennan), or the decentering effect of non-European struggles on the thought of Marx and Engels in their lifetimes (traced by Jani and Nimtz), we see a Marxist legacy that is not only *not* dismissable as Eurocentric, but is not even in any meaningful sense a "possession" of Europe. Thus, this volume maintains not only that Marxism is rightfully a matter of fundamental interest to intellectuals who would unsettle Eurocentrism and critique colonialism and its after-effects, as postcolonial studies purport to do, but also that, especially at this moment of capitalist triumphalism, a Marxist critique is unforgoable.

But if it is indispensable to retrieve Marxism from its contemporary disavowal (not least in postcolonial studies), it is arguably also important not to commit oneself either to an undifferentiating (Marxist) disavowal of postcolonial studies. With such prominent Marxist and neo-Marxist scholars as Arif Dirlik and Aijaz Ahmad, we recognize the structuring conceptual and historical weaknesses of postcolonial studies as a field of inquiry. But we still feel that their categorical repudiation of postcolonial studies is deeply misconceived. (Ahmad, for instance, dismisses *all* postcolonial criticism as "postmodernism's wedge to colonize literatures outside Europe and its North American offshoots" [1995a: 1].) Among many other things, such repudiations make impossible any balanced consideration of the field's genuine intellectual (and ideological) achievements. It seems to us that Marxist theorists can and should engage *with* postcolonial studies in mutual sites of concern, and concede to the field the authentic insights and advances that have been generated within it. Among these we would list the extension of the discussion of subalternity and political representation in the non-metropolitan context; the demonstration that in their aspirations toward unisonance or universalism, many of the most historically resonant "master narratives" of nationalism, secularism, and internationalism have typically been appropriative, neglectful of difference and even of active dissidence; the expansion of the purview of literature departments to include opportunities for the study of a geographically wider range of texts; the provision of detailed knowledges of particular local conditions, situations, and texts; the recognition that the former colonial languages are no longer the possession of the former colonizers alone; the identification of Eurocentric concepts, practices, and habits of thought; etc.

Indeed, the standard critique of Marxism within postcolonial studies pivots on the charge that it is Eurocentric, and it would be foolish to pretend that some concepts – even many – generated in the history of Marxist thought (including by Marx himself) are not guilty as charged here, as it would be foolish to pretend that some – even many, including some of the most decisive – Marxist theorists (especially those with no experience of and no regard for non-European conditions) have not construed their own narrowly conceived horizons universalistically. We need to remember, however, that Marxism is, as Sartre argued, a "living philosophy," and thus that it is continually being adapted and adapting itself "by means of thousands of new efforts" (1968b: 7). The very fact that many of the most brilliant, prominent, and effective anticolonial activists have insistently pronounced themselves Marxists should give pause to postcolonialists who stand poised to dismiss Marxism as a "European" philosophy.

Moreover, to the extent that Marxism has been susceptible to Eurocentrism, so too has postcolonial studies. The constitutive metropolitanism of the field inevitably structures the vision of its agents as well. In other words, the "politics of location" (geographical and historical) – to borrow the preferred postcolonial locution – affects Marxism and postcolonial studies alike. That members of each group have so frequently accused members of the other of "Eurocentrism" should not lead us to attempt to arbitrate the dispute (impossible, in any case). It would be much better to pay attention to the *unequal global politico-economic conditions* in which knowledge itself is produced, no matter what its ideological cast. Thus Ahmad correctly points out that the Euro-American academy and its faculties, as well as the various supporting institutions (e.g., book publishers, libraries), are constituted by forces which tend to position "non-Western" literary works not through reference to their registration of the diverse and discrepant modes of appearance of *capitalism* on the world's stage, but rather as signifiers of "civilizational, primordial Difference" (1992: 64). To be sure, Bart Moore-Gilbert (and others) have pointed out in response to Ahmad that the politics of location are often more complicated than he typically seems to allow: his own institutional position (in India), is also privileged, after all, and he has made use of, and benefited from, the very apparatuses he attacks, in being published for example, in English, by an elite (if oppositional) metropolitan press, and accepting teaching assignments in metropolitan universities (1997: 153–57). But these objections, while not entirely impertinent (especially in their dismay at the personal tone that Ahmad's recriminations seem to take, and their occasional reductiveness) still miss the fundamental point of his argument, which is that any attempt to rectify the genuine widespread ignorance of non-metropolitan situations in the metropole which fails to address itself to the material asymmetries which both structure and sanction this ignorance, is doomed to failure. It can lead only to further appropriation: cooptation and cloying tokenism at best. The dizzying disequilibria (of power, resources, social agency) exhibited in the contemporary world system are, as Enrique Dussel (1997) among other Marxists, has persistently argued, literally *irreducible* without closing the gaps in *material* inequalities among peoples. The contest of cultures with which postcolonial studies has been so preoccupied, in other words, simply cannot be divorced from rigorous critique of the imbalances of global political economy, in which the scandalous fact – circulated each year with depressing predictability in United Nations reports of "human" and "economic" development – remains: 80 percent of the world's wealth circulates among 20 percent of its people, with the use of resources similarly unbalanced. To point this out – and, further, to recognize that these imbalances have real effects on intellectual and cultural (as well as other kinds) of production – is not "crude." On the contrary, it is crude to attempt to ignore, or treat as insignificant, the continuing existence – even expansion – of such levels of inequality.

Global imbalances manifest themselves in a number of ways in the relations between metropolitans and non-metropolitans in intellectual life, through a density of mediations that make their intrication with political economy obscure, but not absolutely unreadable. Take, for example, the institutionalization of *disproportion* in knowledge production, which mandates that while non-metropolitan intellectuals must demonstrate a familiarity with Euro-American scholarship to gain credibility (and not only in the eyes of their metropolitan peers), the reverse does not apply; instead, a state of affairs that Dipesh Chakrabarty terms "asymmetric ignorance" obtains (2000: 28). Arif Dirlik has observed along similar lines that "hybridity" always seems to be assumed in the metropole to describe the fusing of metropolitan with non-metropolitan cultures, never as being an effect of cultural elements shared among non-metropolitan peoples (1994b: 342). In addition, because of widespread ("sanctioned") ignorance of non-metropolitan cultural forms and conditions of existence on the part of metropolitan readers, certain non-metropolitan texts (typically ones which in reference or form seem familiar to metropolitan readers) gain extravagant weight – often being subjected to highly decontextualized assessments (for a critique of this, see Spivak 1993, 1994). For similar reasons, metropolitan cultural forms and works are sometimes celebrated in lieu of less familiar ones, even on matters of most concern to non-metropolitan populations. One notes in general, indeed, that concepts deriving from intellectual circuits outside the metropolitan world often fail to gain currency within this world until put forth, with or without attribution, by metropolitan intellectuals. To offer just one case of the many that could be produced: "transculturation" is widely associated today with Mary Louise Pratt rather than with Fernando Ortiz – even by critics who might be expected to be especially sensitive to its earlier development and widespread use among non-metropolitan intellectuals.[3] As Jean Franco (1988) has noted, it remains a commonplace assumption that theory as such is a metropolitan enterprise (and masculine too, Franco adds), and that its (feminized) non-metropolitan forms therefore require sponsorship and integration in the metropole – rather like the prefaces by white abolitionists that used to accompany slave narratives – to authorize them, and render them visible and available for circulation.

The point here is not to determine priority for its own sake, but to illuminate the vast discrepancies in "being heard" under current conditions, and to assert the intimacy of the connection between the "deafness" of metropolitan intellectuals and their location – economic and ideological, not merely geographical. Taking stock of such imbalances and their root causes, Samir Amin has cautioned against supposing that it is an easy matter to "disengag[e] . . . oneself from the world as it is" when one is benefiting from it in the "developed center" (1989: 141). What might appear to be gestures of openness to alternatives, or solidarity with marginalized cultural forms and peoples, can all too easily become instead marks of the old, familiar dynamic of *appropriation* (Brennan 1997: 8). Those of us who teach postcolonial studies in metropolitan universities might be able to testify to this on the basis of our own experience: it is extremely difficult to bring our students (and ourselves) to read *differently*, in a climate in which the "Third World" has literally been transformed into a battery of (highly regulated) objects for metropolitan consumption. Such commodification, an ineluctable consequence of the globality of contemporary capitalism, goes hand in hand with the greater exploitation, of labor-power and resources, across the international division of labor. Students socially trained to think of the "Third World" in terms of *Rainforest Crunch* cereal, Body Shop soaps and potions, eco-tourism, the dance beats of Deep Forest, salsa or Afropop, will not necessarily abandon the habits of a lifetime when confronted by the work of a Carpentier or a Ngugi, a Kincaid or a Djebar, however brilliant and uncompromising in their critiques such work might be. The fact that such novels are conventionally recuperated either as "Great Family of Man" stories of "growing up" or "facing adversity," or extolled as exemplars of the "mystery" and "wonder" of far away places by their metropolitan marketers, powerfully mitigates their potentially radical effects.[4] In the popular imaginary, such books and other artistic forms become so many "culturalisms" to be celebrated – carefully detached from the material world(s) they inhabit. Exoticized fantasies of the "Third World" in this way displace the one world of relations between exploiters and exploited, which puts sport shoes on the feet, shirts on the backs and microchips in the computers of the students (and teachers) alike in US and European classrooms.

In this context, neither benevolence nor a "one size fits all" paradigm for viewing the world will suffice. Radical metropolitan intellectuals must recognize that it will only be possible to "think globally" as a matter of course when the current global asymmetries, economic, political, institutional, ideological, have been eliminated. The persistence of these asymmetries today, however, makes it doubly important to situate all cultural works and forms in their *specificity*, with reference to their conditions of production and circulation at their point of origin as well as in wider circles. In addition, metropolitan intellectuals in particular must be ever vigilant to the inequality that structures production, circulation and use of cultural forms, and to the various, irreducible effects of this inequality. We emphasize this point because it seems to us that without the tools of political economy, postcolonial studies will never be able to diagnose these conditions and launch effective critiques of them.

Hence, the current volume offers essays which contest the dominant understandings in postcolonial studies on two fronts, with respect to both Marxism and modernity. Regarding Marxism, first, they offer readings which, through their contextualization of Marxist practice and their consideration of the institutional dimensions of Marxist thought make clear that Marxism has indeed served, and served consistently, as an anti-imperialist social project. One of our underlying assumptions in this volume is that Marxism has not only *not* been discredited – still less rendered obsolete – by recent historical developments (most significantly the collapse of Sovietism) or developments in theory (most notably the rise of postmodernism), but in fact remains indispensable to any authentically emancipatory social thought or practice. With respect to modernity, second, our ambition in this volume is to contribute toward the formulation of a different conceptualization of the phenomenon, one critically aligned with Marxism. Harry Harootunian has offered one such possible reconceptualization recently, proposing that Marxist cultural critics develop a sensitivity to

differing *inflections* of the modern . . . not alternative modernities, but coeval or, better yet, peripheral modernities (as long as peripheral is understood only as a relationship to the centers of capitalism before World War II), in which all societies shared a common reference provided by global capital and its requirements . . . In this regard, modernity provided a framework of temporal imminence in which to locate *all* societies.

(2000: 62–63, *emphasis added*)

Certainly the theorization of modernity has been of central interest to both postcolonial studies and Marxism, with the former often focusing on modernity as a "cultural" dilemma, and seeking ways to confront the problem of entry into a "modernity" which has hitherto typically been conceived, erroneously, in terms of "Westernization" alone. Marxism, however, has, in the first instance (as Harootunian's comments suggest), viewed modernity and capitalism as inextricably bound up with each other in the world as we, collectively – though heterogeneously – live it, and sought to understand its variously shaping force throughout the globe. Our hope, and indeed conviction, is that the time has come for a new orientation in postcolonial studies in this direction, capable of challenging the idealist and dematerializing tendencies that have heretofore dominated the field as a whole, while keeping hold of its knowledge of and appreciation for the local differences that continue to matter.

We have chosen to organize and orient the volume under three rubrics – Eurocentrism, Modernity, and "Theory." These mark flash points in the longstanding disputes between "Marxist" and "postcolonialist" scholars, as well, of course, as crucial areas of study and argument within both Marxism and postcolonial studies. The volume's first section, "Eurocentrism, 'the West', and the world," features essays which recognize and address the spatial interests of postcolonial studies (from *Orientalism* onwards), but gives a specifically Marxist inflection to its examinations of the importance of interstitial formations to capitalism (Arrighi), "the West" as a category of thought (Lazarus), and claims by postcolonial theorists that Marx(ism) is Eurocentric (Nimtz, Jani). Section II, "Locating modernity," comes at the vexing problem of the modern from various focal points – the "anomalous" Irish case (Cleary), race (Scott), gender (Gopal), and anticolonial revolution (Parry). "Marxism, postcolonial studies, and 'theory'," our third grouping of essays, insists that Marxism is not the refuge of the crude in relation to poststructuralist sophistication. It tracks the prehistories of "post-"theory to find abandoned paths which the present might productively assess: a recognition of the milieux saturated by Marxism in which "post-"theories themselves emerged (Brennan), the too-hasty abandonment of Marxism as a *project* during the Althusserian moment (Larsen), the loss entailed in the rejection of "authenticity" as a serious theoretical category (Ganguly), and the neglect of the non-metropolitan perspective in Marxist theory (San Juan).

Where do we go from here? The essays that follow are by no means all-inclusive in their range, homogeneous in their perspectives, or representative in their approaches. What they all share, however, is a resistance to the devaluation of Marxism so evident in mainstream understandings of the world today, and, increasingly, in the academy as well – not least in postcolonial studies. Our contributors see the ongoing critique of capitalism as necessary to any project for social justice, and view the Marxist tradition as providing the conceptual tools and analytic frameworks essential to such a critique. Above all, the contributors to this volume see – and attest to – the continuing force of Marxism as a living *project*, neither simply a discourse nor a body of (academic) knowledge. It is this project that they propose as the most fruitful path to take in understanding both the colonial past and the contemporary world order.

NOTES

1 This statement should be taken as *descriptive* rather than prescriptive in its recognition that postcolonial studies in its current form is largely an academic and metropolitan disciplinary formation, practiced by diasporic intellectuals and their students and colleagues in the Euro-U.S., and – with various levels of enthusiasm and resistance – throughout the "commonwealth." From this, it follows that its relation to anticolonial movements and non-metropolitan theory needs to be explored, expanded, and worked through – not assumed or merely asserted. Otherwise, the very real specificity of various forms of (post-)coloniality may be lost to view, and non-metropolitan formulations and ways of seeing silently appropriated or obscured.

2 This advertisement is reproduced (Illustration no. 64) in Hobsbawm (1994).

3 Cf. Loomba's implicit attribution of the concept to Pratt (1998a: 68–70), in a book that calls attention to the continuing dependence of postcolonial studies on Eurocentric theoretical paradigms. The point here is *not* primarily to criticize Loomba – who is among the more careful and scrupulous of scholars in the field today – but to register the formidable difficulties that lie in wait for anybody attempting to negotiate the global theoretical terrain in a consistently critical idiom. In any case, Pratt herself encouraged Loomba's reading by foregrounding the concept in her own *title*, but relegating Ortiz to a slender mention in one *footnote* in her text (1992: 6, 228 n.4).

4 To give two examples: the back cover of Farrar, Straus and Giroux's English edition of Carpentier's *The Kingdom of this World* (a stunning meditation on the violence of colonialism and its aftermath) describes it as "creat[ing] a brilliant improbable world which has the stylized reality of the great myths"; an advertisement for Plume's "New American Library," inserted into Jamaica Kincaid's *A Small Place* (!), presents *Annie John* (among other listed books) as "contemporary fiction for your enjoyment," through which "women especially will learn much about their childhood."

Part I

Eurocentrism, "the West," and the world

2

The rise of East Asia and the withering away of the interstate system

Giovanni Arrighi

I

History continually messes up the neat conceptual frameworks and the more or less elegant theoretical speculations with which we endeavor to understand the past and forecast the future of the world we live in. In the closing decades of the twentieth century, two events stood out as eminently subversive of the intellectual landscape: the sudden demise of the USSR as one of the two main loci of world power and the gradual rise of East Asia to epicenter of world-scale processes of capital accumulation. In recent years, this recentering of world-scale processes of capital accumulation on East Asia has manifested itself in instability rather than growth. As argued elsewhere, however, this follows a well-established historical pattern – the pattern, that is, whereby newly emerging centers of world capitalism tend to become focal points of system-wide financial turbulence long before they acquire the politico-institutional capabilities to promote and govern a system-wide expansion of trade and production. Suffice it to mention the crucial role played by the United States – the emerging center of the early twentieth century – in the making and global propagation of the crisis of 1929–31 (Arrighi et al. 1999).

Although the demise of the USSR and the rise of East Asia have each received more than their due of scholarly attention, it is their *joint* occurrence that has the most significant conceptual and theoretical implications. World-systems studies are as likely to be revolutionized by this joint occurrence as any other field of historical inquiry. Thus, Andre Gunder Frank has claimed that

the recent demise of the "socialist system," and the increasing wealth of many Asian countries provide a new perspective on the origins and development of a world economic system that spanned the globe. It is an appropriate moment to critically reexamine the work of Fernand Braudel and Immanuel Wallerstein, both of whom have advanced the view that a world-economy emerged in Western Europe by at least 1450, then spread outward from Europe to encompass the rest of the world.   *(1994: 259)*

In the new perspective that Frank proposes, the formation of a world-economic system encompassing Eurasia and parts of Africa antedates 1450 by several millennia. Within this ancient world economic system, Europe in the modern era did not "incorporate" Asia. Rather, after 1500 it used American silver to buy its way into an Asian-dominated trading system. Even then, "Europe's incursions into Asia . . . succeeded only after about three centuries, when Ottoman, Moghul, and Qing rule was weakened for other reasons. In the global economy, these and other economies competed with each other until Europe won" (Frank 1994: 273, 275; see also Frank 1998).

Frank does not spell out the dynamic of this "victory." He nonetheless insists on two things. First, at the origins of the victory there is "no dramatic, or even gradual, change to a capitalist economy, and certainly none beginning in Europe in the sixteenth century" (1994: 275). And second, the victory now seems to have been very short-lived. "The contemporary economic expansion in East Asia, beginning with Japan, then in the East Asian NICs and now apparently also in coastal China, may spell the beginnings of a return [to a world system] in which parts of Asia again play a leading role in the future as they did in the not so distant past" (Gills and Frank 1994: 6–7).

Starting from altogether different premises, Takeshi Hamashita and other Japanese historians have recently advanced a reinterpretation of "modernization" in East Asia that converges in key respects with Frank's critique of established views of the formation and expansion of the modern world system. Unlike Frank, Hamashita focuses on East Asian rather than world history. But like Frank, he denies that the expanding European world-economy ever "incorporated" what he calls the Sinocentric tribute–trade system of East Asia.

In Hamashita's conceptualization, the several sea zones that stretch from Northeast to Southeast Asia have constituted for at least a millennium an integrated ensemble of regions, countries, and cities held together by a tribute–trade system centered on China. The regions, countries, and cities located along the perimeter of each sea zone "are close enough to influence one another, but are too far apart to assimilate or be assimilated." The Sinocentric tribute–trade system provided them with a political-economic framework of mutual integration that nonetheless was loose enough to endow its peripheral components with considerable autonomy vis-à-vis the Chinese center (Hamashita 1997: 114–17).

Within this system, tribute missions performed an "imperial title-awarding" function that was both hierarchical and competitive. Thus, Korea, Japan, the Ryukyus, Vietnam, and Laos, among others, all sent tribute missions to China. But the Ryukyus and Korea sent missions also to Japan; and Vietnam required tribute missions from Laos. Japan and Vietnam, therefore, were both peripheral members of the Sinocentric system and competitors with China in the exercise of the imperial title-awarding function (Hamashita 1994: 92).

The system of tribute missions was intertwined and grew in symbiosis with extensive trading networks. In fact, the relationship between trade and tribute was so close that "it is quite legitimate to view tribute exchange as a commercial transaction."

Even the Chinese court ... acted as a party to business transactions. The mode of payment was often Chinese currency, whether paper money or silver. Seen from an economic perspective, tribute was managed as an exchange between seller and buyer, with the "price" of commodities fixed. Indeed, "price" standards were determined, albeit loosely, by market prices in Peking. Given the nature of this transaction, it can be shown that the foundation of the whole complex tribute–trade formation was determined by the price structure of China and that the tribute–trade zone formed an integrated "silver zone" in which silver was used as the medium of trade settlement. The key to the functioning of the tribute trade as a system was the huge [foreign] "demand" for [Chinese] commodities ... and the difference between prices inside and outside China.

(Hamashita 1994: 96–97)

European expansion in Asia did not bring the Sinocentric tribute–trade system to an end. It simply influenced its inner dynamics, most notably, by strengthening the preexisting disposition of peripheral countries to seek better terms for their exchanges with the center or even to replace China as the system's center. But the formation of national identities among these countries long preceded the European impact and was based on their own understanding of Sinocentrism (Hamashita 1994: 94; 1997: 118–24). Thus, through its seclusion policy in the Edo period (1603–1867) "Japan was trying to become a mini-China both ideologically and materially." And Japanese industrialization after the Meiji Restoration "was not so much a process of catching up with the West, but more a result of centuries-long competition within Asia" (Kawakatsu 1994: 6–7; also 1986).

23

To my knowledge, neither Hamashita nor Heita Kawakatsu tell us much about what was left of the Sinocentric tribute–trade system at the end of the Second World War and what happened to it in the Cold War era. Their analyses are nonetheless presented as having important implications for our understanding, not just of East Asian history, but also of the present and likely future evolution of political and economic relations within the region and between the region and the rest of the world (see e.g., Hamashita 1997: 117). These implications are not spelled out but, at least in so far as Hamashita is concerned, it seems to me that they can be summed up in two propositions.

First, the present political, economic, and cultural configuration of East Asia is a legacy of the tribute–trade system that regulated relations among the various political jurisdictions of the region for centuries before its incorporation into the modern interstate system. This incorporation is a very recent phenomenon and cannot be expected to have displaced, let alone erased, shared understandings of interstate relations that have deep roots in the geography and history of the region. These shared understandings will continue to influence the way in which interstate relations operate in East Asia and between East Asian and non-East Asian states.

Second, the legacy of the Sinocentric tribute–trade system can be expected to weigh even more heavily on relations among business enterprises in the region than on relations among governments. For tribute was inseparable from a regional trading system which, over time, became increasingly autonomous from the actual dispatch of tribute missions. The main expression of this autonomy was the growth of large interstitial business communities, most notably an Overseas Chinese business diaspora, that connected the local economies of the region to one another in complementarity and, increasingly, in competition with tribute missions (Hamashita 1994: 97–103; 1997: 125–28). When the Sinocentric tribute system began to wither away under the combined impact of endogenous nationalism and exogenous incorporation in the Eurocentric interstate system, these interstitial business communities did not vanish into thin air. On the contrary, they continued to constitute an "invisible" but powerful connector of the East Asian regional economy.

This conceptualization of East Asian history contains an implicit critique of established world-systems theories that present both analogies and differences with Frank's critique. The two critiques are analogous in their emphasis on the premodern ancestry of the contemporary world system and on the superficiality of Western hegemony in Asia in general, and in East Asia in particular. Since modernity and Western hegemony have been associated in Braudel's and Wallerstein's conceptualizations of world history with the rise and expansion of a Eurocentric *capitalist* world system, this emphasis is tantamount to a rejection of capitalism as a useful notion for the analysis of world historical social change. Frank rejects the notion explicitly (1998: 330–32); but Hamashita does so implicitly by omitting any reference to capitalism in his account of the Sinocentric world system and of its transformation under Western influence.

For all their similarities, the two critiques diverge in one important respect. The main thrust of Frank's critique is to underscore the basic continuity *in time* of a single *global* world system before and after the European discovery and conquest of the Americas (Frank 1994: 273; 1998: ch. 7). The main thrust of Hamashita's implicit critique, in contrast, is to underscore the basic *discontinuity in space* of *regional* world systems that retain their geohistorical identity even after they are incorporated in a single global world system. To put it crudely, the main thrust of Frank's critique is to erase modern (and capitalist) history from the map of the contemporary global economy, while the main thrust of Hamashita's critique is to put regional geopolitics at the center of contemporary world history.

The purpose of this paper is to show that, taken jointly or separately, these critiques go both too far and not far enough. They go too far, because their legitimate preoccupation with the premodern ancestry of the modern world system translates into a negation of the undeniable specificity of the modern era, as defined by the extraordinary expansionary thrust of the Eurocentric system both absolutely and relative to the Sinocentric system. Wallerstein's theory of the rise in Europe of an inherently expansionary *capitalist* system is meant to highlight and explain this phenomenon and, as such, it cannot be dismissed unless we produce an alternative and more plausible explanation.

Neither Frank nor Hamashita do, and that is the reason why their critiques of established world-systems theories do not go far enough. By dismissing (Frank) or neglecting (Hamashita) the role of capitalism in shaping the contemporary world, they cannot see the challenge that the great events of our days pose to our understanding of capitalism as world historical social system. In the next two sections of this paper, I shall sketch the nature of this challenge as can be perceived from an East Asian perspective. I shall then return to the issues raised here to propose a reconceptualization of historical capitalism that accommodates Frank's and Hamashita's legitimate preoccupation with the premodern ancestry of the contemporary world system.

II

As the title of this paper suggests, the rise of East Asia and the present crisis of the system of nation-states are closely related phenomena. By and large, this close relationship has gone unnoticed. Each phenomenon has been debated as if it bore no significant relationship to the other.

Ever since Charles Kindleberger (1969: ch. 6) declared the nation-state to be "just about through as an economic unit," the crisis of the system of nation-states has been associated with, and traced to, the emergence of a system of transnational corporations which, in Kindleberger's characterization, owe to no country more loyalty than to any other, nor feel completely at home in any country (see also, among others, Barnet and Müller 1974: 15–16; Hymer and Rowthorn 1970: 88–91; Reich 1992: 3). In recent years, other facets of the disempowerment of nation-states have been brought into the picture. Thus, Peter Drucker (1993: 141–56) traces the disempowerment to the combined impact of three forces: the "transnationalism" of multilateral treaties and suprastatal organizations, including transnational corporations; the "regionalism" of economic blocs like the European Union and the North American Free Trade Agreement (NAFTA); and the "tribalism" of increasing emphasis on diversity and identity. Either way, the symptoms and the causes of the ongoing crisis of the system of nation-states are sought and found in all regions of the world without any special attention being paid to East Asia.

Accounts of economic expansion in East Asia, for their part, make almost no reference to the disempowerment of nation-states as a significant aspect of the phenomenon (for a partial exception, see Bernard and Ravenhill 1995). Worse still, the neoliberal fantasy of a greater respect for, and reliance on, self-regulating markets on the part of economically successful East Asian governments, has channeled debates on the wrong track. In dismantling authoritatively and effectively this fantasy, Amsden (1989), Evans (1995), Johnson (1987, 1988), and Wade (1990), among others, have conveyed the impression that the crisis of nation-states, if at all real, does not concern East Asia, where states are well and strong.

Leaving aside the question of whether the states of East Asia are well and strong – some are, while others are not – let us begin by noticing how peculiar East Asian states appear when compared with the ideal type of nation-state. Three peculiarities stand out above all others: the "quasi-state" nature of the economically most successful states of the region; the importance of informal business networks in connecting the economies of these quasi-states to one another and to the rest of the region; and the extreme imbalance of the distribution of military, financial and demographic resources among the states operating in the region.

The expression "quasi-states" has been coined by Robert Jackson (1990: 21) to designate states that have been granted juridical statehood, and have thereby become members of the interstate system, but lack the capabilities needed to carry out the governmental functions associated historically with statehood. Jackson uses the expression with special reference to the less successful among the Third World states that have emerged from the post-Second World War wave of decolonization. Nevertheless, to varying degrees and in different ways the five most successful capitalist states of East Asia – Japan and the so-called Four Tigers – all qualify as quasi-states.

For the internal and external aspects of national sovereignty are essentially theories about the legitimacy of authority. National polities organized into states are theorized as the pinnacle of legitimate authority, "neither subordinate to the world polity nor defied by local polities or organizations." The theory, however, "is often violated by the facts" (Boli 1993: 10–11). As we shall see, key facts of the history of the modern world system violate the theory of nation-states as the pinnacle of legitimate authority. But at no time since the sixteenth century have the facts of an emerging center of world capitalism violated the theory more conspicuously than today in East Asia.

Among the region's most successful capitalist states, only the largest, Japan, is a nation-state in the full sense of the term. Regionally and globally, however, even Japan is still a US military protectorate. *Mutatis mutandi*, it fully deserves the designation of "semisovereign state" with which Peter Katzenstein (1987) has characterized the Federal Republic of Germany. South Korea and Taiwan, the two states of intermediate size, are also US military protectorates. In addition, neither of them is a nation-state in the full sense – South Korea living in constant hope or fear of being reunited with its northern half, and Taiwan in constant hope or fear of becoming the master or the servant of Mainland China. Finally, the two smallest but by no means least important states, the semisovereign Hong Kong and Singapore, are not nation-states at all but city-states, exercising in the East Asian region functions not altogether different from those performed by Genoa and Venice in early modern Europe – the commercial-industrial entrepôt functions exercised by Singapore making it resemble Venice, and the commercial-financial entrepôt functions exercised by Hong Kong making it resemble Genoa (Arrighi 1994: 78).

This peculiar configuration of East Asian capitalist states is matched by an equally peculiar configuration of the region's business organizations. Up to very recently, East Asia (Northeast Asia in particular) has been a secondary source and destination of foreign direct investment in comparison, not just with North America and Western Europe, but also with Latin America, Southern and Central Africa, North Africa and the Middle East. As a result, the vertical integration of economic activities across political jurisdictions typical of US corporate capitalism never became as important in East Asia as it did in most regions of the non-Communist world.

Although in the 1970s and, above all, in the 1980s foreign direct investment within East Asia and between East Asia and the rest of the world grew rapidly (Petri 1993: 39–42), the cross-border organization of business enterprise in the region relied heavily on informal networks among juridically independent units rather than vertical integration within a single multi-unit enterprise. In the 1970s and early 1980s, the leading agency in the formation of regional business networks of this kind were Japanese trading and manufacturing companies, which transplanted across the region their domestic multilayered subcontracting system (Arrighi, Ikeda and Irwan 1993). From the mid-1980s onwards, however, the leading role of Japanese companies in the formation of regional business networks was supplemented, and in key areas surpassed, by the activities of the Overseas Chinese business diaspora (Arrighi 1996; Irwan 1995). These two agencies, in the words of a senior economist for Deutsche Bank Capital Markets in Tokyo, "don't really mix, but complement each other well. The Overseas Chinese are the oil – the lubricant that makes deals possible – and the Japanese are the vinegar – the technology, capital, and management that really packs a punch" (qtd. in Kraar 1993: 40).

Po-keung Hui (1995) has documented the derivation of the Chinese capitalist diaspora that is emerging as a leading agency of processes of capital accumulation in East Asia from the business communities that grew in the interstices of the Sinocentric tribute–trade system before and after the European impact. His analysis lends support to Hamashita's contention of the continuing relevance of the Sinocentric tribute–trade system for an understanding of the present and future dynamic of the East Asian region. But it also invites a comparison with similarly structured business agencies that played a critical role in the formation and initial expansion of the Eurocentric capitalist world-economy.

I am referring specifically to the Genoese capitalist diaspora which, in association with the territorialist rulers of Portugal and Spain, promoted and organized the transoceanic expansion of the European world-economy in the late fifteenth and early sixteenth centuries (Arrighi 1994: ch. 2). We shall later return to the significance of this Genoese–Iberian association for an understanding of the origins of the Eurocentric capitalist world system. For now, let us simply underscore two striking similarities between the sixteenth-century Genoese and the late-twentieth-century Chinese capitalist diasporas. First, like the networks of commercial and financial intermediation controlled by the sixteenth-century Genoese diaspora, the business networks controlled by the Chinese diaspora *occupy* places (Hong Kong, Taiwan, Singapore, as well as the most important commercial centers of Southeast Asian countries and Mainland China) but are not *defined* by the places they occupy. What defines the networks is the space-of-flows (the commercial and financial transactions) that connect the places where individual members or sub-groups of the diaspora conduct their business (cf. Arrighi 1994: 82–84). Second, like the business networks of the sixteenth-century Genoese diaspora, the business networks of the Overseas Chinese are an interstitial formation that thrives on the limits and contradictions of very large territorial organizations – organizations whose networks of power are so extensive as to resemble premodern world-empires rather than nation-states.

This brings us to the third peculiarity of the political economy of the East Asian region: the extreme imbalance of the distribution of power resources among political jurisdictions. This extreme imbalance is the obverse side of the two peculiarities we have just discussed. Broadly speaking, the "semisovereignty" of the most successful capitalist states of the region is the obverse side of their incorporation within the networks of power of the United States. And the growing importance of the Overseas Chinese in promoting the economic expansion and integration of the region is but one aspect of the reincorporation of Mainland China in regional and world markets.

The extreme imbalance of military power in the region is primarily a legacy of Japan's defeat in the Second World War and of the US policy of "containment" during the Cold War era. The unilateral military occupation of Japan by the United States in 1945 and the division of the region five years later into two antagonistic blocs created, in Bruce Cumings's words, a US "vertical regime solidified through bilateral defense treaties (with Japan, South Korea, Taiwan and the Philippines) and conducted by a State Department that towered over the foreign ministries of these four countries."

All became semi-sovereign states, deeply penetrated by US military structures (operational control of the South Korean armed forces, Seventh Fleet patrolling of the Taiwan Straits, defense dependencies for all four countries, military bases on their territories) and incapable of independent foreign policy or defense initiatives ... There were minor demarches through the military curtain beginning in the mid-1950s, such as low levels of trade between Japan and China, or Japan and North Korea. But the dominant tendency, until the 1970s, was a unilateral US regime heavily biased toward military forms of communication.   *(Cumings 1997: 155)*

It is interesting to notice how this "unilateral US regime" combined from the start features that made it resemble the premodern Sinocentric tribute–trade system as well as the early modern Genoese–Iberian regime of rule and accumulation. The main resemblance with the Sinocentric system was the interpenetration of tribute and trade relations between an imperial center whose domestic economy was of incomparably greater size than that of its vassal states. In this respect, we may well say that the *Pax Americana* in East Asia transformed the periphery of the former Sinocentric tribute–trade system into the periphery of a US-centric tribute–trade system, through the coercive exclusion of Mainland China from commercial and diplomatic intercourse with most of its East Asian neighbors.

The US-centric East Asian regime, however, fostered a functional specialization between the imperial and the vassal states. This functional specialization had no parallel in the old Sinocentric regime. Rather, it reminds us of the sixteenth-century Genoese–Iberian quasi-imperial regime. The main feature of the latter regime was a relationship of political exchange between an (Iberian) territorialist organization – which specialized in the provision of protection and in the pursuit of power – and a (Genoese) capitalist organization, which specialized in trade and in the pursuit of profit. A similar relationship can be clearly recognized in US–Japanese relations throughout the Cold War era. For "semisovereignty" enabled Japanese capital to externalize protection costs and to specialize in the pursuit of profit as successfully as Genoese capital had done four centuries earlier (Arrighi 1994: 120, 338).

Freed from the burden of defense spending, Japanese governments have funneled all their resources and energies into an economic expansionism that has brought affluence to Japan and taken its business to the farthest reaches of the globe. War has been an issue only in that the people and the conservative government have resisted involvement in foreign wars like Korea and Vietnam. Making what concessions were necessary under the Security Treaty with the Americans, the government has sought only involvement that would bring economic profit to Japanese enterprise.

(Schurmann 1974: 143)

For all its similarities with premodern and early modern modes of rule and accumulation, the post-Second World War US-centric East Asian regime differs radically from its predecessors in at least one respect: the incomparably greater size and technological sophistication of the US military–industrial apparatus. The far-flung network of quasi-permanent overseas bases put or kept in place by the United States after the Second World War "was without historical precedent; no state had previously based its own troops on the sovereign territory of other states in such extensive numbers for so long a peacetime period" (Krasner 1988: 21). Not even in their wildest dreams could the rulers of Imperial China or Imperial Spain imagine that such an extensive and potentially destructive deployment of military muscle could ever materialize.

And yet, it was precisely in the military sphere that the US-centric East Asian regime began to crack. For the Vietnam War destroyed what the Korean War had created. The Korean War had instituted the US-centric East Asian regime by excluding Mainland China from normal commercial and diplomatic intercourse with the non-communist part of the region, through blockade and war threats backed by "an archipelago of American military installations" (Cumings 1997: 154–55). The Vietnam War, in contrast, initiated a reversal of the economic fortunes of the United States and Japan that, over time, made US world power dependent on Japanese finances. More importantly, it forced the United States to readmit Mainland China to normal commercial and diplomatic intercourse with the rest of East Asia (cf. Arrighi 1996).

This outcome transformed without eliminating the previous imbalance of the distribution of power resources in the region. The rise of Japan to industrial and financial powerhouse of global significance transformed the previous relationship of Japanese political and economic vassalage vis-à-vis the United States into a relationship of mutual vassalage. Japan continued to depend on the United States for military protection; but the United States came to depend ever more critically on Japanese finance and industry for the reproduction of its protection-producing apparatus. That is to say, power resources became more evenly distributed between the United States and Japan but the structural differentiation between the two states that was at the basis of their relationship of political exchange, if anything, increased further.

At the same time, the reincorporation of Mainland China in the regional and global market economies brought back into play a state whose demographic size, abundance of labor resources, and growth potential surpassed by a good margin that of all other states operating in the region, the United States included. Within less than twenty years after Richard Nixon's mission to Beijing, and less than fifteen after the formal reestablishment of diplomatic relations between the United States and the PRC, this giant "container" of labor power already seemed on the verge of becoming once again the powerful attractor of means of payments it had been in premodern and early modern times. To be sure, the PRC has been reincorporated in regional and global markets at the lowest levels of the value-added hierarchy of the capitalist world economy. And in spite of the extraordinary expansion of its domestic production and foreign trade over the last fifteen years, its GNP per capita at world market prices has remained among the lowest in the world (Lu 2000: 121–71). Nevertheless, this failure of relative GNP per capita at world market prices to rise, has further increased the attractiveness of the PRC's huge reserves of labor for foreign capital and entrepreneurship, as reflected in the explosive growth of capital flows to China since the late 1980s (Arrighi 1994).

If the main attraction of the PRC for foreign capital has been its huge and highly competitive reserves of labor, the "matchmaker" that has facilitated the encounter of foreign capital and Chinese labor is the Overseas Chinese capitalist diaspora.

Drawn by China's capable pool of low-cost labor and its growing potential as a market that contains one-fifth of the world's population, foreign investors continue to pour money into the PRC. Some 80 percent of that capital comes from the Overseas Chinese, refugees from poverty, disorder, and communism, who in one of the era's most piquant ironies are now Beijing's favorite financiers and models for modernization. Even the Japanese often rely on the Overseas Chinese to grease their way into China.
(Kraar 1993: 40)

In fact, Beijing's reliance on the Overseas Chinese to ease Mainland China's reincorporation in regional and world markets is not the true irony of the situation. As Alvin So and Stephen Chiu (1995: ch. 11) have shown, the close political alliance that was established in the 1980s between the Chinese Communist Party and Overseas Chinese capitalists made perfect sense in terms of their respective pursuits. For the alliance provided the Overseas Chinese with extraordinary opportunities to profit from commercial and financial intermediation, while providing the Chinese Communist Party with a highly effective means of killing two birds with one stone: to upgrade the domestic economy of Mainland China and at the same time to promote national unification in accordance to the "One Nation, Two Systems" model.

The true irony of the situation is rather how premodern "post-modernity" looks in what has become the most dynamic region of the capitalist world system. According to most accounts, one of the main features of post-modernity is the waning of the usefulness and power of nation-states.

The key autonomous actor in political and international affairs for the past few centuries appears not just to be losing its control and integrity, but to be the *wrong sort* of unit to handle the newer circumstances. For some problems, it is too large to operate effectively; for others, it is too small. In consequence there are pressures for the "relocation of authority" both upward and downward, creating structures that might respond better to today's and tomorrow's forces of change.

(Kennedy 1993: 131; emphasis in the original)

If the problem with nation-states is that they are either "too large" or "too small" to operate effectively, gifts of history and geography seem to have provided East Asia with a solution to the problem by endowing it with a variety of territorial and non-territorial organizations that are either something less, or something more, or something different than nation-states. There are city-states, and quasi-states; quasi-empires, and "nations" that are not states, like the Overseas Chinese; and above all, there is a structural differentiation among the most powerful organizations in the region that has left the United States in control of most of the guns, Japan and the Overseas Chinese in control of most of the money, and the PRC in control of most of the labor. In this "messy" but capitalistically highly successful political economic formation there are plenty of nation-states. But either they are peripheral components of the regional formation – as Malaysia, Thailand, Indonesia, Vietnam, Laos, Cambodia, and the Philippines to different degrees and in different ways all are – or they do not fit the image of nation-state with which we have been trying to understand the origins and present dynamics of the modern world.

III

The peculiar political economic configuration of contemporary East Asia poses two main challenges to established world-systems theories. First, is it possible that some or all of its peculiarities are in fact more ordinary features of historical capitalism than we have been willing or able to acknowledge? And second, if that is the case, what kind of theoretical construct would best enable us to grasp the logic and implications of the rise of East Asia and the concomitant demise of nation-states as key actors in world politics? In this section I shall concentrate on the first challenge, leaving the second for brief consideration in the concluding section.

The foregoing description of the peculiarities of the political economy of East Asia has already underscored how difficult it is to disentangle within the East Asian "melting pot" modern from premodern, and Eastern from Western forms of organization. On the one hand, we have pointed out how the strategies and structures of the leading governmental and business institutions of late-twentieth-century East Asia resemble those of their counterparts in sixteenth-century Europe. On the other hand, we have noted some striking resemblances between the US-centric East Asian regime of the Cold War era and the Sinocentric tribute–trade regime of premodern times.

To this we should now add that the political economic configuration of the entire history of the Eurocentric capitalist world system is as "messy," nay, "messier" than the present configuration of East Asian capitalism. In particular, the notion that nation-states have been the key agencies of the process of formation and expansion of the Eurocentric capitalist system obscures as much as it clarifies about that process. City-states, diaspora capitalist classes, quasi-states and quasi-empires have all played as critical a role as nation-states.

In the original formation of the system, city-states led the way. As Braudel (1984: ch. 2), Cox (1959), Lane (1966; 1979), Mattingly (1988), and McNeill (1984: ch. 3) have emphasized in different but complementary ways, the late-medieval system of city-states centered on Venice, Florence, Genoa, and Milan anticipated by two centuries or more many of the key features of the European system of nation-states that was instituted by the Peace of Westphalia of 1648. In fact, according to Mattingly (1988: 178), the Peace of Westphalia was modeled after the Peace of Lodi of 1454 which institutionalized the balance of power among the Italian city-states.

The two-hundred-year period that separates 1648 from 1454 corresponds almost exactly to Braudel's and Wallerstein's "long" sixteenth century. At the beginning of the period, capitalism as mode of rule and accumulation was still embedded primarily in the Italian system of city-states and, as such, it remained an interstitial formation of the European world-economy. At the end of the period, it had become embedded in a European-wide system of nation-states and, as such, it had become the dominant mode of rule and accumulation of the entire European world-economy. The obverse side of this transformation of the inner structure of the European world-economy was an extraordinary expansion of its outer boundaries through the conquest of the Americas, major incursions in the Indian Ocean world-economy, and the establishment of direct contacts with the Sinocentric tribute–trade system (Arrighi 1994: 32–47).

From the vantage point of the present political economic configuration of East Asia, the most interesting aspect of this transformation-*cum*-expansion is that its agencies were either something less, or something more, or something different than nation-states. To be sure, nation-states were the main beneficiaries of the process. But they were not its promoters and organizers.

Initially, its main agency was the previously mentioned Genoese–Iberian complex brought and held together by a mutually beneficial relationship of political exchange between the Genoese capitalist diaspora and the territorialist rulers of what very quickly became Imperial Spain. As the European world-economy was reorganized and expanded under Genoese–Iberian leadership, various forms of proto-nationalism emerged in its midst in opposition to the imperial pretensions of the territorialist rulers of Spain and to the centralizing tendencies of the Genoese capitalist diaspora in European high finance. Even then, however, the leading loci and agencies of this countervailing power were not the more accomplished nation-states, like France, England, and Sweden. Rather, it was the quasi-state of Holland – a semisovereign organization still struggling for juridical statehood and having more features in common with the declining city-states than with the rising nation-states (Arrighi 1994: 109–58, 177–95).

After the Peace of Westphalia, nation-states did become the main agencies of change in the Eurocentric world system. Nevertheless, the nation-state that was most active and successful in promoting the outward expansion of the system, Britain, relied heavily on forms of governmental and business organization that had been pioneered by city-states, business diasporas, quasi-empires and quasi-states. This premodern and early modern heritage became particularly evident in the nineteenth century, when Britain briefly, but almost literally, ruled the entire world through a combination of techniques of power derived equally from Venice and Holland on the one side, and from Genoa and Imperial Spain on the other (Arrighi 1994: 57–58, 167–71, 195–213).

Britain's half-territorialist, half-capitalist world-empire eventually collapsed under the weight of its own contradictions. Nevertheless, by the time of its collapse the world had been transformed out of recognition and the ground had been prepared for the subsequent universal expansion and simultaneous supersession of the European system of nation-states. The "industrialization" of war, transport, and communication led to an unprecedented breakdown of temporal and spatial barriers both within and between the previously discrete regions of the global economy. In its turn, this "time–space compression" – as David Harvey (1989: 240–41) has called the phenomenon – revolutionized the conditions under which states formed and related to one another.

On the one hand, state-making and national-economy-making could now be pursued effectively on a much greater scale than before. As a result, the typical nation-state of the European core came to be perceived as being "too small" to be able to compete militarily and commercially with the continent-sized national economies that were forming in the Russian Empire on its eastern flank and in the United States on its western flank. Germany's obsession with *Lebensraum* – paralleled in the Sinocentric system by Japan's obsession with *tairiku* – was but an aspect of this perception, which soon became a self-fulfilling prophecy by exacerbating the conflicts that led to the First and then to the Second World Wars. Even before the Second World War was over, notes Paul Kennedy (1987: 357), "The bipolar world, forecast so often in the nineteenth and early twentieth centuries, had at last arrived; the international order, in DePorte's words, now moved 'from one system to another.' Only the United States and the USSR counted ... and of the two, The American 'superpower' was vastly superior."

On the other hand, the low-volume, low-density web of exchanges that had linked loosely the world-economies and world-empires of Afroeurasia to one another since premodern times and, in modern times, to the Americas and then Australasia, now grew in volume and density at a speed that had no historical precedent. As a result, the global economy came to be perceived as so highly interdependent as to make national economic independence anachronistic. Ironically, the earliest prophets of global economic interdependence were the founding fathers of that brand of socialism that eventually became the staunchest advocate of national economic seclusion. "All old-established national industries" – proclaimed Marx and Engels (1988: 37) at a time when the great mid-nineteenth-century revolution in world transport and communication had hardly begun – "are dislodged by new industries, whose introduction becomes a life and death question for all civilized nations, that no longer work up indigenous raw material, but raw material drawn from the remotest zones; industries whose products are consumed, not only at home, but in every quarter of the globe . . . In place of the old local and national seclusion and self-sufficiency, we have intercourse in every direction, universal interdependence of nations."

As Robert Wade (1996) has noted, much of recent talk about globalization and the irrelevance of nation-states simply recycles arguments that were fashionable a hundred years ago. There are nonetheless two important differences between the realities, if not the perceptions, of the obsolescence of nation-states today and in the late nineteenth and early twentieth centuries. First of all, a hundred years ago the reality, and to a large extent the perception, of the crisis of nation-states concerned the states of the old European core relative to the continent-sized states that were forming on the outer perimeter of the Eurocentric system, the United States in particular. The irresistible rise of US power and wealth, and of Soviet power, though not wealth, in the course of the two World Wars and their aftermath, confirmed the validity of the widely held expectation that the nation-states of the old European core were bound to live in the shadow of their two flanking giants, unless they could themselves attain continental dimension. The reality, and to a lesser extent the perception, of the present crisis of nation-states, in contrast, is that the giant states themselves are in trouble.

The sudden collapse of the USSR has both clarified and obscured this new dimension of the crisis. It has clarified the new dimension by showing how vulnerable even the largest, most self-sufficient, and second-greatest military power had become to the forces of global economic integration. But it has obscured the true nature of the crisis by provoking a general amnesia about the fact that the crisis of US world power preceded the breakdown of the USSR and, with ups and downs, has outlasted the end of the Cold War.

The second difference between the crisis of the nation-state today and a hundred years ago is that the strategies and structures of US hegemony in the Cold War era have deepened and widened the crisis by transforming small and medium-sized states into quasi-states, and by creating the conditions for a new time–space compression that has undermined the power of even the larger states. To be sure, under US hegemony the nation-state form of political organization became universal. But as the form of national sovereignty expanded, its substance contracted like never before (Arrighi 1994: 66–69).

In part, this was the direct outcome of the institutionalization of the idea of world government and of the actual exercise of world-governmental functions by the United States. The institutionalization of the idea of world government materialized through the creation of the United Nations and Bretton Woods organizations, which imposed restrictions of various kinds on the sovereignty of most of their member nation-states. But the greatest restrictions were imposed by the series of US-centric regional military alliances and by the US-centric world monetary system through which the United States at the height of its power actually governed the world.

In part, however, the evaporation of the substance of national sovereignty was the indirect result of the new forms of regional and world-economic integration that grew under the carapace of US military and financial power. Unlike the nineteenth-century world-economic integration instituted by and centered on Britain, the system of regional and world economic integration instituted by and centered on the United States in the Cold War era did not rest on the unilateral free trade of the hegemonic power and on the extraction of tribute from an overseas territorial empire. Rather, it rested on a process of bilateral and multilateral trade liberalization closely monitored and administered by the United States, acting in concert with its most important political allies, and on a global transplant of the vertically integrated organizational structures of US corporations (Arrighi 1994: 69–72).

Administered trade liberalization and the global transplant of US corporations were meant to serve a double purpose: to maintain and expand US world power, and to reorganize interstate relations so as to "contain," not just the forces of Communist revolution, but also the forces of nationalism that had torn apart and eventually destroyed the nineteenth-century British system of world economic integration. In the attainment of these two objectives, the overseas transplant of US corporations had priority over trade liberalization. Thus, as

Giovanni Arrighi

Robert Gilpin (1975: 108) has underscored with reference to US policy in Europe, the fundamental motivation of US support for Western European economic unification was the consolidation of US and Western power vis-à-vis the USSR. In this pursuit, the US government was willing to tolerate some discrimination against the import of US goods in the newly created Common Market. But it was not willing to tolerate discrimination against the transplant of US corporations within the walls of that market.

In Gilpin's view, the relationship of these corporations to US world power was not unlike that of joint-stock chartered companies to British power in the seventeenth and eighteenth centuries: "The American multinational corporation, like its mercantile ancestor, has performed an important role in the maintenance and expansion of the power of the United States" (141–42). This has been undoubtedly true but only up to a point. The global transplant of US corporations did maintain and expand the world power of the United States by establishing claims on the incomes, and controls over the resources, of foreign countries. The importance of these claims and controls should not be underestimated. In the last resort, they constituted the single most important difference between the world power of the United States and that of the USSR and, by implication, the single most important reason why the decline of US world power, unlike that of the USSR, has proceeded gradually rather than catastrophically (for an early statement of this difference, see Arrighi 1982: 95–97).

Nevertheless, the relationship between the transnational expansion of US corporations and the maintenance and expansion of the power of the US state has been just as much one of contradiction as of complementarity. For one thing, the claims on foreign incomes established by the subsidiaries of US corporations did not translate into a proportionate increase in the incomes of US residents and in the revenues of the US government. On the contrary, precisely when the fiscal crisis of the US "warfare–welfare state" became acute under the impact of the Vietnam War, a growing proportion of the incomes and liquidity of US corporations, instead of being repatriated, flew to offshore money markets. In the words of Eugene Birnbaum of Chase Manhattan Bank, the result was "the amassing of an immense volume of liquid funds and markets – the world of Eurodollar finance – outside the regulatory authority of *any* country or agency" (qtd. in Frieden 1987: 85; emphasis in the original).

Interestingly enough, the organization of this world of Eurodollar finance – like the organizations of the sixteenth-century Genoese business diaspora and of the Chinese business diaspora from pre-modern to our own times – occupies places but it is not defined by the places it occupies. The so-called Eurodollar or Eurocurrency market – as Roy Harrod (1969: 319) characterized it well before the arrival of the information super-highway – "has no headquarters or buildings of its own... Physically it consists merely of a network of telephones and telex machines around the world, telephones which may be used for purposes other than Eurodollar deals." This space-of-flows falls under no state jurisdiction. And although the US state still has a privileged access to its services and resources, the main tendency of the last thirty years has been for all nation-states, including the US, to become the servant rather than the master of extraterritorial high finance.

Equally important, the transnational expansion of US corporations has called forth competitive responses in old and new centers of capital accumulation that have weakened, and eventually reversed, US claims on foreign incomes and resources. As Alfred Chandler (1990: 615–16) has pointed out, by the time Servan-Schreiber called upon his fellow Europeans to stand up to the "American Challenge" – a challenge that in his view was neither financial nor technological but "the extension to Europe of an *organization* that is still a mystery to us" – a growing number of European enterprises had found effective ways and means of meeting the challenge and of themselves becoming challengers of the long-established US corporations even in the US market. In the 1970s, the accumulated value of non-US (mostly Western European) foreign direct investment grew one-and-half times faster than that of US foreign direct investment. By 1980, it was estimated that there were over 10,000 transnational corporations of all national origins, and by the early 1990s three times as many (Arrighi 1994: 73, 304).

This explosive growth in the number of transnational corporations was accompanied by a drastic decrease in the importance of the United States as a source, and an increase in its importance as a recipient, of foreign direct investment. The transnational forms of business organization pioneered by US capital, in other words, had rapidly ceased to be a "mystery" for a large and growing number of foreign competitors. By the 1970s, Western European capital had discovered all its secrets and had begun outcompeting US corporations at home and abroad. By the 1980s, it was the turn of East Asian capital to outcompete both US and Western European capital through the formation of a new kind of transnational business organization – an organization that was deeply rooted in the region's gifts of history and geography, and that combined the advantages of vertical integration with the flexibility of informal business networks. But no matter which particular fraction of capital won, the outcome of each round of the competitive struggle was a further increase in the volume and density of the web of exchanges that linked people and territory across political jurisdictions both regionally and globally.

IV

We are thus back to the rise of East Asia and its "messy" political economic configuration, which now appears to be a special case of the even "messier" political economic configuration of the capitalist world system throughout its history. In both configurations, the leading agencies of the formation and expansion of the capitalist world system appear to have been organizations that are either something less (city-states and quasi-states) or something more (quasi-empires) or something different (business diasporas and other transterritorial capitalist organizations) than nation-states. At a decisive moment of its evolution, the Eurocentric capitalist world system did become embodied in a system of nation-states. But its further expansion continued to depend on the formation in its midst of organizations that resembled their premodern and early modern predecessors. What's more, as the Eurocentric capitalist system came to encompass the entire globe, nation-states gradually lost their centrality as the main loci of world power. World power came instead to be concentrated in structurally differentiated governmental and non-governmental organizations that reproduce on a much larger scale and in incomparably more complex forms many of the traits of premodern and early modern modes of rule and accumulation.

This "messy" historical formation does not quite fit the concept of "capitalist world-economy" that has become dominant in world-system studies. In order to capture the rise and present demise of the system of nation-states, that concept needs to be revised in a way that complements Christopher Chase-Dunn's and Thomas Hall's revision of the concept of "world-empire." According to Chase-Dunn and Hall, Wallerstein's claim that what makes the modern world system unique is that it is the only world-economy (competing polities within a single economic system) that did not transform into a world-empire (a single polity encompassing an entire economic system) does not quite stand up to empirical scrutiny. "The modern world-system *apparently* is the longest lived world-economy, but there have been others that have lasted for several centuries ... Among other things, this suggests that the celebrated interstate system of the capitalist world-economy is not as novel as is sometimes claimed." They accordingly propose to replace the concept of "world-empire" with the concept of "core-wide empire" to allow for the fact that premodern state-based world systems oscillated back and forth between core-wide empires and interstate systems (Chase-Dunn and Hall 1993; Chase-Dunn 1996; see also Chase-Dunn and Hall 1997).

The reconceptualization proposed here, in contrast, concerns the very idea of "capitalist world-economy." Just as Chase-Dunn and Hall have found more "modern" features in premodern world systems than Wallerstein's dichotomy "world-empire" versus "world-economy" allows for, so we have found more "premodern" features in the modern world system than allowed for by that same dichotomy. The reason why the celebrated interstate system of the capitalist world-economy is not as novel as Wallerstein claimed, is not just that several of its features were already present in premodern world systems. It is also that several features of premodern core-wide empires have played a critical role in the formation, expansion and present supersession of the modern interstate system.

As the study of early modern Western Europe and of late-modern East Asia both suggest, we need a concept of "capitalist world-economy" that defines capitalism as an interstitial formation of both premodern and modern times. Capitalism as mode of rule and accumulation did become dominant, first in Europe and then globally. But it never completely lost its interstitial character, which is as evident in today's emerging center of world capitalism (East Asia) as in its original sixteenth-century center (Western Europe). In between, there lies the era of the modern interstate system. But as long as we remain infatuated with the typical "containers" of power of this era, we shall be as ill equipped to predict the future of our world as we are to understand its origins and evolution.

NOTE

1 An earlier version of this paper was presented at the Ninetieth Annual Meeting of the American Sociological Association, Washington, DC, August 19–23, 1995.

3

The fetish of "the West" in postcolonial theory

Neil Lazarus

I

In a commentary entitled "East isn't East," which appeared not long ago in the *Times Literary Supplement*, Edward Said proposed that one of the essential gestures of postcolonial criticism, and one of its enduring achievements, rested in what he called its "consistent critique of Eurocentrism" (1995: 5). In the pages that follow, I would like to put some pressure on this assessment. My intention is not, of course, to suggest that the postcolonialist critique of Eurocentrism has *not* been significant in helping to expose the tendentiousness, chauvinism, and sheer pervasiveness of the ideological formation that Said himself, in his seminal study of 1978, addressed under the rubric of Orientalism. I take it for granted that it *has*, and believe moreover that to argue otherwise would be simply perverse. Rather, my aim in this chapter is to suggest that in the field of postcolonial studies at large, including in the work of some of the field's most audacious and theoretically sophisticated practitioners, Eurocentrism has typically been viewed not as an ideology or mode of representation but as itself the very basis of domination in the colonial and modern imperial contexts. Setting out from this strictly idealist conceptualization, postcolonial theorists have sought to produce an anti-Eurocentric – or, in Gyan Prakash's (1990) preferred terminology, a "post-Orientalist" – scholarship. Some of their achievements have unquestionably been important: I have in mind, for instance, the salutary demonstration that such historically resonant "master narratives" as enlightenment, modernity, progress, and reason – narratives that have almost always been phrased in universalistic terms – have often been mobilized in defense of practices both ethnocentric and intolerant of difference (sometimes murderously so). But to the extent that a plausible account of the structurality of the modern world order has necessarily eluded them, postcolonial theorists have been unable to situate Eurocentrism as an historical problematic, to understand how it has been able to achieve its momentous effects.

One of the anchors of the postcolonialist critique, latent in the very term "Eurocentrism," has been the fetish of "Europe" or "the West." It is this fetish in particular – Tim Brennan calls it "a pamphleteer's fiction" (1997: 61) – that I would like to examine in this chapter. The concept of "the West" as it is used in postcolonial theory, I want to argue, has no coherent or credible referent. It is an ideological category masquerading as a geographic one, just as – in the context of modern Orientalist discourse – "Islam" is an ideological category masquerading as a religious one. As Fernando Coronil has argued, the substitution enacted in the deployment of the concept of "the West" – of a cartographic term for an ideological one – functions to gloss or represent the relatively intangible "historical relations among peoples" in terms of "the material, thinglike, tangible form of geographical entities" (1996: 77). In postcolonial theory, Coronil writes, "the West is constituted as an imperial fetish, the imagined home of history's victors, the embodiment of their power" (78). This construction, which positions "the West" as at one and the same time a mappable zone and a social agent, seems at first glance to resemble the trope, familiar to us from newspapers and television news, in terms of which place names – "Whitehall," "the Vatican," "Beijing," for instance – are used metonymically to designate social and political agencies. But there is an important difference: while the concept of "the West" certainly functions, as does "Beijing" or "the Vatican," to specify a social power, it serves in addition to mystify this power, rendering its social ground opaque. For "the West" references neither a polity nor a state (nor even a confederation of states), but a "civilization," something altogether more amorphous and indeterminate. As Raymond Williams has pointed out, when people speak about "'Western values,' 'Western interests,' and even ... of the President of the United States ... as the 'acknowledged' leader of 'the West as a whole,'" it is impossible to certify even the sociological actuality, still less the unity or transhistorical integrity, of what their discourse so blithely presumes (1983: 201).

To help us situate what is distinctive about the conceptualization of "the West" prevailing today in postcolonial studies, it will be helpful for us first to say a little more about the way in which the category tends to be mobilized elsewhere. Williams outlines a history of fairly radical *dis*continuity. He records that the "earliest European form" of "the West" "comes from the division of the Roman Empire, from the third century"; this "was followed by the division of the Christian churches, from the eleventh century." Both meanings, however, were then "superseded by contrasts between 'the West' as a Christian civilisation and an 'East' defined either as Islam or as the civilisations beyond it from India to China. Western and Eastern (or 'Oriental') worlds were commonly defined in this way from the sixteenth century." And after 1945, with the advent of the Cold War, a further refunctioning gave the binary opposition between "West" and "East" a new geopolitical significance: "This first rested on the evident political divisions between Western and Eastern Europe, but was soon generalised to what was offered as a universal contrast, between political and economic systems of different types" (1983: 200).

In common-sense language today, as Stuart Hall has pointed out, the notion of "the West" characteristically designates not only or even primarily a geographical zone, but "a type of society" or "a level of development." While "it's true that what we call 'the West,' in this . . . sense, *did* first emerge in Western Europe . . . 'the West' is no longer only in Europe, and not all of Europe is in 'the West,'" Hall writes (1996b: 185). His central point is that "the West"

> is a *historical*, not a geographical construct. By "western" we mean . . . a society that is developed, industrialized, urbanized, capitalist, secular, and modern. . . . Nowadays, any society which shares these characteristics, wherever it exists on a geographical map, can be said to belong to "the West." The meaning of this term is therefore virtually identical to that of the word "modern." (*186*)

This common-sense understanding accords substantially with that prevailing in social scientific scholarship. In work after work by theorists as different from one another as Anthony Giddens, James Coleman, and Francis Fukuyama, we find a tendency to situate the global dispersal of capitalist modernity in terms of the universalization of "the West." In all such theorizations, it seems to me, "the West" is construed in a Weberian light, as a *civilization*. In my view, the inevitable result of this construction is a dematerialized understanding of "the West" – and of modernity, its socio-historical ground – as being in a fundamental or primary sense a sort of cultural disposition.

To begin to explore what is at stake here, let us examine briefly two recent additions to the compendious literature on the "rise" and/or predicted "decline" of "the West": Samuel Huntington's *The Clash of Civilizations and the Remaking of World Order* (1998) and Theodore von Laue's *The World Revolution of Westernization* (1987). Both authors write from the hard right wing of the American political spectrum, but their views of global politics are interestingly different. Von Laue's book opens on a portentous if, at the level of syntax, poorly executed note:

> For the first time in all human experience the world revolution of Westernization brought together, in inescapably intimate and virtually instant interaction, all the peoples of the world, regardless of their prior cultural evolution or their capacity – or incapacity – for peaceful coexistence. Within a brief time, essentially within half a century, they were thrust into a common harness, against their will, by a small minority commonly called "The West" – the peoples of Western Europe and their descendants in North America. As a result, the human condition in the present and the future can only be understood within the framework of the Westernized world. *(3)*

Here "the West" – not, as with Giddens, say, a cluster of institutions and forces, but a collocation of people – is phrased as the agent of the cataclysmic socio-historical change that provides the author with his subject. Not only has the specter of *capitalism* been exorcised: there is no mention of any material instance whatsoever. We are left to infer that "the small minority commonly called 'The West'" act in concert because they share an identity, which is to say a difference at least from everyone else in the world. It is this identity that powers the "world revolution of Westernization." Even when, in subsequent paragraphs, von Laue concedes a certain materiality to the conquest of the "non-West" by the "West," he clings to this preliminary conceptualization:

> This massive confluence of the world's peoples, infinitely exceeding in intensity all previous interdependence and transforming the world's ecosystem on which human life depends, was started by irresistible force, by guns, supported by a vast and complex array of cultural skills, adding up to an overwhelming political presence that excelled also in the arts of peace. In creating an interdependent world through conquest, colonization, and expanded opportunities for all, that Western minority imposed its own accomplishments as a universal standard to which all others, however reluctantly, had to submit. *(3–4)*

Our indignation at the sheer ideological meretriciousness of this formulation (the claim that among the modern West's notable accomplishments has been excellence "in the arts of peace" is particularly objectionable, given the bloody historical record of the past 500 years!) should not cause us to fail to reflect on the assumptions that underpin it at the level of method. I want to emphasize two such assumptions in particular here: first, the supposition that the making of the modern world is to be accounted a discrete and autonomous achievement of the "Western minority" who profited most by it; and second, the supposition that the making of the modern world drew upon civilizational attributes ("cultural skills") possessed, uniquely, by "the peoples of Western Europe and their descendants in North America." That neither of these assumptions is tenable ought, it seems to me, to be clear to anyone who has consulted a representative range of the historical and sociological literature produced on this subject over the course of the past thirty years or so. Von Laue's failure to have done so derives all too obviously from his ideological dispositions. But what makes his argument relevant to the present discussion is methodological not substantive. And at this level the mistake he makes is representative of much mainstream writing today, and not just of a conservative stamp. It consists in a neglect of the socio-material basis upon which the modern world was predicated, a neglect which leads von Laue to situate modernity as the effect of the consolidation and subsequent dispersal of a civilization or cultural logic. Modernity is read not in terms of *capitalism*, but in terms of *Westernization*. It is revealing, in this respect, to contrast von Laue's commentary on "the world revolution of Westernization" with that of Marx and Engels on what we might call "the world revolution of capitalism" in *The Communist Manifesto*. For von Laue, the agent of revolution is "the Europeans," who

exploited the world's resources, hitherto mostly dormant, for their own gain; they enlisted the prowess and resilience of people around the world to make themselves masters. The will to power and the capacity for taking advantage of all opportunities for their own aggrandizement . . . sprang from Europe, from the hothouse competition among the Europeans themselves. In expanding around the world and enlarging their base from Europe into "the West," they foisted their singular qualities on the unwilling and unprepared majority of humanity, dynamically transforming the entire world in their own image and establishing a hierarchy of prestige defined by the success of imitation. (4)

Nothing that is described here is not also featured in Marx and Engels's description of the coming of "the epoch of the bourgeoisie": exploitation of resources; the imposition of the market; competition between capitals; the generation of historically unprecedented social wealth; enrichment of a few and immiseration of most; "universal interdependence of nations"; the "battering down" of "all Chinese walls"; the compelling of "all nations, on pain of extinction, to adopt the

47

bourgeois mode of production"; and so on (1988: 33–38). The categorical difference between von Laue and Marx and Engels, of course, is that the latter phrase the capitalist mode of production, and the bourgeoisie as a *class*, not "the West," and "Westerners" as a geographically identified *population*, as the agents of revolution.

In the case of Huntington, it is different and the same. Different because, unlike von Laue, Huntington insists that "modernization is distinct from Westernization and is producing neither a universal civilization in any meaningful sense nor the Westernization of non-Western societies" (1998: 20). Sixty years ago, in his famous essay "The American Century," Henry Luce proposed that the world's future was – or ought to be – American. The "abundant life" would be universally available if only people everywhere would commit themselves to "America's vision": "It must be a sharing with all peoples of our Bill of Rights, our Declaration of Independence, our Constitution, our magnificent industrial products, our technical skills. It must be an internationalism of the people, by the people and for the people" (qtd. in Cumings 2000: 16). At the dawn of the twenty-first century, however, Huntington sees global politics as having become "both multipolar and multicivilizational." *The Clash of Civilizations* is written under the paranoid political delusion that, far from corresponding to the realization of the Lucean dream, the ever-increasing "modernization" of the world at large poses a threat to the "Western way of life." So severe is this threat, indeed, that "the West's" very survival is at stake: today it hangs in the balance, depending "on Americans reaffirming their Western identity and Westerners accepting their civilization as unique not universal and uniting to renew and preserve it against challenges from non-Western societies" (1998: 20–21).

Huntington differs from von Laue, therefore, in his evaluation of the world-historicality of "the West." But like von Laue, he believes that the *differentia specifica* of "the West" are civilizational and, accordingly, that what has made "the West" what it is is a function of the unique "values" and "beliefs" – in a word, the culture – that people in "the West" have and hold, and have had and have held, more or less since time immemorial. Huntington writes, thus, that

Western civilization emerged in the eighth and ninth centuries and developed its distinctive characteristics in the following centuries. It did not begin to modernize until the seventeenth and eighteenth centuries. The West was the West long before it was modern. The central characteristics of the West, those which distinguish it from other civilizations, antedate the modernization of the West. (69)

Operating from the dogma that "[h]uman history is the history of civilizations. It is impossible to think of the development of humanity in any other terms" (40), Huntington produces an analysis that is ironically as unsustainable historically as, in its gross partiality, it is ideologically transparent. It is not only that he proves altogether incapable of telling us how the "characteristics" that distinguish "Western" from other "civilizations" are constituted and historically sedimented or – having been so – how and why they resist further mutation, transformation and reconstruction in the face of the myriad pressures to which they are, presumably, continually exposed as historical forms. (Huntington seems never to have read about the *inventedness* of traditions, never to have contemplated the idea that what he ponderously labels "civilization consciousness" might be the *effect*, rather than the cause, of social conflicts.) The poverty of his analysis stems, at a deeper level, from the conjoint operations in it of a thoroughgoing essentialism and a thoroughgoing culturalism: the former prevents Huntington from recognizing the discontinuity of the historical narrative of "the West" and the perduring porousness of the border between the various "Wests" and their Others over the centuries; the latter prevents him from coming to terms in any plausible manner with what "the West" *is* as a "civilization." As Arif Dirlik has put it in a compelling critique, Huntington

> reifies civilizations into culturally homogeneous and spatially mappable entities, insists on drawing impassable boundaries between them, and proposes a fortress EuroAmerica to defend Western civilization against the intrusion of . . . unassimilable Others. What is remarkable about his views is his disavowal of the involvement of the "West" in other civilization areas . . . [Huntington erases] the legacies of colonialism, [insisting] that whatever has happened in other societies has happened as a consequence of their indigenous values and cultures.[1]   (*1999: 17*)

II

In his 1989 study, *Eurocentrism*, Samir Amin offers a brilliant summary statement of what he terms "the Eurocentric vision" – a "vision," incidentally, that he believes emerged very belatedly, "only in the nineteenth century, as a defensive response to the unfolding critique of bourgeois society," even if it was "then predicated on (and served to rationalize, to systematize, to render coherent) three centuries of bourgeois social practice" (89). The pertinence of his encapsulation to a text like von Laue's is almost uncanny. From the standpoint of the Eurocentric thinker,

The fetish of "the West" in postcolonial theory

The European West is not only the world of material wealth and power, including military might; it is also the site of the triumph of the scientific spirit, rationality, and practical efficiency, just as it is the world of tolerance, diversity of opinions, respect for human rights and democracy, concern for equality – at least the equality of rights and opportunities – and social justice. It is the best of the worlds that have been known up until this time.

(Amin 1989: 107)

Amin adds that the first of the theses elaborated here – that concerning the material wealth and power of the "West" – is, in the Eurocentric imagination,

reinforced by the corollary thesis that other societies . . . have nothing better to offer on any of the levels mentioned (wealth, democracy, or even social justice). On the contrary, these societies can only progress to the extent that they imitate the West . . . Consequently, it becomes impossible to contemplate any other future for the world than its progressive Europeanization . . . The progressive Westernization of the world is nothing more than the expression of the triumph of the humanist universalism invented by Europe. *(107–08)*

Confronted by this schema not merely as a set of ideas, but as a more or less systematic and more or less systematized set of practices and institutions – let us recall Said's definition of Orientalism as "the corporate institution for dealing with the Orient – dealing with it by making statements about it, authorizing views of it, by describing it, by teaching it, settling it, ruling over it . . ." (1979: 3) – we can readily appreciate just how central the critique of Eurocentrism must be to any intellectual project seeking seriously to answer to the name of (and aspiration for) the *post*colonial. But the production of a coherent anti-Eurocentric *theory* has, historically, been fraught with quite as many difficulties as has been the production of a coherent anticolonialist *practice*, and it remains so today.

Consider in the historical context, for instance, the pitfalls associated with the position that Aijaz Ahmad (1992) has identified under the rubrics of "cultural nationalism" and "Third Worldism," but which I would want also to situate as correlative to the politico-theoretical problematics of "dependency" and "development of underdevelopment." The conceptual displacements from "class" to "nation" and "capitalist" social relations to "core/periphery" or "First World/Third World" social relations, which characterize these problematics, had as their inevitable consequence the reconceptualization of the agency and geopolitical vectors of imperialism. A steady drift from the vocabulary of "class struggle" to that of "Third World revolution" can be discerned as the 1960s lengthen and spill over into the 1970s. In the African context, for example, the initial phase might be marked by Kwame Nkrumah's *Neo-Colonialism: the Last Stage of Imperialism,* published in 1965 (1980). The transitional phase might then be represented by Walter Rodney's 1972 study, *How Europe Underdeveloped Africa,* in which a theoretical project and vocabulary derived from dependency theory exists rather uneasily alongside a project and vocabulary defined in classical Marxist terms. On the one hand, thus, Rodney will write that his key term, underdevelopment, "expresses a particular relationship of exploitation: namely, the exploitation of one *country* by another" (1982: 14; emphasis added). On the other hand he will also point out that "most of the people who write about underdevelopment... confuse the issue [by placing] all underdeveloped countries in one camp and all developed countries in another camp irrespective of different social systems; so that the terms capitalist and socialist never enter the discussion" (23). The latent contradiction between these two modes of conceptualization is never finally resolved in *How Europe Underdeveloped Africa.*

By the time of Chinweizu's *The West and the Rest of Us,* however, the erstwhile Marxist problematic has been definitively displaced by a Third Worldism which eschews any focus on capital and class in favor of a thoroughly culturalist definition of the neocolonial world order. Published in 1975, *The West and the Rest of Us* offers an exact, if inverted, reflection of the Eurocentric vision, to which it therefore remains steadfastly loyal. Compare the opening of Chinweizu's volume with the opening paragraphs of von Laue's, to which we have earlier given our attention:

For nearly six centuries now western Europe and its diaspora have been disturbing the peace of the world. Enlightened, through their Renaissance, by the learning of the ancient Mediterranean; armed with the gun, the making of whose powder they had learned from Chinese firecrackers; equipping their ships with lateen sails, astrolabes and nautical compasses, all invented by the Chinese and transmitted to them by Arabs; fortified in aggressive spirit by an arrogant, messianic Christianity of both the popish and Protestant varieties; and motivated by the lure of enriching plunder, white hordes have sallied forth from their western European homelands to explore, assault, loot, occupy, rule and exploit the rest of the world. And even now, the fury of their expansionist assault upon the rest of us has not abated. (3)

Von Laue sees the West as the bringer of peace, Chinweizu sees it as the disturber of peace. Von Laue sees the West's technical resources as having been developed internally, Chinweizu sees them as having been expropriated from non-Western sources. Von Laue prizes Western people's supposed competitiveness, their "will to power and... capacity for taking advantage of all opportunities for their own aggrandizement," Chinweizu excoriates these supposed attributes as aggressive, arrogant, messianic, and grasping. The two writers, in other words, construe the logistics of modern historical development in pretty much the same way; they merely value them differently. Chinweizu's "West" is as much a civilizational abstraction as von Laue's. It is therefore susceptible to criticism on exactly the same grounds, namely that, failing to register the structuration of the modern world by *capitalism*, it can only present modernity under the sign of culture.

Even when Chinweizu refers explicitly to capitalism, his language gives the game away:

> When Europe pioneered industrial capitalism, her demands upon the resources of the world increased tremendously. In addition to obtaining spices for her tables and manpower for her mines and plantations in the Americas, Europe set out to seize for her factories the mineral and agricultural resources of all the world. Her need to take African manpower to the Americas declined. She needed instead to put African labor to work in Africa, digging up for her the riches of African mines. The trading companies that had for centuries bought and sold on Africa's coast were found inadequate for seizing and carting off the raw materials of the African hinterland. Europe now felt a need to export her power into Africa's interior to reorganize the farms, mines and markets for Europe's greater profit. Her adventurers banded together, obtained charters from their national governments, and came to seize the African markets from the African middlemen with whom for centuries Europe had been content to trade.
>
> *(1975: 35)*

In this passage "Europe" is dematerialized through personification – gendered female, racially coded "white," de-differentiated and then re-differentiated on the axis of class, so that divisions within are flattened out entirely, only to make their reappearance as a Manichean divide between "West" and "Rest." Imperialist "predation" is driven by the *personality* of "the West," its essential – hence unchangeable – *identity*. On Chinweizu's account, "Europe" is not only already "Europe" prior to "her" "pioneering" of capitalist modernity, "she" is always-already "Europe."

Perhaps it is too easy to criticize Chinweizu. After all, his work is so patently reactionary, so transparently reductive in its methodology and essentialist in its assumptions, as to have hardly any serious intellectual adherents today. But consider then some of the recent writings of Ngugi wa Thiong'o, unquestionably a great novelist, and the very celebrated proponent, besides, of a hugely influential argument as to the essential – that is to say, foundational and ineradicable – alienness of European languages to African culture (Ngugi 1987). Recently, Ngugi has written:

Over the last four hundred years we have seen Africans in the West lose their names completely so that our existence is in terms of Jones, James, Jones, and Janes [*sic*]. Now every achievement in sports, in academia, in the sciences and the arts goes to reinforce European naming systems and cultural personality. Language is of course the most basic of naming systems. With the loss of our languages will come the loss of our entire naming system and every historical intervention no matter how revolutionary will thence be within an European naming system, enhancing its capacities for ill or good. Thus in whatever she or he does, they will be performing their being for the enrichment of the cultural personality of white Europe.
(2000: 8)

"The West" as "the imagined home of history's victors"; "the West" as "the embodiment of their power" (I return to Coronil's suggestive formulation): for Ngugi, "the West" (a locus, a "white" people, a geopolitical imperative) "has" (in the sense of "is endowed with") a "cultural personality" (a fixed disposition, a programmatic way of "performing its being"). The essentialism of the conception is abundantly clear – and is remarkable only insofar as its active denial of the historicality of social forms seems so obviously to contradict Ngugi's self-identification as a Marxist. But I am struck also by the fact that although Ngugi situates his narrative of conflicting cultural personalities within a temporal register ("Over the last four hundred years ..."), he fails to mark the historical specificity of this time frame. The central process identified in his historical narrative is that of the slow death of African selfhood, its subordination to the civilizational logic of "the West." Capitalism and colonialism feature in this narrative only as aspects of "the West's" "cultural personality" – and therefore as traces of "Westernization" – not as the total social forms in which and through which diverse "Western" powers arrayed themselves before and projected themselves onto "non-Western" polities and peoples. Ngugi cannot in general be accused of neglecting the material basis upon which Eurocentric thought has rested. But is this not demonstrably the tendency of his discourse, when, as here, he speaks of the "cultural death" of Africans in the imperialist era, or when, elsewhere (1987: 3), he maintains that what he calls "the cultural bomb" – whose

53

"intended results are despair, despondency and a collective death-wish" – is "the biggest weapon wielded and actually daily unleashed by imperialism against [the colonized population's] collective defiance"?

One cannot hope to displace or overturn Eurocentric reason by inversion, not least since such a strategy merely replicates, rather than challenges, the thoroughgoing essentialism of the dominant optic. What I have been trying to suggest in addition, however, is that, to the degree that Eurocentrism both derives from and helps to produce and legitimize imperialist power, it is vital in developing anti-Eurocentric theory to "get *imperialism* right," that is, to understand what imperialism is and how it works. And here, it seems to me, the weaknesses of the arguments and theories we have been examining thus far are exemplary, for they point to the adverse consequences that follow from the bracketing, displacement, or euphemization of the specific agency of capitalist social relations in imperialist development. Such bracketing, displacement, and euphemization are easy to detect in cultural nationalist discourse, perhaps – even, as in the case of Ngugi, where they derive from avowedly Marxist premises. But it is my conviction that they are a pervasive feature also of much of the best, and certainly the most influential, work currently being carried out in postcolonial studies.

III

In such texts as Said's magisterial *Orientalism* and Chandra Talpade Mohanty's widely read and frequently anthologized essay, "Under Western Eyes: Feminist Scholarship and Colonial Discourses," for instance, the category of "the West" comes to stand in for imperialist power; but since what is thus named is preeminently a civilizational value rather than a mode of production or a social formation, this alibi of "the West" serves to dematerialize what it tacitly references. In the case of Said, consider again a key formulation from *Orientalism*, already referred to above. Orientalism, Said writes, is "the corporate institution for dealing with the Orient – dealing with it by making statements about it, authorizing views of it, describing it, by teaching it settling it, ruling over it" (1979: 3). So far, brilliant: comprehensive, succinct, superbly realized. But Said continues: "in short, Orientalism as a Western style for dominating, restructuring, and having authority over the Orient." This evocation of a "Western style" has long puzzled me. What exactly does it mean? I take it that one of Said's intentions in *Orientalism* is to demonstrate that the notion of "the West" was given form, consolidated, sedimented, and institutionalized through the processes of conquering, dominating, administering, and governing "the Orient." Within the historical context of modernity, that is to say, "the West" was as much an effect of imperialist practice and theory as was "the East"; it was the self (or the conception of self) that was constituted not so much through the imperial powers' material subjection of African, Asian, Australasian, and American peoples as through their otherizing of them. "The West" is the name by which the authors of this process of otherization came to identify their provenance and to legitimize and justify their practice.

But this, of course, is to situate the concept of "the West" precisely *within* Orientalist discourse, and to render it unusable by any putatively post-Orientalist criticism – at least until it had been refunctioned or deconstructed. (I am thinking, here, of Robert Young's argument [1990: 19] that "[i]f one had to answer, therefore, the general question of what is deconstruction a deconstruction of, the answer would be, of the concept, the authority, and assumed primacy of, the category of 'the West.'") The problem, however, is that no refunctioning of the concepts of "Europe" or "the West" is attempted in *Orientalism*. On the contrary, despite having compellingly demonstrated the ideological character of these concepts, Said proceeds to use them relatively unselfconsciously throughout his study. It is not, of course, that Said's own use of the concepts of "Europe" and "the West" is susceptible to the charge of being Orientalist. My suggestion, rather, is that the dematerialization and abstraction inherent in the Orientalist conceptions carries over into Said's own discourse – as when, for instance, in the sentence that follows the formulation we have been considering, he refers to "the enormously systematic discipline by which European culture was able to manage – and even produce – the Orient politically, sociologically, militarily, ideologically, scientifically, and imaginatively during the post-Enlightenment period" (3). "European culture" as the agent of this process? It seems to me that both terms, "European" and "culture," are inadequate here. As Samir Amin has argued,

the critique of Orientalism that Edward Said has produced has the fault of not having gone far enough in certain respects, and having gone too far in others. Not far enough to the extent that Said is content with denouncing Eurocentric prejudice without positively proposing another system of explanation for facts which must be accounted for. Too far, to the extent that he suggests that the vision of Europeans was already Eurocentric in the Middle Ages. *(1989: 101–02)*

Might we ask what Said gains by his description of Orientalist theory and practice as "Western"? Specifically, do Orientalist theory and practice warrant our criticism and refutation because they are *"European"* (*"Western"*) or because they are *Eurocentric*? Pace Chinweizu or even Ngugi, one would not, I think, presume in general today to describe a body of thought or an ensemble of practices as "white." Why "Western," then? What analytical work does this term do? What terms are *not* specified because the terms "Western" or "European" *are* specified in Said's analysis? Recall, if you will, Ahmad's critique of the concept "Third World," a term, he writes, which,

even in its most telling deployments, [is] a polemical one, with no theoretical status whatsoever. Polemic surely has a prominent place in all human discourses, especially in the discourse of politics, so the use of this term in loose, polemical contexts is altogether valid. But to lift it from the register of polemics and claim it as a basis for producing theoretical knowledge, which presumes a certain rigour in constructing the objects of one's knowledge, is to misconstrue not only the term itself but even the world to which it refers. *(1992: 96)*

I find it hard to exempt Said's "Western" from the force of an analogous challenge. And what is true of *Orientalism* is true, too, *mutatis mutandis*, of Mohanty's "Under Western Eyes," in which the modifier "Western" is used to purely rhetorical ends – there is no plausible analytical justification for its deployment – to lend support to a tendentially third worldist argument that colonial domination inheres in "Western" thought and practice.

There is a contradiction between two lines of argument in "Under Western Eyes." On the one hand, Mohanty proposes – and convincingly demonstrates – that even when it derives from avowedly feminist or otherwise progressive political premises, writing on the "third world" by scholars "who identify themselves as culturally or geographically from the 'west'" is often vitiated by "assumptions of privilege and ethnocentric universality" (1994: 199, 197). Studies that are ostensibly intended to give a voice to "third-world women," to register solidarity with them, ironically end up "[robbing] them of their historical and political *agency*" (213). Mohanty's suggestion here is that, especially when one takes into account its sociological and institutional conditions of production, the ethnocentrism such scholarship betrays cannot but be referred to a wider "colonialist discourse which exercises a very specific power in defining, coding and maintaining existing first/third-world connections" (214). At this level, Mohanty's argument is impeccably anti-essentialist. Indeed, she insists that she is "not making a culturalist argument about ethnocentrism." Not all "Western" feminists are ethnocentrically universalist – Maria Mies is cited as one who is not; and not all "third-world" feminists contrive to steer clear of this methodological pitfall.[2] "As a matter of fact," Mohanty writes, "my argument holds for any discourse that sets up its own authorial subjects as the implicit referent, i.e. the yardstick by which to encode and represent cultural Others" (199).

What is being described, in other words, is a scholarship that – for all its liberal or even radical pretensions – is in fact reductionist, appropriative, colonizing. (Mohanty uses all three terms.) But this is precisely where a second, and discrepant, line of argument enters the frame of "Under Western Eyes." For having produced her excellent analysis of how the feminist writing under review functions to "discursively colonize the material and historical heterogeneities of the lives of women in the third world" (197), Mohanty then moves to identify this writing through reference not to its ideological character or disposition, but to its geographical provenance. The word "Western" is used on literally dozens of occasions in the essay (thirty times in the first five pages, for instance, another twenty in the concluding three pages) to gloss, qualify, characterize and, of course, taint and disparage the feminist scholarship that provides her with her subject and critical target. We must then ask of Mohanty the same questions that we asked of Said: why "Western" rather than "Eurocentric" or even "Orientalist"? What does the term "Western" offer that the term "Eurocentric" would not? The answer, I suspect, has something to do with the fact that for all the manifest criticality and vaunted politicality of her argument, Mohanty draws no explicit ideological distinctions – as between bourgeois and socialist, for instance – whatsoever. We would be safe to infer, I think, that this is because, for her, the term "Western" and its counterpart, "third world," stand in for such distinctions. In other words, we find ourselves confronted, once again, with "the West" as alibi in the determinate absence of a plausible conceptualization of capitalism and imperialist social relations. Witness the final paragraphs of her essay, in which Mohanty rushes ahead in paradigmatically postmodernist fashion to align "Western feminist writings on women in the third world" with "humanism" (described

57

as a *"western* ideological and political project which involves the necessary recuperation of the 'East' and 'Woman' as Others") and "scientific discourse" (another *"western* ideological and political project," one must suppose?) as planks in the "latent economic and cultural colonization of the 'non-western' world" (214–16; emphasis added). Not only does the sweeping reductionism and transparent partiality of such formulations render them analytically worthless in a general sense (One could with at least equal justification and evidential basis argue that "humanism" and "science" have been decisive to "third-world" struggles *against* colonialism – does one need to do more in this respect than to refer to Fanon's exhortation of a new humanism in the concluding sentences of *The Wretched of the Earth*?[3]), but it also seems to me, more narrowly, that to refer the dominative propensities of "science" or "humanism" or ethnocentric feminism to "the West" is to insure that an understanding (and redress) of them remains systematically unavailable.

IV

In *The Philosophical Discourse of Modernity*, Jürgen Habermas refers to an "anarchist" strain in contemporary thought which does not critique the pseudo-universalism of the conventionally received theory of modernity – that is, does not argue that despite this theory's own universalistic pretensions, it has in fact been partial, Eurocentric, masculinist, and so on – but instead performs a strange double disavowal. First, it asserts that the conventional theory is the only one to have been elaborated in the modern West – that all modern Western thought has in fact been modern*ist*, Eurocentric, and rational*ist*. Then it moves, on the basis of this false inference, to disavow modernity, Europe, rationality – and behind these, of course, universalism – themselves, as all inherently imperialistic and totalitarian. For these "anarchist" theorists, Habermas writes, not just rationalist thought but reason itself – and, for the purposes of this essay, we might add: not just Eurocentric thought but Europe itself, and not just modernist thought but modernity itself – "becomes unmasked as the subordinating and at the same time itself subjugated subjectivity, as the will to instrumental mastery" (1987: 4). The misguided attempt then becomes to "pull . . . away the veil of reason [or of modernity or "the West"] from before the sheer will to power." Reason, modernity, and "the West" are construed by these "anarchist" thinkers only as so many masks over the face of domination.

Habermas has in mind here the various proponents of a revisionary Nietzscheanism in contemporary social theory, and above all Foucault. But one can readily see the applicability of his critique to leading theorists in the field of postcolonial studies, and not only because, as Harry Harootunian has recently put it, an "obsessive Foucauldianism" obtains there (2000: 46). The postmodernist address of Mohanty's conclusion to "Under Western Eyes" fits the bill perfectly, for instance, with its dematerialization of modernity, its corresponding fetishization of "the West" as the super-agent of domination in the modern world, and its totalizing and undifferentiating conceptualization of "reason," "enlightenment," "science," and "development" as nothing more than grimly functional instruments of "the West's" brutal rise to hegemony – what the eminent sociologist, Zygmunt Bauman, writing in precisely this context (1994: 10–11), has called the "new, fully operative enchantment kit" which, at the dawn of the modern age, enabled the "priests of science" to replace the "priests of God."[4]

In the field of postcolonial studies, two distinctive gestures proceed from this general fetishization of "the West." The first consists in the desire to "provincialize Europe" – that is, to dismantle Eurocentrism by demonstrating that the enabling concepts upon which it has been founded are not (or at least are not all, or are not always) "obvious" or "transparent" or "universal" or positively "true," as is invariably supposed within the Eurocentric imaginary, but are instead situated, contingent, the products of specific projects and contexts. As Dipesh Chakrabarty – who first coined the phrase, "provincializing Europe" – puts it, the object is to document and explain "how – through what historical process – [Enlightenment]...reason, which was not always self-evident to everyone, has been made to look obvious far beyond the ground where it originated" (2000: 43). The second gesture, closely related to the first, consists in the argument that, within the problematic of "modernity," there is no space or act or utterance which is not Eurocentric. The argument is that it is necessary to break with all the traditions of modern thought in order to break with their Eurocentrism, for modern thought is constitutively Eurocentric.

Within postcolonial studies – a field of scholarship with an *a priori* commitment to the "unthinking" of Eurocentrism (Shohat and Stam 1994) – the call to "provincialize Europe" sounds irresistible. Who in the field would *not* be in favor of "cutting Europe down to size," exposing the arrogance of Eurocentric thought and practice, doing across the board intellectually what the new, equal-area maps and atlases – which show that Britain is not the size of India and that the entire African continent cannot fit snugly into a corner of north-western Europe! – have done for our understanding of geographical space? Yet it seems to me that the way in which "Europe" has been conceptualized by the "provincializers" fatally undermines the efficacy of their critique. For in their hypostatization of "modernity" and "the West" – their dematerialization of capitalism, their misrecognition of its world-historical significance, their construal of it in civilizational terms, as "modernity" – these theorists (a representative short list might include, say, Nick Dirks, Lisa Lowe, Jan Nieerveen Pieterse, Gyan Prakash, and Tsenay Serequeberhan in addition to Chakrabarty) seem to me to render the *structurality* of the global system either arbitrary or unintelligible.[5]

What is at issue here is a radicalization of an argument initially made by Said in *Orientalism*. In his study, Said had written that so "authoritative" was Orientalist discourse during the post-Enlightenment period, that "no one writing, thinking, or acting on the Orient could do so without taking account of the limitations on thought and action imposed by [it]" (1979: 3). Technically, at least – and irrespective of the position that Said himself actually took up in *Orientalism* (about which there has been much disagreement) – there is an important difference between this claim and a further claim that *all discourse on "the Orient" is Orientalist*, that is, that Orientalism is the necessary ground and tendency of all such discourse. Yet it is this latter claim that one typically encounters in postcolonial theory today, whether in reductionist postmodernist theses about the Eurocentric absolutism of modern thought *in toto*, or in Chakrabarty's more sophisticated thesis (2000) concerning the constitutive Eurocentrism of history and, by implication, of all modern discourses of society.

Central to these lines of argument is a genealogical placement of Marx as a nineteenth-century thinker "without remainder" – that is, a thinker whose deepest conceptions were at one with those of all the other thinkers of his time – and a corresponding dismissal of all Marxist claims to provide a "total" critique of capitalist society. These impulses derive their imprimatur, of course, from Foucault's snide and venomous statement to the effect that "Marxism exists in nineteenth century thought like a fish in water: that is, it is unable to breathe anywhere else" (1973: 262). But it is worth registering their sheer ubiquity in postcolonial theory today. Witness Robert Young, who argues that "Marxism, as a body of knowledge itself remains complicit with, and even extends, the system to which it is opposed . . .

Marxism's standing Hegel on his head[6] may have reversed his idealism, but it did not change the mode of operation of a conceptual system which remains collusively Eurocentric" (1990: 3); or Tsenay Serequeberhan, who reads Marx as "triumphantly celebrating" the "globalization of Europe" in the opening pages of the *Communist Manifesto* and then goes on to propose that for Kant, Hegel, and Marx, "no matter how differently they view the historical globalization of Europe, what matters is that European modernity is the *real* in contrast to the *unreality* of human existence in the non-European world" (1997: 143); or even Arif Dirlik, who – seeming to contradict other statements of his, which suggest the continuing cogency of Marxist critique – maintains that "historical materialism in its very structure presupposed Eurocentrism" (1994a: 23–24).

The postcolonialist disavowal of Marx and Marxism is mandated, I take it, by the need to demonstrate that there are no resources within the conceptual universe of modernity adequate to the task of unthinking Eurocentrism. Nobody supposes that Kant's thought, or Locke's, or Rousseau's, or even Tom Paine's, contains the capacity to explode the world that it itself inhabits. But different claims are often made for Marxism as, on Lukács's famous formula, the "self-knowledge of capitalist society." If it can be demonstrated that even *Marxism's* vaunted criticality is in fact a mere ratification of an overarching narrative or condition, to which it is as deeply committed as any bourgeois philosophy, then one may safely conclude, as Dirlik does, both that "the political history of Marxism has been part of the narrative of capitalism," and that "it is no longer possible to sustain convincingly that Marxism as we have known it in any serious sense points to a future that may transcend the capitalist mode of production" (1994a: 39–40).

Let us consider these views on one of their best representations – that advanced by Chakrabarty in his essay, "Postcoloniality and the Artifice of History."[7] In this essay, Chakrabarty argues that "insofar as the academic discourse of history . . . is concerned, 'Europe' remains the sovereign, theoretical subject of all histories, including the ones we call 'Indian,' 'Chinese,' 'Kenyan,' and so on. There is a peculiar way in which all these other histories tend to become variations on a master narrative that could be called 'the history of Europe'" (2000: 27). As a critique of colonialist, elitist, or Eurocentric history, this claim would be unimpeachable. But the distinctive force of Chakrabarty's argument derives from his determination to prosecute it against "history" (and "social science") *as such*. He considers that "history" and "social science" are *constitutively* Eurocentric, and, given that they are *modern* intellectual practices, cannot be anything but. From the standpoint of "history" or "social science," Chakrabarty claims, "[o]nly 'Europe' . . . is *theoretically* . . . knowable; all other histories are matters of empirical research that fleshes out a theoretical skeleton which is substantially 'Europe'" (29).

Concerning Marx and Marxism, Chakrabarty pays lip service to earlier writings in the Subaltern Studies project that had emphasized the degree to which Marx's concepts and methods break decisively with those of bourgeois science. "Marx's vision of emancipation," he concedes, "entailed a journey beyond the rule of capital, in fact beyond the notion of juridical equality that liberalism holds so sacred" (30). Yet Chakrabarty expressly relegates this fact, which for such earlier Subalternists as Ranajit Guha had been of epochal significance, to the status of a 'parenthesis.'" "Marx's methodological/epistemological statements have not always successfully resisted historicist readings. There has always remained enough ambiguity in these statements to make possible the emergence of 'Marxist' historical narratives" (31). And it seems that, for Chakrabarty, historicism and "narrativization" are in fact characteristic of Marxism as such: for the reading of Marx's writings that he produces collapses them seamlessly into Eurocentric "history":

> The coming of the bourgeois or capitalist society, Marx argues in the *Grundrisse* and elsewhere, gives rise for the first time to a history that can be apprehended through a philosophical and universal category, 'capital' . . . All past histories are now to be known (theoretically, that is) from the vantage point of this category, that is in terms of their differences from it. Things reveal their categorical essence only when they reach their fullest development, or as Marx put it in that famous aphorism of the *Grundrisse*: "Human anatomy contains the key to the anatomy of the ape." (29–30)

Thus where Marx, in his Introduction to the *Grundrisse*, had written that "[b]ourgeois society is the most developed and the most complex historic organization of production" (1993: 105), Chakrabarty chooses to read contrariwise: "For 'capital' or 'bourgeois,' I submit, read 'Europe' or 'European'," he writes, thereby simply dismissing from consideration Marx's express insistence, both that 'capital' and 'bourgeois society' are categories specifying *global* phenomena, and that history does not come to an end or "reach [its] fullest development" with capitalism but has an as-yet-unscripted future to look forward to. At this level, Chakrabarty's reading is no better than Serequeberhan's, which, confronted by Marx and Engels's studied references to "modern bourgeois society," "the epoch of the bourgeoisie," and "the bourgeoisie" in the *Communist Manifesto*, concludes, as we have already seen, that they celebrate "the globalization of *Europe*" (1997: 143; emphasis added).

In Chakrabarty's programmatic formulation, the idealist inclination to replace a concrete *ideological* specification ("bourgeois," "capitalist") with a pseudo-geographical one ("Europe," "the West") is elevated to the status of a methodological principle. Chakrabarty admits that his mobilization of the concept of "Europe" is, as he puts it, "hyperreal." "Europe" for him is the name not of a continent but of an epistemo-political imperative: this "Europe," he writes, "reified and celebrated in the phenomenal world of everyday relationships of power as the scene of the birth of the modern, continues to dominate the discourse of history" (2000: 28). Indeed, on his reading, "Europe" more than *dominates* the discourse of history. There is no historical discourse that is not centered on this "Europe."

But against Chakrabarty and Serequeberhan, I want to insist that not all historical narrativization is teleological or "historicist," and that at least one crucial modern narrative of modernity – the Marxist one – does *not* "point to a certain 'Europe' as the primary habitus of the modern." In calling for the "provincialization" of Europe, Chakrabarty fails to accord the instance of capitalism *within* modernity due centrality. But he also fails to reckon with the unprecedentedness, the *difference* of (capitalist) modernity from all previous universalizing projects. The critique elaborated by Chakrabarty and those aligned with him is directed against a progressivist conception of modernity – one that privileges "the West" and views the "non-West" as its non-modern remainder. But this critique wrongly assumes the internality of Marxism to "modernist" narratives of modernity. It sits very poorly, therefore, with Marx's paradigmatic insistence on the globality of capitalism as an historical formation. This is a point that Marxists need to emphasize strongly in their ongoing contestation of the prevailing concepts in postcolonial studies.

NOTES

1 Actually, Dirlik misreads Huntington when he writes that Huntington "proposes a fortress EuroAmerica to defend Western civilization against the intrusion of *unmodernizable* and unassimilable Others" (emphasis added). Huntington does not deny the "modernizability" of non-Western civilizations. On the contrary, he insists that they *have*

modernized. This is precisely his point: for their modernization does not proceed along the path of Westernization. This is what licenses his view that non-Western civilizations are unassimilable to Western civilization.

2 What she says about the "presuppositions or implicit principles" of ethnocentric "western feminists," Mohanty writes, also "holds for anyone who uses these analytical strategies, whether third-world women in the west, or third-world women in the third world writing on these issues and publishing in the west" (1995: 199). The elaborate specification begs the further question: what about third-world women in the third world writing on these issues and publishing *in the third world*? I cannot tell whether Mohanty wishes to keep open the idea of an uncontaminated space somewhere beyond the reach of what she terms "the hegemony of western scholarship" (198).

3 "For Europe, for ourselves, and for humanity, comrades, we must turn over a new leaf, we must work out new concepts, and try to set afoot a new man" (Fanon 1968: 316).

4 Elsewhere, Bauman debunks modernity as a "locally conceived" conception – specifically, European – "which in its global hubris and ecumenical ambition" laid unwarranted claim to the status of universality (Bauman 1995: 144).

5 I have developed my critique of Chakrabarty more fully in Lazarus 1999b. See also Dirlik 1999, Dussel 1998, and Harootunian 2000, all of whom offer materialist critiques of Eurocentrism while continuing to insist on the paramount centrality of capitalism to any history of the past five hundred years.

6 Marx actually wrote that he was standing Hegel right side up, of course! With Hegel, he wrote, the dialectic "is standing on its head. It must be inverted to discover the rational kernel within the mystical shell" (Marx 1990: 103).

7 First published in *Representations* 37 in 1992, this essay has been reprinted in *Provincializing Europe* (2000).

4

The Eurocentric Marx and Engels
and other related myths

August Nimtz

Europe's failed revolutions of 1848–49 were followed by a decade-long lull in the class struggle. Karl Marx and Frederick Engels, like others who had been brought into active politics during those two momentous years, were always on the look out for new revolutionary initiatives – a posture that could sometimes lead to wishful thinking. When developments in Russia at the end of 1858 suggested that the revival might begin there and then spread to Western Europe, Marx, writing from London to his comrade in Manchester, advised caution this time. Given capitalism's still ascendant trajectory in other areas of the world, such a revival might "be crushed in this little corner of the earth" (Marx-Engels 1975a, *40*: 347).[1] The fate of the revolutionary process in Western Europe was not only dependent now on developments elsewhere but its own weight in that process had diminished. Contrary, then, to what has come to be a staple in much of the literature, Marx and Engels, at least by 1859, had begun to look beyond the "little corner" in which they lived to the rest of the world for revolutionary initiatives.

This article disputes the charge that Marx and Engels were Eurocentric – a charge that has roots in the long-established marxological enterprise and has since been embraced by postcolonialists and postmodernists to varying degrees – and argues that they were first and foremost revolutionaries who viewed the entire globe as their theater of operations. To make my case I begin by showing how the Marx–Engels partnership began with a global perspective and then, when presented with new political opportunities in the aftermath of the post-1848–49 lull, sought to realize their vision. Along the way I challenge two related myths: "England as the model" and "Marx against the peasantry." Rather than England, I argue that they looked

increasingly, certainly after 1870, to Russia as the revolutionary vanguard, an overwhelmingly peasant country that had only one foot in
Europe and not the Europe that the Eurocentric charge refers to, that
is, its most developed western flank. Lastly, I speculate briefly about
what they might say about today's political reality.

Communism – a "world-historical" process

Long before 1858, Marx and Engels had looked beyond their "little corner" in explaining and making political judgments about the revolutionary process. Though Hegel's philosophy of world history no doubt
prepared them to think globally, it was when they became conscious
communists and formed their revolutionary partnership in 1844 that
they concretized their own position. In *The German Ideology*, where
they presented for the first time their "new world view," i.e., the "materialist conception of history," they argued that only with the "universal
development of productive forces" would it be possible for "a *universal*
intercourse between men [to be] established . . . making each nation
dependent on the revolution of others, and finally [putting] *world-
historical*, empirically universal individuals in place of local ones."
Thus, "communism . . . can only have a 'world-historical' existence"
(5: 49). Shortly afterwards, this and other fundamental premises of
their new perspective would find their way into the *Manifesto of
the Communist Party*. The draft from which Marx worked, Engels's
catechized "Principles of Communism," was more explicit. To the
question, "Will it be possible for this revolution to take place in one
country alone?" the reply is: "No . . . It is a worldwide revolution and
will therefore be worldwide in scope" (6: 351–52).[2] Written on the
eve of the 1848–49 revolutions, Marx and Engels clearly understood
that only the "real movement" could provide the actual answer to
the question. Nevertheless, the global orientation with which they entered those upheavals served as their frame of reference in making
political assessments along the way.

Within a couple of weeks of the *Manifesto*'s publication, the long-
anticipated revolutions of 1848–49 began. For present purposes, the
most significant aspect of Marx and Engels's very rich and instructive practice in those events over the course of fifteen months is that
they gave active support to national liberation struggles, particularly
those of the Poles, Hungarians, and Italians. By the end of 1848, they
had concluded that the fate of the German revolution was linked to
the successful outcome of a worldwide revolutionary process that

combined national liberation, anti-feudal and anti-capitalist struggles "waged in Canada as in Italy, in East Indies as in Prussia, in Africa as on the Danube" (*8*: 215).[3] In the relative calm of London and the British Museum in 1849–50 they undertook research that allowed them to strengthen this judgment. Their findings made clear that the world's economic center had by then shifted from Western Europe to the United States. "The most important thing to have occurred [in America], more important even than the February [1848] Revolution, is the discovery of the California gold-mines.... [As a result the] centre of gravity of world commerce, Italy in the Middle Ages, England in modern times, is now the southern half of the North American peninsula ... [T]he Pacific Ocean will have the same role as the Atlantic has now and the Mediterranean had in antiquity and in the Middle Ages – that of the great water highway of world commerce" (*10*: 265–66).

This assessment, apparently the first ever made,[4] would have, they predicted, further revolutionary implications for the peoples of Asia, especially the Chinese. News of the Taiping Rebellion in 1850, the result in part of British commercial penetration into coastal areas, suggested that "the oldest and least perturbable kingdom on earth [was on] the eve of a social upheaval, which, in any event, is bound to have the most significant results for civilisation" (*10*: 267). Marx and Engels could barely conceal their joy about the possibility of a bourgeois democratic revolution in China and the world-shaking repercussions it would have. If Western Europe had once been at the center of their worldview, this was certainly no longer true after 1850. Their global orientation allowed them to see clearly beyond "this little corner of the earth" without a hint of nostalgia.

Marx and Engels's practice during the revolutions reveals their actual position on the peasant question. When the first revolutionary outbreak occurred in Germany in March 1848, they quickly supplemented the *Manifesto* with an addendum which addressed the issue explicitly. (The *Manifesto*'s failure to cover this subject is often taken to justify the widely held misperception that they discounted the peasantry.[5]) The oft-ignored document, the *Demands of the Communist Party of Germany*, basically a program for a bourgeois democratic revolution in Germany, spoke to the immediate needs of the peasantry – an ending of all feudal obligations and a radical land reform. The program informed Marx and Engels's practice throughout the course of their involvement in the upheavals, especially their ceaseless – but in the end unsuccessful – efforts to forge a worker–peasant alliance. This perspective forever informed their revolutionary strategy and tactics, especially for countries in which the social and political weight of the peasantry was decisive (Nimtz 2000). During the Paris Commune in 1871 (about which I shall have more to say later), for example, Marx did all he could from afar to convince its leadership that the insurgency's survival depended on getting the support of the peasantry. After his death, it fell to Engels in 1894 to write the most comprehensive programmatic statement that they ever produced on the subject, *The Peasant Question in France and Germany*.

The failure of the 1848 revolutions allowed Marx and Engels to give more detailed attention to developments beyond Europe. Three settings are instructive for our purposes here, Algeria, India, and Mexico. Regarding the first, a month before the *Manifesto* was published Engels applauded the French conquest of Algeria and defeat of the uprising led by the religious leader Abd-el Kader saying that it was "an important and fortunate fact for the progress of civilization" (6: 471). Nine years later in 1857 he had completely reversed his stance and now severely denounced French colonial rule and expressed sympathy for religious-led Arab resistance to the imperial power (18: 67–69). Their historical materialist perspective explains Engels's initial position. However, the real movement of history, especially the lessons of 1848, had taught that, however progressive French imperialism may have been prior to then, it had outworn its usefulness; the opposition of the colonial subjects was now the movement to be supported. Shortly before his death in 1883, Marx visited Algeria in the hope that its climate would improve his health. A comment to his daughter Laura about the situation of the colonized reveals that his identification with them as fellow fighters had not waned: "they will go to rack and ruin without a revolutionary movement" (46: 242).[6]

Marx's first sustained writing on India strikes a similar tone to that sounded by Engels about Algeria in 1848. He described in 1853 England's undermining of local industries and social structures as "causing a social revolution," however "sickening . . . it must be to human feeling to witness" the effects of such policies (12: 132). But by the time of the Sepoy Mutiny against British rule in 1857–59, Marx and Engels's sympathy for the anticolonial struggle was unquestionable. As Marx told his partner: "In view of the DRAIN OF MEN and BULLION which she will cost the English, India is now our best ally" (40: 249).[7] For both of them, therefore, the uprisings in these countries were exactly what Marx had forecast at the end of 1848 about the global interdependency of the revolutionary movement. Later in

1871, the International Working Men's Association, which Marx effectively headed, reported that a request had come to it from Calcutta to establish a branch of the body in the city. The secretary for the organization's executive committee in London, the General Council, "was instructed ... to urge the necessity of enrolling natives in the Association," thus making clear that the new affiliate was not to be an exclusively expatriate branch (*General Council* 1974: 258).

Finally, there is the case of Mexico. For Engels in 1849 the US conquest of Northern Mexico was "waged wholly and solely in the interest of civilisation," particularly because the "energetic Yankees" – unlike the "lazy Mexicans" – would bring about the "rapid exploitation of the California gold mines" and, hence, for the "third time in history give world trade a new direction" (8: 365).[8] Subsequent history and research forced them to qualify this assessment. With the US Civil Wars looming, Marx wrote in 1861 that in "the foreign, as in domestic, policy of the United States, the interests of the slaveholders served as the guiding star." The seizure of Northern Mexico had in fact made it possible to "impose slavery and with it the rule of the slaveholders" not only in Texas but later in present-day New Mexico and Arizona (**19**: 36–37).[9] The benefits that came with California were compromised by the "barbarity" of slavery's extension.

One of the alleged problems with Marxism and one to which Marx himself succumbed, according to Stuart Hall, is its "Eurocentric take" on the "origins of capitalism as organically growing out of feudalism... peacefully evolving out of the womb of feudalism." This view, says Hall, is belied by the experiences of anyone "from anywhere in the periphery of the capitalist system" (Terry 1995: 56–57). For Hall, of course, the problem is symptomatic of the limitations of what he and others often call "classical Marxism" – in this instance, apparently, the fact that "Marx took [England] as his paradigm case in *Capital*" (Hall 1986: 15). While it is not exactly clear what Hall is getting at he seems to suggest that however "peaceful" the European origins of capitalism might have been, this was definitely not the case with what would later be called the periphery. This is an odd criticism since Hall certainly knows what Marx wrote in *Capital* about the emergence of capitalism in the center, especially England, let alone the periphery: Marx's chapter, "The Genesis of the Industrial Capitalist," with its famous last sentence, "capital comes [into the world] dripping from head to toe, from every pore, with blood and dirt," indicted a process that was no less horrible in the center than in the periphery.

A new revolutionary era

From their global posture, Marx and Engels were predisposed to look for revolutionary initiatives beyond Western Europe. Hence they concluded in the beginning of 1863 that "the era of revolution has now fairly opened in Europe once more" (41: 453). The basis for this judgment was the peasant uprising in Poland that year; thus, "the lava will flow from East to West." However, even before then other signs had already appeared on the political horizon that gave cause for optimism. At the beginning of 1860, Marx declared "that the most momentous thing happening in the world today is the slave movement – on the one hand, in America, started by the death of Brown, and in Russia, on the other" (41: 4, 7). He was referring, of course, to the abortive rebellion of the abolitionist John Brown at Harper's Ferry, Virginia, a few months earlier, which in turn had stimulated at least one slave uprising in its aftermath. As for Russia – the "lava from the East" – its "slaves," i.e., serfs, had since 1858 also been on the march for emancipation. A year later, in a move to preempt a revolt from below, the Czar abolished serfdom. Because Marx and Engels viewed the class struggle globally they gave more weight to the conjuncture of struggles in various countries than to isolated ones. The fight against slavery and other precapitalist modes of exploitation was obviously key in labor's struggle against capital. In his preface to *Capital*, written seven years later and after the Civil War, Marx would be even more explicit: "As in the eighteenth century, the American War of independence sounded the tocsin for the European middle class, so in the nineteenth century, the American Civil War sounded it for the European working class." Political reality had revealed by 1867 that of the two "slave movements" in 1860, the one on the other side of the Atlantic was more decisive. Six decades later, however, in 1917, "the lava [would] flow from East to West."

With the determination that a new revolutionary era had opened, Marx and Engels were primed to return to active politics when the opportunity presented itself. In 1864, at an international meeting of trade unionists in London, Marx was invited to represent the German movement, and soon emerged as the guiding force in what came to be called the International Working Men's Association (IWMA), or First International – the first truly international proletarian organization. Though the International's influence and legacy was enormous, it came to an effective end in 1873. A major reason was ruling-class attacks against it for its well-known support, with Marx leading the way, for the Paris Commune of 1871. An important casualty of this campaign was the participation of English trade-union officials in the organization's leadership body, the General Council, based in London. Their departure is instructive and reveals how Marx and Engels reassessed the revolutionary potential of the English working class.

More than a year before the Paris Commune, Marx commented to Engels on the prospects for revolution: "I am firmly convinced that although the first blow will come from France, Germany is far riper for a social movement, and will grow far over the heads of the French" (*43*: 429). While the "first blow" did indeed come from France in the form of the Commune, Marx and Engels were still convinced that the axis of world revolution had moved east of Paris. Implicit in their view was a downgrading of the importance of the English movement. They indeed had once looked to the latter as the vanguard of the workers' movement owing to the advanced character of capitalism in England and the existence of a genuine workers' party, the Chartists. What explains, therefore, their reevaluation of the English movement?

As early as 1858 Engels began to have second thoughts about the revolutionary potential of England. When the Chartist leader Ernest Jones sought to maneuver with the liberal bourgeoisie by watering down the historical demands of the Chartist program, Engels wrote that it was symptomatic of "the fact that the English proletariat is actually becoming more and more bourgeois." He then offered an explanation: "In the case of a nation which exploits the entire world this is, of course, justified to some extent" (*40*: 344). The booty of British imperialism had begun to compromise England's workers. It was exactly this point that Marx responded to in his comment that the revolutionary movement might be "CRUSHED in this little corner of the earth" because capitalism, with Britain in the lead, was still "ascendant" globally.

The English trade-union leaders who were instrumental in the International's foundation came almost exclusively from the building trades, and skilled crafts. The latter, in particular, were mainly concerned about their survival in the face of industrial capitalism. Both the building trades' and skilled crafts' officialdom were motivated to participate in the IWMA on the basis of narrow economic and political interests and not proletarian internationalism.[10] In his *Inaugural Address* for the IWMA, Marx had alluded to the stratification in the English working class by noting that "a minority [had gotten] their real wages somewhat advanced" during the unprecedented expansion of British capitalism in the third quarter of the nineteenth century. The political repercussions of these differences within the working class would only become clear in the course of the IWMA's experience in England. More than anything it was the suffrage question and electoral politics that first revealed to Marx the reality of the trade unionists' participation on the General Council (GC), specifically, their decision to block with British liberals – in contravention of GC policy – in the electoral arena to support household instead of universal male suffrage.

If the trade unionists on the GC had sold out the English working class on the suffrage issue, Marx made sure that they would not be able to do the same on the Irish question. His strategy was to craft a GC policy position which made clear that the IWMA's support of the recently jailed Fenian prisoners and Irish self-determination was unequivocal while attempting, at the same time, to drive a wedge between the trade unionists and the liberal Gladstone government. If Marx's resolution on the Irish question was difficult for the trade unionists to swallow, his now famous homage to the Communards, *Civil War in France*, proved to be indigestible. Their disagreement with its line forced those who were still formally members of the GC to completely sever their ties with the IWMA. Under pressure from their liberal allies they chose to distance themselves from the fallen Communards and Marx's uncompromising defense of them. Whatever hopes, therefore, Marx and Engels had once pinned on the English movement had clearly been dispelled by the reaction of their leaders to the demise of the Commune.

At The Hague in 1872, effectively the last congress of the IWMA, Marx left little doubt about what he thought of the trade-union leaders. When one of them questioned the credentials of one of the delegates with the charge that he didn't represent English workers, Marx retorted: "it does credit to [him] that he is not one of the so-called leaders of the English workers, since these men are more or less bribed by the bourgeoisie and the government" (*Documents* 1978: 124). Although his widely publicized remarks led to a complete rupture with the reformists, Marx was still unapologetic two years later: "I knew that I was letting myself in for unpopularity, slander, etc., but such consequences have always been a matter of indifference to me. Here and there people are beginning to see that in making that denunciation I was only doing my duty" (45: 18).[11]

In an analysis of the parliamentary elections in 1874 Engels returned to the point that he and Marx had raised in 1858 to explain the political backwardness of English workers. "This is understandable in a country in which the working class has shared more than anywhere else in the advantages of the immense expansion of its large-scale industry. Nor could it have been otherwise in an England that rules the world market" (**23**: 613).[12] While politics was also determinant – the willingness of the ruling class to grant the historical demands of the Chartists was particularly important – the impact of imperialism on the consciousness of English workers was still for Engels, as late as 1883, decisive. "Participation in the domination of the world market was and is the economic basis of the English workers' political nullity" (**47**: 55). Only when the world monopoly of Britain's rulers would be challenged by competitors, with the resulting diminution of the booty, would English workers begin to move. Contrary, therefore, to the standard marxological portrait, Marx and Engels had long abandoned – at least by 1871 – their earlier optimism about the exemplary role of English workers.

In no place was the reality of British imperialism and its domestic repercussions clearer than in its continuing subjugation of the Irish people. Marx's comment in 1869 that the "English working class... will never be able to do anything decisive here in England before they separate their attitude towards Ireland...from that of the ruling classes" (**43**: 390) is as relevant today as then. The comment, in fact, represented a key shift in his and Engels's strategy for the Irish movement for self-determination. Prior to then they had held that the overthrow of capital in England was the precondition for Ireland's liberation. Implicit in this stance was the assumption that the Irish struggle should take its lead from that of the English workers. But the initiatives taken by the Fenians in 1867 forced them to reconsider this assessment.

The relegation of Ireland to a giant farm to meet England's food needs was the fundamental reason for the revision Marx made in his political stance; the process gave England's landlord class a new lease on life with all the resulting negative social and political effects – in effect, the first detailed analysis of a process that would be generalized throughout the world, the phenomenon of underdevelopment. It was in response to the landlordism factor, more than any other, that Marx would write to Engels in 1869: "The lever must be applied in Ireland." As he observed: "quite apart from international justice, it is a *precondition to the emancipation of the English working class* to transform the present *forced union* (i.e., the enslavement of Ireland) into *equal and free confederation*, if possible, into *complete separation* if need be" (*43*: 390). This revised view became the basis for the positions the GC took on the amnesty campaign for the Fenian prisoners that year.

The Russians in the vanguard

Just as Marx and Engels were concluding that the English working class was not "the model," they were beginning, not coincidentally, to look further eastward – to Russia. Proposing in 1863 that a new revolutionary era had begun they pointed to the peasant movement then under way in Polish Russia. But it would take about seven years before they made direct contact with Russia's nascent revolutionary movement. In the meantime, and symptomatic of developments there, revolutionaries in Moscow took the initiative in 1872 to have *Capital* published in Russian, its first translation into another language.

To gain a better appreciation of Russia's importance Marx began in early 1870 to learn Russian. "He has begun," according to his wife, "studying Russian as if it were a matter of life and death" (Rubel 1975: 252). After reading *The Condition of the Working Class in Russia* by N. Flerovsky, the Russian Narodnik socialist – a work that Marx described to Engels as "the most important book published since your work on the *Condition of the Working Class*" (*43*: 424) – "one feels deeply convinced that a most terrible social revolution... is irrepressible in Russia and near at hand. This is good news. Russia and England are the two great pillars of the present European system. All the rest is of secondary importance, even *la belle France et la savante Allemagne*" (*43*: 450).[13] Five years later Engels accurately foresaw – though it would clearly take longer than he expected – that the social revolution in Russia would "have inevitable repercussions on Germany" (*45*: 103).[14] From this point to the very end of their lives both Marx and Engels prioritized developments in Russia, a fact ignored by almost all marxologists.

Due in part to the enormous impact that *Capital* had in Russia – the Russian edition sold better than any other – as well as his renown in connection with the IWMA, Marx was asked in March 1870 by a group of Russian émigrés in Geneva to represent them on the GC in the IWMA, thus beginning his formal links with the generation of Russian revolutionaries from whom the leadership of 1917 would emerge. It's instructive to note that the Geneva exiles wanted Marx to be their representative because "the practical character of the movement was so similar in Germany and Russia, [and] the writings of

Marx were so generally known and appreciated by the Russian youth" (*General Council*: 220). Although the standard charge is that Marx and Engels's perspective did not address the reality of underdeveloped settings such as Russia, radicalizing Russian youth in the 1870s saw otherwise. They sought out his views on the prospects and course of socialist revolution in their homeland. Specifically, would Russia have to undergo a prolonged stage of capitalist development or could it proceed directly to socialist transformation on the basis of communal property relations that prevailed in much of the countryside at that time?

Exactly because of the socio-economic changes that Russia was then undergoing, Marx was reluctant to make any categorical judgments. It was in his letter to a group of Russian revolutionary democrats in 1877 that he made his oft-cited warning against turning his "historical sketch of the genesis of capitalism in Western Europe [in *Capital*] into a historical-philosophical theory of general development, imposed by fate on all peoples, whatever the historical circumstances in which they are placed" (*24*: 200). What he was willing at that time to say about Russia was that if it "continues along the path it has followed since 1861, it will miss the finest chance that history has ever offered to a nation, only to undergo all the fatal vicissitudes of the capitalist system" (*24*: 200).

When Vera Zasulich, one of the founders of the Marx party in Russia, asked him in 1881 whether the Russian peasant commune could survive in the face of the ever-expanding capitalist mode of production, Marx was again cautious. In order for it to be saved and be the basis for socialist property relations, "it would first be necessary to eliminate the deleterious influences which are assailing it from all sides" (*24*: 359); in other words, as one of the drafts of his letter put it, "to save the Russian commune, a Russian revolution is needed" (*24*: 371). The drafts upon which this reply was based went into far greater detail on the peasant question and revealed how closely Marx had been following developments in Russia, especially on rural social relations.

As for the politics and strategy of socialist revolution in Russia, it was Engels who first predicted what would be involved. Rejecting the Blanquist view that the Russian peasant was "instinctively revolutionary," he warned against "a premature attempt at insurrection" since "Russia undoubtedly is on the eve of a revolution." He provided a most accurate sketch of what did in fact occur, if significantly later than he expected:

... a growing recognition among the enlightened strata of the nation concentrated in the capital that ... a revolution is impending, and the illusion that it will be possible to guide this revolution among a smooth constitutional channel. Here all the conditions of a revolution are combined, of a revolution that, started by the upper classes of the capital, perhaps even by the government itself, must be rapidly carried further, beyond the first constitutional phase, by the peasants, of a revolution that will be of the greatest importance for the whole of Europe.   *(24: 50)*

Marx saw a similar scenario and when the Russo-Turkish War broke out in 1877 both he and Engels thought it would precipitate Russia's social revolution. They got the algebra if not the mathematics right – it would indeed be a war, the Russo-Japanese War of 1905 that would initiate the developments leading up to 1917. Both Marx and Engels also held that the opening of the social revolution in Russia would spread westward, leading to *"radical change throughout Europe"* (45: 296). In fact, the "overthrow of Tsarist Russia ... is ... one of the first conditions of the German proletariat's ultimate triumph" (24: 103). To a close party member in Germany in 1882 Engels counseled that the next international should only be formed when the moment was right:

such events are already taking shape in Russia where the avant-garde of the revolution will be going into battle. You should – or so we think – wait for this and its inevitable repercussions on Germany, and then the moment will also have come for a big manifesto and the establishment of an *official*, formal International, which can, however, no longer be a propaganda association but simply an association for action.   *(46: 198)*

This was most prophetic since it was indeed the Russian Revolution in 1917 that led to the formation in 1919 of the Third or Communist International which proudly proclaimed its adherence to Marx's program.

Finally, in the "Preface" to the second Russian edition of the *Manifesto* in 1882 Marx and Engels wrote that "Russia forms the vanguard of revolutionary action in Europe." To the end of his life, which was only fifteen months away, Marx continued to devote his attention to the peasant question in Russia – the same subject to which the young Lenin addressed his initial research.[15] After Marx's death, Engels continued to believe that the ingredients existed for Russia to play a vanguard role in the revolutionary process. Hence, the beginning of regular correspondence and contact with Zasulich, Plekhanov, and other leaders of the recently formed Emancipation of Labor group, the first explicitly Russian Marxist organization. As he and Marx had earlier noted, the seriousness with which the Russians took their writings was exceptional. They sought his views on the key theoretical issue that Marx had earlier been asked to address – whether Russia could bypass capitalist development and proceed directly to socialism based on the common ownership of property of the traditional peasant commune. There were of course enormous political implications to this most vital question.

Engels returned to the subject of Russia in 1894, almost a decade and a half after he and Marx had last thoroughly discussed it. Russia's development in the intervening years, he observed, had been decidedly capitalist and the "proletarianisation of a large proportion of the peasantry and the decay of the old communistic commune proceeds at an ever quickening pace." Whether enough of the traditional communes remained for a "point of departure for communistic development," Engels could not say:

> But this much is certain: if a remnant of this commune is to be preserved, the first condition is the fall of tsarist despotism – revolution in Russia. This will not only tear the great mass of the nation, the peasants away from the isolation of their villages ... and lead them out onto the great stage ... it will also give the labour movement of the West fresh impetus and create new, better conditions in which to carry on the struggle, thus hastening the victory of the modern industrial proletariat, without which present-day Russia can never achieve a socialist transformation, whether proceeding from the commune or from capitalism. (27: 433)

Thus, indisputably, and contrary to all of the future Stalinist distortions of Marx and Engels's views, Russia could "never achieve a socialist transformation" *without* the overthrow of the bourgeoisie in Western Europe by its own proletariat. Russia would not only be the "impetus" for the socialist revolution in the West, but its own revolution was inextricably linked to that outcome. This forecast would be profoundly and tragically confirmed by subsequent history.

The Russian case reveals unequivocally, therefore, that Marx and Engels could be as programmatically at home in an overwhelmingly peasant country, characterized by extremely uneven and combined development, in transition from one mode of production to another, as in the more industrialized social formations of Western Europe – doing, in other words, everything that "classical Marxism" is incapable of doing according to postcolonial and postmodernist critics. Such fables can persist as long as the real Marx and Engels – their writings, pronouncements, and actions in their entirety and not just what academics or others who might have spoken in their names afterwards have designated as their canon or "classics" – are ignored.[16]

Conclusion

Engels's very prescient observation in 1894 that socialist transformation in Russia could not be achieved without the overthrow of the bourgeoisie in the advanced capitalist countries of Western Europe is worth revisiting. It was consistent with everything that he and his partner had argued from the very beginning of their endeavor: the revolutionary process is a "world-historical" event. The Russian Revolution of 1917, arguably the most influential event of the twentieth century, appears to have embodied in both its glory and agony exactly what Engels was getting at. While it might be possible to overturn capitalist relations of production in one country, to advance beyond that point to socialist transformation required revolutionary transformation in more advanced capitalist countries. That didn't happen and therein lies the explanation for the retrogressions that increasingly unfolded in the aftermath of the 1917 revolution (Nimtz 1993).

The Irish case had similar lessons. In revising their view about the direction of the revolutionary process, that is, looking to the Irish nationalists rather than the English working class for initiatives, Marx and Engels were under no illusion that developments in England were irrelevant. To the contrary, the success in the long run of the Irish struggle depended on whether it got a positive hearing from the producing classes in England because it was there that the material prerequisites for an egalitarian society – the basis of real self-determination – existed. But the Irish did not have to wait for the English working class to go into action; their initiative might in fact inspire England's working classes into revolutionary motion. It was also from this perspective that Marx and Engels viewed the insurgencies in Algeria and India.

If the twentieth century taught anything, it's that although a revolutionary initiative can more easily be undertaken in an underdeveloped than in an advanced social formation, it is less likely to be consummated in such a setting. In declaring as they did in 1882 that "Russia forms the vanguard of revolutionary action in Europe" Marx and Engels did not assume that socialist transformation was on the immediate agenda in an underdeveloped country like Russia. Rather, the transition would begin there through the democratic revolution but could only be consummated as a socialist revolution if it spread to a more advanced capitalist country, particularly Germany. Socialist Germany could then assist Russia in its transition. Between the Russian Revolution in October 1917 and the failure of German socialists to take power in 1923 – coming on the heels of two previous failed attempts – this seemed like a real possibility.

The conclusion that Marx reached at the end of 1848 about the global interdependency of the revolutionary process rings even truer now than then. It is worth repeating his declaration that only with the "universal development of productive forces" would it be possible for "a *universal* intercourse between men [to be] established . . . making each nation dependent on the revolution of others." What is so striking about the world in which we live today is exactly the "universal development of productive forces" which the much overused term "globalization" tries in part to capture. If it were true in 1858 that the success of the socialist revolution in the "little corner of the earth" in which Marx and Engels lived was inextricably linked to the revolutionary process elsewhere, it is all the more true today. Furthermore, their claim that socialist transformation could begin in the underdeveloped world but had to extend to advanced capitalist countries to be successful is more relevant today than ever. Evidence continues to mount that the post-WWII third-world revolutionary process, often in the name of "Marxism," may have reached an impasse that can only be resolved in the advanced capitalist world – the site of the material prerequisites. That the producers of the world today have more in common with one another than at any time in their history, and can engage in "*universal* intercourse" unlike ever before gives the final lines of the *Manifesto* a currency that they have never had: "The Proletarians have nothing to lose but their chains. They have a world to win."

NOTES

1 Hereafter, citations from the *Collected Works* will be designated by volume (as here, *40*, for example) and page number(s).
2 Though the specifics of Engels's exposition refers only to "civilised countries," that "America" is one of them makes clear that even at this stage their perspective went beyond the European arena.
3 Marx's notebooks indicate that a year earlier he had been reading intensively about British imperialism in Africa and elsewhere in what is currently called the third world. See Marx and Engels 1975b: IV Bd. 6.

4 In a subsequent issue of their *Neue Rheinische Zeitung Revue*, Marx and Engels wrote that "we have already pointed out, before any other European periodical, the importance of the discovery and the consequences it is bound to have for the whole world trade" (**10**: 504).

5 The oft-quoted comment in the *Manifesto* about the "idiocy" of the peasantry and the famous likening of them to a "sack of potatoes" comment in The *Eighteenth Brumaire* have been extensively cited in this respect. Concerning the former, Draper (1984: 110–11) has argued convincingly that what is at issue is primarily an issue of mistranslation: it would have been more accurate to have translated "idiocy" as "isolation." As for the latter, it is mainly a problem of taking Marx's words out of context and failing to read further what he had to say; see **11**: 187–89.

6 Though his visit was only for recuperative purposes, it's instructive to note that Marx couldn't help but take an interest in learning about "communal ownership among the Arabs" (**46**: 210–11). Lastly, about a half year before his death, Marx reported favorably on anti-imperialist activities in France against British moves in Egypt (**46**: 298).

7 Edward Said's failure to acknowledge this side of Marx's views of India, that is, his unequivocal solidarity with Indians who struggled against British rule, leads him to treat Marx erroneously as a nineteenth-century Orientalist (1979: 153–57).

8 See **6**: 527 for a similar and somewhat more insightful comment made in 1847. Note also Marx and Engels's comment cited above, about the import of the California discovery.

9 In an otherwise faithful and sympathetic reading of their views Jeffrey Vogel (1996: 40–41) fails to note this reassessment.

10 See Collins and Abramsky (1965: 59–81) for details on the composition and limitations of the British trade-union participation in the IWMA.

11 For evidence that substantiates Marx's charges see Collins and Abramsky (1965: 260); Harrison (1965, ch. 4).

12 In their otherwise useful discussion of the difficulties of the IWMA in England, Collins and Abramsky, unfortunately, do not address this factor.

13 In 1870 Marx foresaw that a war with Germany would be "the midwife of the inevitable social revolution in Russia" (**44**: 57).

14 I am referring, of course, to the revolutionary upheavals in Germany that followed in the wake of the Russian Revolution in 1917.

15 Also noteworthy is the fact that Marx spent his final years reading and taking notes on precapitalist societies from the Americas to Europe and Asia – giving the lie once again to the Eurocentric charge. For details see Krader 1972.

16 The 48 volume (as of this writing) *Collected Works* is the most accessible record. For the more ambitious, the projected 114 volume *Marx-Engels Gesamtausgabe* (New Edition), which is about half-completed, is the definitive account.

5

Karl Marx, Eurocentrism, and the 1857 Revolt in British India

Pranav Jani

> England, it is true, in causing a social revolution in Hindostan, was actuated only by the vilest interests, and was stupid in her manner of enforcing them. But that is not the question. The question is, can mankind fulfill its destiny without a fundamental revolution in the social state of Asia? If not, whatever may have been the crimes of England she was the unconscious tool of history in bringing about that revolution.
> (*Karl Marx, "The British Rule in India," New York Daily Tribune, 25 June 1853*[1])

> By and by there will ooze out... facts able to convince John Bull himself that what he considers a military mutiny is in truth a national revolt.
> (*Karl Marx, "The Indian Question," New York Daily Tribune, 14 August 1857*)

The 1857 Revolt in British India was unique in that it was a "convergence of various strands of resistance" on a vast and intense scale, involving mutinies of sepoys (soldiers), mass insurrections of peasants, revolts of princes in central India, and *taluqdars* (landholders) in newly annexed Avadh (called "Oude") and spreading across northern India (Bose and Jalal 1998: 88).[2] In May 1857, a group of soldiers, recently mutinied from the Bengal Army at Meerut, and the rebellious villagers who joined them, entered Delhi and placed an unwilling Bahadur Shah II, the nominal heir of the old Mughal Empire, on the throne. Until April 1859, when the last guerrillas were crushed or driven away, the pattern of mutiny–rebellion was reproduced around the country, claiming the allegiance of more than 50 percent of the army, and the support of peasant masses and ruling elites across caste, religious, and regional lines. Despite the tremendous solidarity of the rebels, the Revolt ultimately suffered from great weaknesses: the failure of soldiers in Bombay and Madras to mutiny, the inferiority of arms, the lack of military leadership (most officers in the Indian Army were British), the absence of a clear political agenda, and the breakup of fragile cross-class and cross-communal alliances.

Far away in England, the young Karl Marx, a journalist for the *New York Daily Tribune (NYDT)*, paid close attention to the Revolt. He had already completed ten *NYDT* articles on India in 1853 and would write thirty-one more articles over the course of the insurrection, analyzing its causes, its progress, and its final defeat. While Marx's journalistic pieces do not represent a rigorous historical study, they have gained a new importance by becoming central to criticisms – most notably by Edward Said (1979) and Bill Warren (1980) – that Marx was a Eurocentric thinker who saw the destruction of precapitalist Asian societies as progressive and tragically necessary for the advancement of capitalism.[3] On the other hand, some Marxist scholars have over-emphasized Marx's description of 1857 as a "national revolt," making an unproblematic connection between the India articles and Lenin's theory of national liberation, formulated sixty years later. Aijaz Ahmad has intervened in these debates by defending the anticolonial politics of the India articles while also exposing the errors and theoretical weaknesses contained in them, namely, that precolonial India consisted of static village communities, and that the brutality of British capital was a historical necessity (1992; 1996). Ahmad also contextualizes Marx's theories within the conditions of their production in the 1850s, including the undeveloped nature of colonialism itself, the lack of information about Asian societies, and the continuing hold of philosophical abstractions on Marx's thought (1996: 18–21; 1992: 231–32).

While I agree that Marx's arguments about colonialism in India are a "mixed bag: great insights mixed with ideological blinkers and fanciful fictions" (Ahmad 1996: 19), I argue that there is a deeper logic operating here, a more dialectical relationship between the development of Marx's ideas and the 1857 Revolt. I maintain that under the impact of the Revolt, Marx's articles increasingly turned from an exclusive focus on the British bourgeoisie to theorize the self-activity and struggle of colonized Indians. Further, the struggle between the paradigm of the "Asiatic mode of production" (AMP) and Marx's growing sympathy for colonized Indians is eventually resolved in an anticolonial direction.[4] My defense of Marx's treatment of colonialism against the allegation of Eurocentrism seeks to move beyond a simple declaration of Marx's anticolonial politics by establishing how his historical-materialist methodology allowed him to transcend some weak theoretical formulations and prejudices in early pieces on India and move toward a more complex understanding of the relation between colonizer and colonized. Such conceptual shifts, products of the dialectical relationship between theory and class struggle in Marxism, have been crucial throughout its development; the Revolt functioned for Marx's ideas on colonialism in much the same way as the Paris Commune did for his theory of the state, forcing him (however unconsciously) "to re-examine his theory in the new light it afforded" (Lenin 1943: 32).

Before the Revolt, Marx's standpoint was always derived from the British perspective: "Indian progress," when discussed, was seen as being joined to the advances of British colonialism. Indeed, Marx never rejected the idea that colonialism was essential for bringing capitalism to Asia. However, after the insurrection and the ranting of the racist, jingoistic British press, he began to see colonized Indians as agents in their own history, who, as in the classic model of the bourgeois–proletarian relation, needed to struggle *against* the colonizers to win their liberation. It is on the basis of these economic and political critiques of colonialism and the resulting contradiction in Marx's own thought that later Marxists understood national liberation struggles to be an integral part of the socialist revolution globally, and not just its junior, non-European partner.

The revolutionary, swinish colonizers

The first of the epigraphs cited at the head of this essay is from "The British Rule in India," cited widely by critics for its claim that "England...was the unconscious tool of history in bringing about [a social] revolution" (Marx 1968: 89). Four days after writing these words, Marx wrote in a letter to Engels that he had "continued... hidden warfare [against the *NYDT* and its "socialistic humbug"] in a first article on India, in which the destruction of the native industry by England is described as *revolutionary*. This will be very shocking to them. As for the rest, the whole rule of Britain in India was swinish, and is to this day" (430; Marx's emphasis). While Marx's note does not revoke the word "revolutionary" in his description of the British role, in acknowledging that it will be "shocking" to some, it asks that it also be read as "swinish." The revolutionary, swinish colonizers are portrayed in more analytical terms in a passage from "The Future Results of British Rule in India" (8 August 1853), explaining their historic task: "England has to fulfill a double mission in India: one destructive, the other regenerative – the annihilation of Asiatic society and the laying of the material foundations of Western society in Asia" (125).

At first glance, Said seems right to argue that these passages portray British capitalism as a necessary medicine, however bitter, for the stagnant villages of India (1979: 153–57). Indeed, the AMP paradigm is in full effect, with the British colonists as the agents of change, charged by history to carry out the "annihilation of Asiatic society."[5] Phrases like mankind's "destiny," history's "unconscious" tool, and the "mission" that England "has to fulfill" turn colonialism into a supra-historical process, and then link the inevitability of colonialism with its world-historical necessity, making Britain's "vile" interests, stupidity, and "crimes" extraneous and forgivable. As Gayatri Spivak points out in her critique of Marx, capitalist development in India *required* colonialism because, according to the AMP paradigm, there existed no revolutionary dynamic in static Asia (1999: 97). However, such conclusions about Marx are incomplete because they analyze neither the intellectual conditions of his India articles nor his anticolonial politics.[6] By situating the passages within Marxist dialectics, rather, Ahmad shows how the idea of the "double mission" is certainly not Eurocentric in itself. For instance, Marx's descriptions of the role of the European bourgeoisie in the European countryside *also* evoked the paradigm of the "double mission," calling it "revolutionary" when emphasizing the upheaval in the productive forces and "swinish" when emphasizing its brutality (Ahmad 1996: 19; 1992: 225). The "double mission" followed the framework of Marx's theory of history (not a racist discourse) and was even a common idea among later anticolonial nationalists (1992: 226, 234).

Ahmad's holistic view of Marx's ideas, in fact, allows him to make a useful critique of Marx's portrayal of an historical occurrence (what happened) as an historical necessity (what had-to-happen). Ahmad argues that Marx's analysis itself was mistaken since, according to the historical record, neither was precolonial India as backward as Marx imagined, nor was colonialism as progressive in terms of establishing capitalism, as it often destroyed indigenous venues of transportation and communication (1996: 18–21).[7] Going further than Ahmad, however, I maintain that the AMP paradigm continues to be dominant in these passages because Indian agency remains outside the dialectical progress of the British bourgeoisie in India. Although the passage from "The British Rule" emphasizes the British role as "revolutionary" (though swinish) and the letter to Engels calls it "swinish" (though revolutionary), in each case the "tool of history" is still the British, however "unconscious" it may be. Indeed, there is a crucial aspect of the dialectical term "revolutionary" that is missing in the 1853 articles. In the *Communist Manifesto*, the catastrophic progress of the bourgeoisie opens up the possibility that the proletariat – forged out of the advance of the bourgeoisie and on the basis of whose labor the bourgeoisie's great wealth is created – could take its place on the stage of history (Marx and Engels 1988). But if the British bourgeoisie is "revolutionary" in India, there is no sense of what its nemesis will look like. India seems to be an empty space; its conditions of progress are, it seems, submitting quietly to the civilizing British.

Between "The British Rule" and "The Future Results," the first and last of the 1853 articles specifically on Indian society, many texts reiterate the "swinish" theme and refrain from progressivist exuberance. For instance, "Parliamentary Debate on India," published on the same day as "The British Rule," repeatedly uses forms of the term "scientific barbarism" to describe the colonizing project and its agents, creating a rhetorical effect that reverses the discourse of "civilization" and "barbarism" inherent in the AMP paradigm. Further, by discussing the difficulties of Indian cotton-workers and other Indians under the restrictions of a colonial economy (Marx 1968: 81), Marx begins an analysis of the modern mechanisms of colonial exploitation that is quite different than simply pitying Indians as the representatives of a dying civilization (e.g., "The British Rule" 88–89). The moment of conquest itself is described as being "in every respect as hideous as the Slave trade" and the brutalization of Ireland (77–78). In this scathing critique of the British, Marx identifies the contending forces in colonialism and chooses the side of the colonized. On the one hand, he counters the glorified accounts of the colonizing process by politicians like Lord Macaulay who speak in the "richest slang of highwaymen and cutthroats" (81), and, on the other, he links the Indian situation with those of Africans and the Irish. Unfortunately, however, this fiery anticolonialism does not produce an Indian agent that can defeat those British: in a final, ambiguous analogy with Ireland, India – though potentially a locus of revolt – is cast in the accursed isolation of "complete and universal poverty" (81–82).[8]

If "Parliamentary Debate" emphasizes the "degenerative" role of the British, "The Future Results" begins to address the question of "regeneration" seriously, both in terms of capitalist development and Indian agency. Marx produces a list of the benefits of British rule that is strewn with ambiguities: political unity that is "imposed by the sword," a strong army that is "the *sine qua non* of Indian self-emancipation," education given to reluctant Indians "sparingly," and "abominable" systems of land tenure that produce private property, "the great desideratum of Asiatic society" (1968: 126). Marx argues that the ruling classes of Britain – thus far maintaining only an "accidental, transitory" interest in India in order to "conquer it," "plunder it," and "undersell it" – would develop infrastructure for conveying and exchanging goods and for irrigating land in India in order to keep it profitable (126–29); despite the intentions of the capitalists, the "railway system will therefore become, in India, truly the forerunner of modern industry" as a whole, as industrial processes introduced would expand far beyond the immediate needs of the railways (128–29). In turn, running the machinery would require hiring and training Indians, whose "capabilities and expertness" were already being revealed by engineers and mechanics in northern India (129). The expansion of capitalist industry and Indian employment within it would mean, finally, the dissolution of the "hereditary divisions of labor, upon which rest the Indian castes, those decisive impediments to Indian progress and Indian power" (129). Leaving aside the question of historical accuracy – the growth of the railways was as embedded in the contradictory processes of "development" as any industry – we can see that the article is still firmly ensconced in the discourse of capitalism-as-progress, Indian agency-as-reactive, and, implicitly, of colonialism-as-necessary. But there is a new ideological dimension through which Marx clearly opposes the interests of the colonizers to those of Indians: the end of caste divisions, gradual proletarianization and, in some vague way, "Indian power."

In the following paragraphs Marx tries to outline the dialectic of structure and agency operating in colonial India and its relation to the British and, for the first time in the articles, envisions "Indian progress" as a product of *struggle* against colonialism. The "double mission" is explained again, but in a way that emphasizes the "degenerative" and "regenerative" aspects differently. First, the bourgeoisie itself "will neither emancipate nor materially mend the social condition of the mass of the people," not only in terms of "the development of the productive powers," but also "their appropriation by the people" (Marx 1968: 129). On the other hand, what the capitalists "*will not fail to do is lay down the material conditions for both*" (129; Marx's emphasis); as the "unconscious tool," they must establish the basis for capitalism and Indian appropriation even if it is against their immediate interest. Once again, Marx reminds us, these are the historical limits of bourgeois "progress":

Has the bourgeoisie ever done more? Has it ever affected a progress without dragging individuals and peoples through blood and dirt, through misery and degradation?

The Indians will not reap the fruits of the new elements of society scattered among them by the British bourgeoisie, till in Great Britain itself the new ruling classes will have been supplanted by the industrial proletariat, *or* till the Hindoos themselves shall have grown strong enough to throw off the English yoke altogether (129–130; my emphasis).[9]

Indian liberation is neither an automatic by-product of British rule – a position shared by both British imperialists and the new, English-educated indigenous elites – nor is it solely dependent on the socialist revolution in Britain. Undoubtedly, the British bourgeoisie and proletariat have revolutionary primacy over the ill-defined rebellion of the "Hindoos," posited in some distant future. But we also have the outlines of Indian action, both in coordination with the British – as workers, landowners, peasants, soldiers – and in opposition to them. Further, Marx's ideas about Indian independence, unavailable to Indian nationalists themselves until fifty years later (Ahmad 1992: 236), and his implication that Indians and the British working class share a common enemy in the British bourgeoisie, contradict the entire colonialism-as-progress narrative. The brutality of colonialism as described in "The Future Results" is no longer justified as a necessity but described as only an expression of the horrors of capitalism: "The profound hypocrisy and inherent barbarism of bourgeois civilization lies unveiled before our eyes [in India], turning from its home, where it assumes respectable forms, to the colonies, where it goes naked" (Marx 1968: 130). The passage is a clear forerunner of a similar one from *Capital*, in which Marx argues that the proof of capitalist exploitation is in the colonies, where the myth that capitalist relations are natural relations is "torn aside" (1990: 935).

The major deficiency of the pre-Revolt articles is not their lack of anticolonial sentiment or lack of human sympathy, but that they do not produce an understanding of colonialism that is as sophisticated and dynamic as Marx's theory of capitalism in Europe. Even when British domination is shown to effect some Indian response, the dynamic of class struggle inherent in the bourgeois–proletariat dyad is absent here, as the colonizers simply act upon the colonized. Indians appear as victims of the colonial process but are as yet not seen as makers of their own history. This is not because of racism or Eurocentrism but because – as with his early views on Ireland – Marx did not think that revolts in regions with precapitalist societies would be of *primary* importance in overthrowing capitalism itself. In effect, the Marx of the India articles is influenced by precisely the sort of abstraction that he would decry in his (unsent) letter of 1877 to the editors of *Otechestven-niye Zapiski*, a Geneva-based Russian socialist journal. Marx argues against the inclination of N. K. Mikhailovsky, to "metamorphose [his] historical sketch of the genesis of capitalism in Western Europe to a historico-philosophic theory of the general path every people is fated to tread, whatever the historical circumstances in which it finds itself" (444–45). It took the Revolt itself to force Marx to develop a better understanding of the agency of the colonized subject.

Towards a new dialectic: the post-Revolt articles

Unfortunately, most of the theorists who label Marx as Eurocentric based on his India articles do not incorporate the post-Revolt articles into their analyses; those who do strategically suppress the anticolonial portions of his writings and read the Revolt as a "reactionary" threat to a colonialism marked by Marx as "progressive" (e.g., Avineri 1968: 22–24). My reading implicitly critiques both perspectives by taking up Marx's unique position with regard to both the "civilizing" British and the "anti-modern" insurgents. Through his analysis of the structure of colonial institutions and his new, dialectical understanding of the colonizer/colonized relation, Marx substantiates the notion of "Indian power" that was only imagined in "The Future Results." At the same time, however, I caution against reading too much into Marx's phrase, cited in my second epigraph above, that the Revolt was a "national revolt" (196). Given the general rejection of nationalism and national liberation in postcolonial studies, it is important for contemporary Marxists to reject the Stalinist legacy that equates the support for national liberation struggles with the support for nationalism (Lazarus 1999a: 68–143). Marx's ultimate defense of the Indians' right to revolt should neither be misconstrued as a theoretical perspective on anticolonial nationalism nor as a political stance for the rebels' victory.

Mass struggles are touchstones for gauging the ideological position of historians and commentators. All British imperialists agreed that the Revolt needed to be subdued, but Whig politicians, defending their aggressive "reform" policies, claimed that it was merely a "military mutiny," whereas the Tories, attempting to show that the mutiny expressed Indians' deeper dissatisfaction with Whig policies, called it a "national revolt" (Metcalf 1964: 72–74). The British press condemned the insurgents and whipped up hysteria; as Marx observed, "John Bull is to be steeped in cries for revenge up to his very ears" in order to scapegoat the Indians and "make him forget that his Government is responsible . . . for the colossal dimensions" of the Revolt (1968: 215). Educated Indians in northern India who were alienated from English cultural institutions joined the anti-foreign revolt, but the new Bengali, English-educated intelligentsia, reformist yet with ties to the landlord class, regarded the Revolt as a movement of "feudal oligarchs" and remained loyalist (Metcalf 1964: 85; Bose and Jalal 1998: 91–92). Seeing themselves as "the chosen instruments of European civilization in Asia," they understood the Revolt, in fact, within an AMP-type paradigm as a clash between a progressive European civilization and "Asiatic stationaryism" (Metcalf 1964: 83–84). Finally, the ideological propensities of the insurgents themselves were many, ranging from popular struggle against all class oppression (British or Indian), to a clear anti-British, anti-communal perspective, to millenarian ideas about the imminent fall of the British one hundred years after their rule began, to a localized struggle between Indian caste and ruling groups to right earlier wrongs and reclaim ancestral property (Guha 1983: 25–27, 117–18, 314–30; Metcalf 1964: 65). But the clear presence of a strong anti-British sentiment did not translate into nationalism; the idea of a modern, independent nation was notably absent from the rebels' proclamations (Majumdar 1963: 406–32; Bayly 1988: 178).[10]

In this context, Marx's analysis of the Revolt carves out a complex and entirely unique perspective. On one level, he seems to share much with both the British analysis and that of the Bengali intelligentsia. He makes passing stereotypical remarks, for instance, on the Asian desire for "blissful anarchy" ("State of the Indian Insurrection" 1968: 203), or on the poor military skills of ignorant and undisciplined Indian soldiers when faced with a "civilized" army ("How Lucknow was Taken" 1968: 283).[11] Similarly, though Marx always analyzed European religion as ideological, he mistakenly saw Indian religion as essential to the population (Ling 1980: 75), easily conflating Indians' continuing anti-British sentiment after the Revolt with their hatred of the "Christian intruder" ("The Failure of the Insurrection in Oude – Final Defeat of the Indian Revolt" Marx 1968: 331). Finally, Marx shared with the Bengali elites some notion of the Revolt as the expression of a (necessary) battle between "modern, civilizing" and "traditional, barbaric" civilizations, despite the fact that he never explicitly championed the British. While it is true that both precapitalist elites and religious ideas played an important role in shaping the Revolt, it is one thing to derive this picture from a detailed analysis of Indian society in the mid-nineteenth century – virtually impossible for Marx to conduct – and another to draw it from an idea of Asian essences.[12]

However, Marx's conclusions in the post-Revolt articles – directed, once again, by his incessant critique of British capitalism – also contradict the AMP paradigm and forge a unique unity with the rebels' perspective. The passing comments described above do not interfere, ultimately, with Marx's analysis that the Revolt was a product of socioeconomic conditions and the resistance of an oppressed people, and not simply an isolated event or an "Asiatic" reaction. In article after article, Marx openly contests British justifications for counterinsurgency by showing how colonial policies themselves laid the groundwork for a revolt that involved all levels of Indian society: peasants (high taxation), artisans (destruction of handicrafts), employees of the British (discriminatory promotions), landlords (confiscation of property), and princes (annexation of land).[13] Marx developed a widespread critique of British hypocrisy, Indian victimization, and the political immaturity of the Revolt all at the same time, seeing neither Whigs, Tories, loyalist Indian elites, or insurgent Indians (princes, landowners, or poor peasants) as offering alternatives to the situation of colonialism.

In his best writings on the Revolt, on the other hand, Marx outlines a new, dialectical relation between the colonizer and the colonized, which approaches that of the classic bourgeoisie–proletariat model; the latter is seen as both the product and "gravedigger" of the former. One example is Marx's brilliant analysis of the central question of the Revolt: the relationship between the military mutinies and the popular uprisings due to the social character of the colonial army. He writes that "[t]he allegiances of the Indian people rests on the fidelity of the native army, in creating which the British rule simultaneously organized [their] first center of resistance" ("The Revolt in the Indian Army," Marx 1968: 181); at the same time, the mutineers were the "acting instruments only"of a more general anger among Indians against heavy taxation ("The Indian Question," Marx 1968, 193).[14] Similarly, in three articles between 1857–58, Marx refutes racist representations of Indian violence in the British press by drawing a sharp division between the violence of the oppressed and that of the oppressor, and dialectically linking the two. Line by line, Marx portrays the Indian rebellion as the necessary, dialectical product of British rule:

"Torture formed an organic institution in [Britain's] financial policy. There is something in human history like retribution; and it is a rule of historical retribution that its instrument be forged not only by the offended but by the offender himself" (212). The statement echoes the logic of the *Communist Manifesto*. The Indian mutineers are being seen not simply as "agents" in the casual sense of "people who can act" but in the Marxist sense of "historical agents," forged by the double-edged "revolution" of the colonizers, and acting against them in struggle. While "The Future Results" outlines such an agency, "The Indian Revolt" substantiates it.

The articles on British atrocities transform Marx from a mere observer of the battle to an active participant in the ideological struggle over the meaning of the Revolt. They record the particular kinds of torture used by the British and the racist rhetoric surrounding them, expressing how "the halter rather than the sword had become the favorite weapon of British officers" (Marx 1968: 266). In "[Investigation of Torture in India]" (17 September 1857), searching for "the antecedents which prepared the way for this violent outbreak" (216), Marx develops his analysis of colonial institutions through actual complaints by Indians to the Torture Commission in Madras about the punishments they had received for being unable to pay the land-tax. Without interpretation or interjection, Marx quotes a long passage from the testimony of peasants from the southwestern coast and concludes:

We have here given but a brief and mildly-colored chapter from *the real history* of British rule in India. In view of such facts, dispassionate and thoughtful men may perhaps be led to ask whether a people are not justified in attempting to expel the foreign conquerors who have so abused their subjects. And if the English could do these things in cold blood, is it surprising that the insurgent Hindoos should be guilty, in the fury of revolt and conflict, of the crimes and cruelties alleged them?   *(221)*

On one level, in the face of ruthless counter-insurgency and imperialist propaganda, Marx begins to investigate colonial institutions more thoroughly and concludes that Indians were "justified" in their efforts to "expel" the British. But he also recognizes the ideological battle as a historiographical one; reading against the grain of the colonizers' own text, he frees the subaltern testimony trapped within them as the unmediated "truth" of the matter, the "real history" of colonial India. Marx's condemnation of the whitewashing of British atrocities in their newspapers (subsequently repeated in imperial histories of the Revolt), anticipates the work of Nehru and other anticolonial historians in reading the specific instances of British violence in terms of the institutionalized violence of colonialism.[15] The outright justification of the Revolt implies that the path to liberation from this "real history" will not come through collaboration with the "revolutionary" British, but through struggle against them.

In effect, the Revolt forced Marx to set aside his *own* advice that readers postpone "whatever bitterness the spectacle of the crumbling of an ancient world may have for our personal feelings" in the interest of the historical "progress" of colonialism ("The British Rule," Marx 1968: 88). Within the logic of Marx's articles, of course, the "real history" of colonial India does not necessarily contradict the earlier idea that pre-colonial India had "no history" ("The Future Results" 125). But what is important is that Marx's failure to provide an appropriate history of the development of capitalism in 1853 does not prevent him from recognizing the "real history" of 1857; in fact, the process of searching for "real history" in the post-Revolt articles means that the AMP can emerge here only as a series of petty prejudices, not a conceptual albatross. Stereotypes appear in "The Indian Revolt," for instance, but are overcome by the strong anticolonial critique. Marx speculates that acts of cruelty and "horrid mutilation" might appear "natural" to Hindus, whose "religion has made [experts] in the art of self-torturing," but that such acts "must appear still more so to the English" who not only "draw revenue from the bloody rites of Juggernaut festivals" but even applaud the "throwing of a red-hot shell on Canton dwellings by a Secretary of the Manchester Peace Society [during the 1856 rebellion in China]" (214). While the spreading Revolt evoked the most racist metaphors from the colonial government, who called it a "contagion" and "infection" (Guha 1983: 220–24) and the British press, which portrayed Indians as savages and children (Metcalf 1964: 75), and while it pushed Indian elites, regardless of their criticisms of the government, into confirming their loyalism, that same event provoked, in Marx, a more detailed look at colonial institutions and a critical solidarity with the movement of the oppressed.

Marx's critique of British colonialism and the defense of Indian resistance in the post-Revolt articles is so powerful that some Marxists have mistakenly drawn a straight line from these articles to Lenin's "national self-determination" theses of the 1910s to the general Left support for decolonization after World War II. The editors of the Moscow anthology of the India articles, published at the centenary of the Revolt and entitled *The First Indian War of Independence, 1857–1859*, argue that Marx and Engels "describe the movement from the first as a national revolt – a revolution of the Indian people against British Rule" (Marx and Engels 1959b: 10). Indian Marxists have characterized it as a popular revolutionary movement with a "solider–peasant democracy" as its prime achievement (Joshi 1957: 192–204) or have implied that only a properly revolutionary leadership was required for victory (Panikkar 1989: 39). Even Ahmad, though far more nuanced and explicitly critical of the "inordinately imposing title" of the Moscow anthology, draws too much from Marx's term (1992: 338 n.14, 229).

It should be remembered that Marx lifted the phrase about the "national revolt" from a speech by Benjamin Disraeli, who was establishing the Tory position that the Revolt was a product of Whig misgovernance ("The Indian Question" Marx 1968: 196). Indeed, Marx had a complex relationship with Tory ideas on India; although he clearly realized their class basis and opportunism, his lack of accurate information about Indian society led him to accept some of their conjectures about land laws in India (e.g. "[The Annexation of Oude]"). This is not to say that the term "national revolt" should be ignored, but that it be appropriately contextualized. Given his clear political differences with the Tories regarding the "civilizing mission," for instance, Marx put the idea of "national revolt" to a different use: investigating the ways in which the military mutinies and popular uprisings were connected and gained "national" breadth and depth. Yet, this is still a loose definition of the "national," falling quite short of the rigorous discussions between Lenin (1975a; 1969) and Luxemburg (1976).

Marx articulated the idea that "Indian progress" would ultimately be achieved through struggle against the British bourgeoisie, but the fundamental limitation of his perspective came not from the AMP paradigm but the absence of any rebellious class that seemed geared towards establishing a modern bourgeois democracy. The "most significant general line of distinction" between Indians who remained loyalist and those who joined the Revolt was between "magnates who had broadly survived the onset of colonial trade and administration, and those who had been steadily losing land rights" since the turn of the century (Bayly 1988: 193); the nascent national bourgeoisie that was looking to establish capitalism, in other words, awaited a British victory. In this light, Marx and Engels's defense of the rights of people of Avadh to fight for their "national independence" (Marx 1968: 288) or of the Chinese to defend their "nationality" (Ahmad 1992: 229; 1996: 21–22) in the middle of the nineteenth century is quite different from Lenin's declaration in the early twentieth century that supporting a war of an oppressed nation would be "legitimate, progressive,

and just" (1975b: 185). Whereas it is extremely difficult and speculative to imagine (even today, not only in the 1850s) what paths Indian
development would have to have taken, in the aftermath of a victorious Revolt, to achieve the political and economic gains of a bourgeois
revolution, the explicit goal of most anticolonial revolts in the twentieth century was the establishment of (state) capitalism and a modern
nation-state. As Trotsky bluntly put it in his study of the Chinese
revolution of 1925–27, "a war of a colonial nation against an imperialist nation is a bourgeois-revolutionary war" – neither more nor less
(1974: 130). The uncritical readings of Marx's phrase "national revolt,"
merely strengthen the nationalist interpretation of the Revolt (Metcalf
1964: 58) and avoid the difficult questions about the development of
a specifically national consciousness.

Conclusion

If "Eurocentrism" connotes a sustained discourse and worldview that
makes (Western) Europe the center of the globe – politically, economically, theoretically and, thus, racially – then the Marx of the India articles is not Eurocentric. While the paradigm of the "Asiatic mode of
production" is certainly a product of the Eurocentric context of Marx's
theoretical development, the critique of capitalism that drives his politics and methodology leads him to results that openly contradict the
static AMP. The charge of Eurocentrism, overemphasizing the impact
of the AMP paradigm, misses Marx's real focus, the development of
capitalism and the possibility of its overthrow, minimizes the anticolonial dimension of his politics, and does not allow for that fact that the
AMP as a paradigm has been rejected by Marxists as the "real history"
of colonialism has become apparent. Later writings by Marx and
other Marxists contradict the center/periphery model that is the first
premise of a Eurocentric argument.

By the time of *Capital I* (1867), Marx's description of "primitive
accumulation" in both the European countryside and the European
colonies had lost all vestige of the progressivism of "The British Rule."
In terms of the peasantry, Marx points out the error of bourgeois historians who are enthusiastic about the "emancipation" of the serfs without seeing that "these newly freed men became sellers of themselves
only after they had been robbed of all their own means of production,
and all the guarantees of existence afforded by the old feudal arrange-
ments. And this history, the history of their expropriation, is written in
the annals of mankind in letters of blood and fire" (1990: 875). Turning

to the European conquests, Marx establishes that "the dawn of the era of capitalist production" was drawn from "the discovery of gold and silver in America, the expatriation, enslavement and entombment in mines of the indigenous population of that continent, the beginnings of the conquest and plunder of India, and the conversion of Africa into a preserve for the commercial hunting of blackskins" (915). Thus began, simultaneously, the development of modern colonialism and modern capitalism: "The colonies provided a market for the budding manufactures, and a vast increase in accumulation which was guaranteed by the mother country's monopoly of the market. The treasures captured outside Europe by undisguised looting, enslavement and murder flowed back to the mother-country and were turned into capital there" (918). "Capital," Marx asserts, "comes dripping from head to toe, from every pore, with dirt and blood" (925–26).

If *Capital* contains the consolidation of Marx's thoughts on the economic roots of colonialism, his writings on Ireland represent his best political conclusions on the question. Between 1858 and 1869, with the rise of Fenian republicanism and British repression and his own efforts to mobilize English workers to defend the Fenians, Marx was fully won to the idea that the Irish liberation movements had to be supported both out of principle itself and for raising the political level of the British working class by fighting national chauvinism. In the course of his writings on Ireland, Marx consciously shifted from a stagist position, in which a socialist revolution in England would then cause Irish liberation, to one in which fighting for Irish freedom was a prerequisite to accomplishing "anything" in England. These writings provide a theoretical basis for the position that internationalism requires a free association of nations.

It was Bukharin's (1972) and Lenin's (1939) theories of imperialism that laid the material basis for the socialist internationalist's critical support of national liberation, making it more than a matter of humanitarianism. By 1916 it was possible to say that many different kinds of movements with different ideological bents – "revolts by small nations in the colonies and in Europe . . . revolutionary outbursts by a section of the petty bourgeoisie *with all its prejudices* . . . movement[s] of the politically non-conscious proletarian and semi-proletarian masses against oppression by the landowners, the church, and the monarchy, against national oppression" – all "objectively . . . attack *capital*" (Lenin 1969: 190–91; emphasis in original). Lenin and later Marxists thus provided a stronger theoretical footing to the economic and political conclusions on colonialism developed unevenly in Marx. Their ideas might not have emerged directly from Marx's writings but they were nevertheless shaped by his study of the 1857 Revolt, the Irish resistance, and the struggle against slavery and the US Civil War. Arguments about Marx's and Marxism's "Eurocentrism" not only fail to account for the complexity of this historical development of the national question, but in doing so, reject the very theories through which the end of imperialism has been, and needs to be, imagined.

NOTES

I would like to thank Anthony Arnove, Purnima Bose, Patrick Brantlinger, William Keach, Neil Lazarus, Ramdas Rao, Nagesh Rao, Phil Rosen, Mytheli Sreenivas, and Lee Sustar for their direct and indirect contributions to this paper.

1 All *New York Daily Tribune* articles and personal letters are quoted from Marx 1968, edited by Avineri. Brackets indicate that Avineri has provided the title.

2 The following historical sketch has been drawn from Bayly 1988, Bose and Jalal 1998, Guha 1983, Majumdar 1963, Metcalf 1964, and Panikkar 1989.

3 Said's criticism is part of the twenty-year trajectory in postcolonial studies away from Marxist methodology and politics. Marxists like Jameson (1990b: 47), Amin (1989: 121), and Benedict Anderson (1991: 3) have also argued that Marxism is deficient in understanding, respectively, the crippling aspect of imperialism, uneven development, or the unique hold of nationalism. Yet Lenin (1969; 1975a; 1975b), Luxemburg (1976) and Trotsky (1997; 1974) wrestled precisely with these questions.

4 I invoke the AMP as a "paradigm" here because its first formulation appears *after* the India articles in *A Contribution to the Critique of Political Economy* (Marx 1971a: 21). The Indian "village community," in fact, forms an important basis of the AMP.

5 See P. Anderson (1974: 462–549) on the contradictions embedded in the AMP idea and Habib (1995: 29–35) on Marx's later reconsiderations of it.

6 Both Warren and Said base their interpretations on "The British Rule" and "The Future Results," the most widely anthologized of the forty-one articles.

7 See Washbrook (1988), Bayly (1988), Subramaniam (1996), and Kumkum Chatterjee (1996) for studies on the level of development in pre-colonial India in terms of both the presence of indigenous merchant capital and the extent of its integration with and/or destruction by British capital. I thank Mytheli Sreenivas for pointing me towards these texts. For specific discussion on Marx and pre-colonial India see the debate between Mukhia, Habib and other Indian historians (Ahmad 1992: 232–4, 338 n12) and Habib (1995: 14–58).

8 Other excellent articles include "Sir Charles Wood's East Indian Reforms" (22 June 1853), exposing the hypocrisy of the discourse of

"reform" employed in all sides of the heated parliamentary debates over the renewal of the East India Company's twenty-year charter (Marx 1968: 74) and "The East India Company – Its History and Results" (11 July 1853), investigating the trajectory of colonial economics and divisions between the British ruling class around the 1853 Charter.

9 Compare with Ahmad's reading of these passages (1992: 235–36).

10 Historians' own ideological positions on nationalism determine what relationship they trace between the Revolt of 1857 and the (elite, loyalist) Indian National Congress of 1885. See especially Majumdar (1963), a deeply nationalist critique of the Revolt, Nehru (1989: 322–27) on its psychological impact on Indian nationalism, Bayly (1988: 170, 196) on the modern character of the Revolt, and Guha (1983: 330–31) for his attempt to link pre-nationalist and nationalist subaltern consciousness.

11 Written by Engels. At Marx's request, Engels wrote the *NYDT* articles most closely connected to military analysis and strategy as the Revolt continued, while Marx focused on politics and economics.

12 See Bose and Jalal (1998: 92–93), Guha (1983: 270–74), Majumdar (1963: 398–406), and Metcalf (1964: 88–89) on the role of religion, rumor, and prophecy in the Revolt.

13 Later historical research has provided a more precise picture of the causes of the Revolt. See Bayly (1988), Guha (1983), Majumdar (1963), Metcalf (1964), and Stokes (1978).

14 Lord Dalhousie, the governor-general of India just before the Revolt, received a warning from a military officer: "If you infringe [on] the institutions of the people of India, that army will sympathize with them; for they are part of the population" (Panikkar 1989: 35).

15 A "false and perverted history" was written about the Revolt and its suppression (Nehru 1989: 325), as "every school-boy, both in India and England" read about Indian atrocities, but few had heard of the massacre of Indians (Majumdar 1963: 192).

Part II

Locating modernity

6

Misplaced ideas? Locating and dislocating Ireland in colonial and postcolonial studies

Joe Cleary

I

The emergence of colonial and postcolonial studies within the Irish academy as a distinct mode of critical analysis can be dated to the start of the 1980s. In retrospect, the Field Day Theatre Company's staging of Brian Friel's *Translations* in 1980 seems a formative moment: the play dealt with the state-sponsored mapping and the Anglicization of the nineteenth-century Irish landscape, provoking questions about the relationship between knowledge, language, and power that would soon be taken up in Irish postcolonial studies also. Later in the decade, the small but growing body of work that shared this colonialist interest received considerable stimulus when Field Day commissioned pamphlets by Edward Said (1990), Fredric Jameson (1990b) and Terry Eagleton (1990) which examined modern Irish culture within the context of colonialism, imperialism, and anticolonial nationalism. At the same time, David Cairns and Shaun Richards published their seminal *Writing Ireland: Colonialism, Nationalism, and Culture* (1988) – the first extended historical survey of Irish literature to draw explicitly on the wider international body of postcolonial criticism inspired by Said's *Orientalism*. The topic's increasing significance in Irish cultural studies was indicated at the start of the 1990s when essays by Luke Gibbons (1991), David Lloyd (1991) and Clair Wills (1991) appeared in a special issue of *The Oxford Literary Review* devoted to the subject of colonialism. Since then a substantial body of criticism by some of Ireland's most distinguished cultural critics has appeared, drawing extensively on the theoretical resources of postcolonial studies (e.g., Boylan and Foley 1992; Lloyd 1993, 1999; Kiberd 1995; Deane 1997; Bourke 1999).

Locating and dislocating Ireland

Although nowadays sometimes identified exclusively with cultural criticism, the emergence of postcolonial studies in Ireland ought not to be seen simply as a literary or cultural studies phenomenon. The work that appeared in the 1980s built on earlier scholarship and intersected with several other intellectual currents, especially the historiographic enterprise generally described as "the history of the Atlantic archipelago." This model stressed the interconnections between English state formation and the extension of English control over the rest of the British Isles and over the westward colonies in North America and the Caribbean, thus challenging the dominant modes of twentieth-century British historiography that tended to maintain an insular amnesia about Britain's imperial enterprise.[1] Long before postcolonial studies came to prominence in the 1980s, therefore, some distinguished Irish historians working with the Atlantic model of history, most notably David Beers Quinn and Nicholas Canny, had stressed the connections – in terms of personnel, trade, political practices, and mentalities – that linked the early modern Tudor and Stuart plantations in Ireland with the contemporaneous establishment of British colonies in the North Americas (Quinn 1966, 1991; Canny 1973, 1976, 1987, 1988, 1998; Andrews, Canny, and Hair, 1978). This historical enterprise has not been without its critics, but by challenging the state-centrism of both British and Irish nationalist historiography, and by locating Ireland within the wider narrative of early modern European imperial expansion, it resituated Irish historical scholarship in ways to which Irish postcolonial studies remains deeply indebted.[2]

The emergence and the reception of postcolonial studies in Ireland must ultimately be linked, however, not simply to contemporary intellectual currents but also to the prevailing political climate on the island in the 1980s. Since the early 1970s, both Northern Ireland and the Irish Republic had experienced sustained crises that unsettled the political orders that had emerged on the island since partition. The well-publicized Northern "Troubles" conditioned the whole political and intellectual climate in the Irish Republic, while the crisis that most immediately affected the South during these decades was essentially an economic one. Since the early 1960s, when it abandoned the autarkic policies adopted after independence, the Irish Republic has pursued a policy of dependent development that involved the assiduous courting of multinational, mostly American, investment and the political integration of the country into the European Community. In the wake of the so-called "oil crisis" of the early 1970s, this strategy seemed destined to prove no more successful, however, than its protectionist predecessor. In the 1970s employment levels fell to their lowest since independence and by the 1980s the Republic had the highest rate of international debt in the EEC (Jacobson 1994: 111, 167). With unemployment rates constantly escalating, emigration from the Republic had risen by the 1990s to rates estimated at approximately thirty to forty thousand people per annum, something not witnessed since the 1950s (MacLaughlin 1994: 261). It was in this context that a small but significant body of dissident economic studies, drawing on various forms of dependency and world-systems theory appeared (e.g. Crotty 1986; Jacobson 1994). These argued that while the history of modern Irish economic development appeared anomalous by Western European standards, it shared much with development patterns in other colonized regions of the world.

The dominant intellectual response to these crises, however, was essentially shaped by variants of modernization theory and revisionist historiography. Most modernization theories rest on a crude dichotomy between "traditional" and "modern" societies, and are designed to elucidate the means whereby "traditional" societies can acquire the attributes of "modernity" (Larrain 1989: 85–110). From this perspective, the problems besetting Irish society since independence – whether they be political violence in the North or conservative Catholic nationalism or economic inefficiency in the South – are interpreted as evidence that the country has yet to complete the transition from a "traditional" to a properly "modern" social order. For many, one of the attractions of postcolonial studies in Ireland as it has emerged since the 1980s has been its attempt to destabilize the cultural dominant represented by modernization discourse. From the perspective of postcolonial studies, modernization discourse is a rearticulation of the nineteenth-century bourgeois ideology of evolutionary progress, the occluded side of which has always been the colonial subordination of the greater part of the world to metropolitan domination. By focusing overwhelmingly upon variables relating to indigenous aspects of social structure and culture, modernization theories generally have displayed indifference to the whole issue of imperialism and have usually ignored or underplayed many important external forces or constraints upon change within given societies. Where modernization discourses, then, consistently locate modern Ireland within an apparently self-contained Western European context and within a foreshortened timespan in which the past is consistently understood as calcified "tradition" that simply impedes progress, postcolonial discourse insists on the need to understand Irish historical development in terms both of the *longue durée* and the wider geographical span of Western colonial capitalism. Where both modernization discourse and Irish revisionist historiography stress the reactionary nature of Irish nationalism, postcolonial discourse has suggested that Irish nationalism can only be understood contextually, as the complex outcome of local interactions with an aggressively expanding imperialist "world" economy. Where revisionist historiography and modernization studies have both concentrated on the political elites that shaped Irish political institutions and state apparatuses, postcolonial studies has sought to develop a more critical understanding of the various forms of subaltern social struggles that have largely been written out of the dominant debates in Irish history, whether in their bourgeois nationalist or revisionist versions (see Lloyd 1999: 37–52, 77–88).

That said, Irish modernization discourse, revisionist historiography or postcolonial studies ought not to be credited with more internal coherence than they deserve. All have been colored to some degree by the extended conjuncture of economic crisis in the South and military stalemate in the North, and how any of these intellectual formations will adapt to the altered conditions of the new century, which commences with the South enjoying a dramatic economic boom and with the tentative establishment of a new political dispensation in the North, still remains to be tested.

II

For many Irish and international academics, the contention that the Irish historical experience has been closer to that of other colonized countries than to that of most Western European societies is simply a species of auto-exoticism with little conceptual merit. Three principal objections to the conception of Irish history in colonial terms are typically cited. The first is that in geographic, religious, racial, cultural, and economic terms Ireland was always an intrinsic part of Western Europe and hence attempts to assess Irish historical development in terms of non-European colonies must inevitably obscure the intricate network of connections that bind Ireland to its immediate geocultural locale. A second objection is that Irish nationalists rarely conceived of their historical experience in colonial terms and even more rarely identified the Irish situation with that of non-European colonized peoples. Irish dissent to British rule, it is argued, was informed by the languages of Jacobitism, English radicalism, and French republicanism, even abolitionist discourse, but only very rarely was it articulated in a specifically anticolonial vocabulary. Where Irish nationalists before the twentieth century did assert analogies between Ireland and other colonial sites, they tended on the whole, it is contended, to compare Ireland's situation with that of other white European settlers in the British Empire rather than with that of the indigenous peoples. A third objection to the colonial model is that not only did the Irish not usually identify with the non-European peoples in the colonial world, but that they were effectively enthusiastic co-partners, like the Scots, in the British imperial enterprise. The British Empire, this argument runs, provided enormous opportunities for Irish people and these were willingly embraced. The massive emigration from Ireland to colonies such as Australia, Canada, and New Zealand and Ireland's significance as a supplier of manpower to the British military machine as well as its extensive contribution to the Catholic missionary enterprise in Latin America, Asia, and Africa are usually cited to support this argument. Thus Thomas Bartlett has wondered whether "Ireland so far from being a colony, should be considered a mother country in her own right?" (Bartlett 1988: 47). From this perspective, though not formally an imperial center like Britain, France, Belgium, Portugal, or Spain, Ireland nevertheless has more in common with its colonizing neighbors than with the colonized peoples of the European empires.

These are important points that carry considerable weight, but none constitutes a decisive objection to the thesis that Ireland was a colony. It will be useful to begin with the question of Ireland's place within Europe here; the other objections will be engaged later in the essay. With regard to the issue of location, it is important to note that the thesis that Ireland was a British colony does not at all rest on the assumption that the country was somehow, culturally or otherwise, "outside" of Europe and hence part of the "Third World." No serious scholar will dispute that the major social, intellectual and cultural transformations that shaped Western Europe's society over the past several centuries – the Reformation and Counter-Reformation, the Enlightenment and French republicanism, the British industrial revolution and German romanticism – were decisive to the development of modern Irish society. What those who would contend that Ireland was a colony would suggest, however, was that in Ireland's case these wider European developments were mediated through a society which was in its structural composition – class and ethnic relations, land tenure systems, state order and relationship to Britain, and so on – objectively colonial in character.

Locating and dislocating Ireland

In his classic essay, "Misplaced Ideas," the Brazilian cultural critic, Roberto Schwarz speaks of what he describes as the besetting "experience of incongruity" that continually obsesses commentators on Brazilian society (1992: 25).[3] Schwarz's attempt to account for this "experience of incongruity" centers on a contrast between the ideological function of liberal ideas in Europe (their location of origin) and Brazil (one of their places of adoption). For Schwarz, an ideology is "in place" when it constitutes an abstraction of the social processes to which it refers. While in Europe, therefore, liberal ideology constituted an abstraction of industrial capitalism, in Brazil the imported liberal ideas were elaborated in a social order of a very different kind. The contrast between, on the one hand, the realities of the slave trade, economic dependency, a political system based on clientalism and favor and, on the other, a liberal discourse which proclaimed universal equality before the law and the virtues of the impersonal state created, he contends, an effect of ill-assortedness, dissonance and distortion that has obsessed commentators on Brazilian life ever since. For Schwarz, then, the "experience of incongruity" that obsesses these commentators ought not to be construed in terms of a clash between European "modernity" and Brazilian "backwardness" nor explained away by a poststructuralist relativism that attributes the problem to the inadequacies of the European methodologies and not to Brazilian reality. Instead, that experience must ultimately be attributed to the constitutive paradox of Brazilian social order: a slave-owning latifundist economy structurally integrated on a dependent basis into the "liberal" capitalist world-economy.

From the theoretical perspective that shapes Irish postcolonial studies, Irish history discloses a constitutive paradox of a similar kind. The suggestion is not, patently, that nineteenth-century Ireland and nineteenth-century Brazil were alike. What is suggested, rather, is that although Ireland belonged to the same geocultural locale and to the same orbit of capital as the major European imperial powers, it was structurally integrated into that orbit of culture and capital in a very different way to its main European neighbors. Those who contend that Western Europe represents the obvious and appropriate comparative framework for the evaluation of Irish society assume an essentially homologous relationship between the country's spatial location, its socioeconomic composition, and its culture. They assume, in other words, a fundamental congruence between the country's economic "base" and its political and cultural "superstructures." Conceived in this way, such differences as existed between Ireland

and Europe are invariably structured by the conceptual couplet of "backwardness" and "advance." The postcolonialist perspective, in contrast, suspends the notion of homologies, and attempts to investigate the *discrepant* ways in which Irish political and cultural life, which were obviously shaped and textured by European developments, were at the same time over-determined by the country's dependent socioeconomic composition. Contrary to what its critics would claim, then, postcolonial studies is not a misplaced or out-of-place idea in Irish circumstances. On the contrary, it might be argued, following Schwarz, that an obsessive "experience of incongruity" – occasioned by the fact that dependent cultures are always interpreting their own realities with intellectual methodologies created somewhere else and whose basis lies in other social processes – is indeed a typical characteristic of postcolonial societies.

III

If the controversy as to whether Ireland can legitimately be considered a colony is to be seriously advanced, it is imperative to understand that this question can be posed on two *analytically* discrete levels that require different methods and procedures of investigation: one that has to do essentially with matters of consciousness and discursive epistemes; the other with material structural and sociocultural correspondences – though ultimately the relationship between these two "levels" also needs to be theorized. On the first level, the question that is essentially being posed is: To what extent, and at what times specifically, did those charged with British government in Ireland as well as Irish nationalists and unionists consciously consider the Irish situation a colonial one? Since British rule in Ireland extended over several centuries, during the course of which British Empire and wider capitalist world systems changed dramatically in economic character and geographical composition, what is called for here is a very challenging kind of intellectual history: one capable of tracking the changing ways in which the various British governing classes, Irish political elites and insurgent social movements conceived of the Irish situation, and the degree to which a consciousness of the wider colonial world informed attitudes and behavior on all sides.

While the value of a history of *mentalités* of this kind is evident, some important caveats need to be entered. As mentioned earlier, scholars sometimes argue that Ireland was not really a colony at some or other stage in its history because the Irish did not deploy the language of colonialism, and that opposition to British domination was coded instead in the language of tyranny and denied citizenship, or argued on the constitutional grounds that the country was a separate kingdom. The difficulty with this line of argument is that it assumes as already available the historical development of a concept whose full range of meanings emerged only gradually through the nineteenth and into the twentieth century (Lloyd 1999: 7). The fact that peasants in medieval Europe did not consciously think of themselves as living in a feudal system does nothing to diminish the theoretical value of the term "feudalism." Similarly, the theoretical value of the term "colonialism," which historically emerges as a conceptual rationalization of European overseas rule and only later as part of a wider oppositional critique of that enterprise, can never be made to rest simply on the subjective consciousness of the colonized.

The argument that eighteenth- and early nineteenth-century Irish nationalists looked mostly to the white settler colonies to highlight their own grievances, and less so to the indigenous native peoples of America or Africa, also needs to be weighed in this context. The fact is that in this period the most decisive struggles with which the European imperialist metropoles had to contend were frequently not with the native peoples in their colonies but with their own white settlers (Emmanuel 1972). The dramatic reconfiguration of the contemporary capitalist world-system brought about by Britain's disputes with her North American settlers and by Spain's quarrels with her creole populations in South America in this period testifies to the wider global significance of such conflicts. In other words, the earliest and most successful anticolonial nationalist struggles were those of the white settler and creole populations in the Americas, and given the international significance of such movements it is hardly surprising that their influence was acutely felt in Ireland at the time. The fact that many prominent Irish nationalists – John Mitchel and Arthur Griffith are exemplary cases – considered it outrageous that Ireland should be treated as a colony because this put an ancient European people on the same level as non-white colonial subjects in Africa or Asia is well established. Examples of Irish nationalists who did identify the Irish predicament with that of non-white colonized peoples can always be produced to counter those who did not. But to try to determine the ratio of those individual nationalists who did and who did not make such identifications is only to compound the conceptual confusion inherent in this whole mode of argument. The extent to which *some* versions of anticolonial nationalism reinscribe the imperialist mentalities they oppose is a well developed theme in postcolonial studies, and Irish nationalism, in this and other respects, offers considerable evidence of the limits of nationalism as an oppositional discourse. But the fact that some Irish nationalists were capable of only a very restricted and conservative critique of British imperialism does not mean that Ireland was not a colony. Were the class-consciousness and solidarity of the oppressed across the world not something that has continuously to be struggled for, rather than something that automatically attends the subaltern condition, then oppression would not be the problem it is in the first instance.

If the concept of colonialism has a theoretical value that cannot be reduced to the subjective consciousness of the colonizer or the colonized, then it might be asked if it matters at all whether either the Irish or the British conceived of Ireland in colonial terms. Even if British administrators or some Irish nationalists discerned parallels between the Irish situation and that in various British colonies this, it might be suggested, does not mean that the objective conditions were actually commensurable. Nevertheless, as Luke Gibbons remarks, it is also the case that: "Understanding a community or a culture does not consist solely in establishing 'neutral' facts and 'objective' details: it means taking seriously *their* ways of structuring experience, their popular narratives, the distinctive manner in which they frame the social and political realities which affect their lives" (1996: 17). Once we allow for this, it is clear that the attempt to trace the changing ways in which Ireland was conceived in relation to other parts of the colonial world does have its own intrinsic importance because this is the domain through which historical experience is lived.[4]

That established, no historical materialist could be content to pose the question as to whether Ireland was a colony simply at the level of systems of representation. To do so would be to allow a one-sided concern with political consciousness and discursive epistemes to dispose with the question of deciding whether the avowed correspondences between Ireland and other colonies are compelling as an explanatory historical framework. For this reason, the question must also be posed at a level that tries to determine whether there are illuminating sociocultural correspondences between Ireland and other colonial situations. But this immediately leads to the question: with which colonies might Ireland productively be compared?

Naive objections to the thesis that Ireland was a colony seem often to assume that there is such a thing as a typical colony and a standard colonial experience against which Ireland's claims might be assessed.

The real difficulty, on the contrary, is that colonial practices, structures, and conditions around the globe have been of the most varied and heterogeneous kind. Indeed, the sheer diversity of the lands that comprised the British Empire alone was so pronounced that some scholars have questioned whether any substantive similarities between colonial polities can be deduced, and some have even queried whether the term "colonialism" itself has any analytical value (Hind 1984). In order to avoid surrender to such positivism, Irish postcolonial studies might do well to devote more attention to the task of generating a serviceable typology of colonies.

The American comparative sociologist of race relations, George Fredrickson (1985), building on the work of the conservative historian of empire, D. K. Fieldhouse (1965), has divided overseas colonies into four categories: administrative, plantation, mixed settlement, and pure settlement. Often the most prized imperial possessions, *administrative colonies* aimed at military, economic, and administrative control of a politically strategic region and were never settled by Europeans on a mass scale. Settlement colonies, as distinct from their administrative counterparts, fall into three general types. *Plantation colonies* usually attracted relatively few white settlers, but these acquired large tracts of land, found that the indigenous population did not meet their labor needs, and imported a slave or indentured and usually non-European labor-force to work the monocultural plantations (Watts 1987; Curtin 1990). In the *mixed settlement colonies*, of which the clearest examples are the highland societies of Latin America, the indigenous peoples were not annihilated but the Iberian settler culture became the dominant one. The racial and class stratifications that emerged in such situations were typically very complex, but miscegenation normally occurred and gave rise to racially mixed groups that served as buffers between those of settler and indigenous descent. Labor exploitation in such situations usually took the form of a coercive form of landlord–peasant relationship – with the indigenous peasantry left in place but required to pay tribute to European landlords or political authorities in the form of labor or commodities (Lockhart and Schwarz 1983; Burkholder and Johnson 1994). In the *pure settlement colonies*, of which the United States, Canada, and Australia are the exemplary instances, the native peoples were either totally exterminated or their remnants moved onto reservations in areas of little interest to white settlers. The North American and Australian colonial economies depended in their initial phases on indentured labor, but because land was usually relatively cheap by contemporary European standards, and labor consequently comparatively expensive, the economies that developed over the longer term in the pure settlement colonies were usually based not on large "feudal" estate systems but on farmer-settlement and free white labor (Harris 1977; Harris and Guelke 1977).

Used crudely, typologies such as these can obviously freeze into Weberian ideal types. But they can also be used more productively to bring into focus dominant settlement patterns, economic systems and state structures that emerged in particular colonial situations, and they can be adapted to account for historical transformations within given colonies in response to larger mutations in the world capitalist system. The real value of such typologies is that they can help to distinguish the new compositions of land, labor, and capital relations that typically predominated in different colonial situations. As such, they may have at least the potential to take postcolonial theory beyond the bad theoretical abstractions for which it is sometimes legitimately criticized. The point of distinguishing between different types of colonies, it must be stressed, is not to enable the proper cataloguing of this or that colonial society. Colonialism was an integral part of the creation of a tendentially global capitalist order, but for a whole variety of reasons – ranging from the vagaries of precolonial social orders to the differentials of anticolonial resistance – there are no identical colonial situations. The purpose of colonial typologies, then, is to allow scholars to situate specific colonial societies within a more materialist theoretical framework that can highlight both what colonial societies had in common as well as the peculiarities and distinct social textures of individual situations.

Analytic discriminations of this sort may also have the capacity to contribute to the development of Marxist social analysis. Marxist political economy has produced a rich corpus of theoretical scholarship on imperialism, but imperialism is usually conceived in this scholarship in essentially economic terms (for a useful survey, see Brewer 1984). Hence these theories of imperialism have usually had little to say about distinct historical compositions of land, labor, and capital or about the modalities of state formation within specific colonial situations. While such theories have much to tell us about wider international circuits of capital investment and extraction, the actual historical development or social texture of colonial societies obviously cannot simply be "read off" this economic datum. The object of colonialism, as Lloyd observes, is normally the wholesale transformation of the colonized society: the eradication of its indigenous structures of feeling, the institutionalization of the colonizer's modes of legality and property relations, and the displacement of indigenous social institutions by those of colonial modernity (1999: 2, 11). The argument here, then, is not that colonialism and imperialism are totally distinct phenomena but that the false theoretical identification of the two should also be avoided.

Viewed in this frame, some elements essential to any evaluation of Ireland in comparative colonial context become evident. First, Ireland was systematically colonized (in the modern sense of that term) in the early modern period, roughly contemporaneous with the Spanish and Portuguese colonies in South America and the English ones in North America. In the sixteenth century comprehensive schemes of plantation by Englishmen in the Gaelic areas of Ireland were underway, and Ireland was gradually redefined in this period as a crucial strategic site in the European struggle to control the Atlantic and the New World. In the same period, the island also became one of the epic battlegrounds in the struggle between Reformation and Counter-Reformation Europe (Smyth 2000: 158–86). It was possibly for this reason that religion became the major index that distinguished between colonizer and colonized in early modern Ireland, with the Old English settler-descended communities from the pre-Reformation period ultimately relegated by the New English Protestant arrivals in the seventeenth century to the same inferior social status as the Gaelic Irish.

The dominant economic mode of production that underpinned the early modern colonial system was state-regulated merchant capitalism (or mercantilism). Like the West Indies and the Americas, Ireland in this period underwent an exceptionally violent and hugely accelerated process of colonial modernization in which every aspect of the indigenous society was almost wholly transformed. All of these colonial sites were commercially orientated toward the emerging Atlantic economy, but imperial mercantilist policy dictated that trade had to be channeled through the British and Spanish imperial centers, inhibiting independent economic development within the colonies over the longer term.[5] One of the distinguishing characteristics of the colonial outposts of this emergent Atlantic economy is the velocity of their transition from various forms of precapitalist society to mercantile capitalist modernity, without experiencing what Kevin Whelan (1993: 205) has called the long conditioning of other medieval European societies. Thus at the beginning of the seventeenth century, Ireland was a lightly settled, overwhelmingly pastoral, heavily wooded country, with a poorly integrated, quasi-autarkic and technologically backward economy. By the century's end all that had changed: as it was commercially reoriented to service the expanding English mercantilist state and concurrently integrated into the world of North Atlantic trade, Ireland underwent "the most rapid transformation in any European seventeenth-century economy, society and culture" (Whelan 1993: 204).

In all the colonial sites in this new Atlantic world this precociously accelerated process of modernization was accompanied, however, by what would ultimately appear, from the perspective of a more fully developed nineteenth-century industrial capitalism, to be economic and legal-juridical "archaisms." These include the slave plantations in the West Indies, the southern United States, and parts of South America; the Spanish *encomienda* and *hacienda* system in South America; and the oligarchic landed estates system in Ireland – which nineteenth-century Irish political economists of all shades by then regarded as the single greatest impediment to "proper" capitalist development in the country. In all of these situations, moreover, the native populations were subjected for extended periods to legal and political constraints – though these varied enormously – designed to secure the privileges of the immigrant settler communities.

The sense of incongruity between, on the one hand, the precocious modernity of these colonial societies and the extent of their integration into the emergent capitalist world system and, on the other hand, some of their more "archaic" characteristics has generated considerable controversy among Marxists as to how they can best be described. From one position, associated with the work of Paul Baran, Andre Gunder Frank, and Immanuel Wallerstein, capitalism as a mode of production is equated with the penetration of capitalist market relations. From this perspective, as capitalism comes into contact with other modes of production through trade, all economic activity is increasingly subordinated to the profit-maximizing imperatives of the market. As such, all essential distinction between the capitalist mode and modes initially outside the capitalist sphere is rapidly eroded and the problem that then poses itself is that of analyzing the relationships of unequal exchange that subsequently emerge between capitalist core and periphery. An alternative position, associated with the works of Ernesto Laclau and Robert Brenner, holds that while capitalist expansion is often accompanied by the expansion of capitalist class relations, it may also result in the combination of capitalist and noncapitalist modes of production in ways that contribute to underdevelopment. For Brenner

(1977: 27), accounts such as Wallerstein's that equate capitalism with the extension of the capitalist market will "fail to take into account either the way in which class structures, once established, will in fact determine the course of economic development or underdevelopment over an entire epoch, or the way in which these class structures themselves emerge: as the outcome of class struggles whose outcomes are incomprehensible in terms merely of market forces."

These different methodologies point to strikingly different conceptualizations of Irish history. From the first perspective (the one which comes nearest to that shared by most Irish economic historians), a hallmark of the Irish economy as it developed in the seventeenth century is the velocity of its enforced capitalist modernization through conquest and colonization and the extent to which the country is incorporated as a producer of agricultural exports into an emergent Atlantic economy. From the alternative perspective, a minority position argued by Eamonn Slater and Terence McDonough (1994), the British conquest allowed for the creation of a landlord class that was able to control the Irish legal system to a degree unparalleled in England. Depending on the theoretical model applied, it is argued then that Ireland either underwent an unusually rapid enforced transition to a form of dependent capitalism constrained within a colonial relationship mediated through London or, alternatively, that it evolved by way of a bastardized variety of "colonial feudalism" that allowed only for a very late development of capitalism by Western European standards. Despite their differences, both approaches suggest, however, that Irish historical and economic development poses theoretical questions for Marxism that cannot be grasped within the feudalism–absolutism–capitalism sequence usually applied to the core centers of Western European imperialism (Anderson 1974). Though modern Ireland is located in the same orbit of capital as these core centers, its social development has been in crucial respects very different. Both of the theoretical models sketched above suggest, therefore, that the assumption that Western Europe constitutes the natural frame of comparative analysis within which Ireland should be located is open to question.

If Ireland is included in the category of settlement colonies as outlined above, then it evidently belongs to a quite limited set of situations where the settlers did not over time become a demographic majority. South Africa (partially settled in the same historical epoch as Ireland was), Algeria, Rhodesia, Kenya and Palestine (all settled much later when industrial capitalism proper had already developed) are other major examples of the same phenomenon. As in the South American colonies, in Ireland the native population was not expelled but was retained as a peasant labor force within a land system now almost totally monopolized by the settler elite. But in contrast to South America, where the indigenous Indian population suffered a drastic decline, in Ireland the native population actually increased in the early modern colonial period and remained a demographic majority throughout the island except in the northeast.

The fact that Ireland was a settlement rather than an administrative colony is a matter of some significance. Within the administrative colonies, colonialism did not create totally new societies – instead it intervened to restructure existing "traditional" societies. In such cases, the social distance between the metropolitan colonial rulers who remained a tiny demographic minority and the majority indigenous society was usually very clearly marked. In these colonies, the metropolitan society was a mere sociological bridgehead of the metropolis and had no local "creole" identity and hence packed its bags and vanished when the tide of nationalist resistance could no longer be stemmed. The settler colonies, in contrast, were characterized by a much larger metropolitan-affiliated population of both sexes intended for permanent residence and in such cases the colonist and indigenous societies were much more closely intermeshed. In these situations, the settlers became an independent third factor that intervened between the imperial mother-country and the colonized native peoples. These settler communities were typically engaged throughout their history in a struggle on two fronts: on the one side, against the natives of the occupied territories who constituted the most immediate threat to their privileged position within the colony; on the other, against the metropolitan mother-state whenever the latter's trade monopolies or "native policies" seemed to jeopardize settler control. Politically, the relative weight of the settlers and their capacity to act independently differed widely from one colony to the next, but their structural positions and attitudes were nonetheless often quite similar (Emmanuel 1972: 39–40). Since their manner of integration into the colonial society was different than that in the administrative colonies, settlers defended their position, which was based on immobile property, much more aggressively than administrators did: it is no accident that decolonization movements in settler colonies such as Algeria and South Africa met with much more violent resistance than they did in most of the administrative colonies such as India or Egypt.

IV

In Irish nationalist discourse it is regularly asserted that Ireland was the first British colony to win independence, thus paving the way for India and the other colonies. The claim has some validity: in his theoretical survey of colonialism, Jürgen Osterhammel (1997: 37) states that "[t]he endorsement of 'home rule' in Ireland in 1922 may be regarded as the first major act of colonial liberation of the twentieth century." Nevertheless, this emphasis on Irish precedence in the twentieth century seems in some ways to misconstrue the real interest of the Irish situation in comparative colonial terms, which might better be construed perhaps in terms of belatedness. After all, the twentieth-century decolonizations in Asia and Africa were only the third phase in the wider territorial dismantling of the European empires. The first wave of decolonization between 1776 and 1825 saw the national emancipation of most of the European possessions in the New World. The second wave began in Canada in 1839 and inaugurated the slow transformation of the pure settlement colonies in places such as Australia and New Zealand into de facto autonomous states, generally known as "dominions" within the British Empire after 1907 (Osterhammel 1997: 37). Since Ireland was colonized during the first phase of European expansion, the real question, it might be argued, is why the development of colonial–settler nationalism there did *not* follow the same trajectory that it did in the American colonies. Had this happened, then Ireland might have been expected to win its independence in the first major phase of decolonization when the American colonies from the United States to Argentina won theirs. The creole nationalisms that emerged in the American colonies at this time constitute, as Benedict Anderson (1991: 47–65) has argued, the first successful anticolonial independence movements.

As is well known, an Irish Protestant nationalism did indeed emerge precisely in this period, more or less "on cue" therefore with that in the other settler colonies that had their genesis in the same historical moment. This Irish Protestant nationalism was, moreover, inspired to a large extent by events in North America, the region of the British Empire with which Irish Protestants then had the closest religious, cultural, and trading connections. Nevertheless, unlike its sister movements in the Americas, Irish colonial settler nationalism did not succeed in winning independence and, after the 1798 rebellion, Ireland's semi-autonomous colonial parliament was abolished and the country was integrated into the British State. Hence the real peculiarity of

the Irish situation perhaps is that Irish Protestant colonial nationalism began to peter out just when its American colonial counterparts
prospered.

One major difference between Ireland and the Spanish colonies in
South America at this time was that whereas Spain was overrun by
Napoleon's armies and could thus offer little support to the loyalists
in its colonies, Britain suffered no such fate and emerged instead as
the supreme European power after the Napoleonic Wars. Despite the
loss of much of its First Empire when the North American colonies
seceded, Britain as it moved into the nineteenth century was, in complete contrast to Spain, entering into its imperial heyday. Moreover,
almost all of the struggles that resulted in the independence movements in Hispanic America between 1810 and 1824 were motivated
as much by a fear of what would happen if the masses revolted as
by dissatisfaction with Spanish imperial control. Concerned to insure against such insurrection, some of the South American creole
elites seem to have concluded that given the shakiness of the Spanish
monarchy their interests could best be maintained by taking control
of the colonies directly into their own hands. In many instances creole
attitudes towards Spain were indecisive; even after they had seized
control from the royal governors in several South American capitals
when Spain was occupied by Napoleon in 1808, many continued to
proclaim their loyalty to the Spanish throne. It was only after the
restoration of the Spanish monarchy in 1814 and its determination
to return to the *status quo ante* that many creoles opted, finally, for
independence (Burkholder and Johnson 1994: 290–334).

The mixture of creole anxiety concerning the dangers of mass insurrection from below, on the one hand, and self-assertiveness in the face
of imperial crisis, on the other, offers some suggestive parallels with
Irish Protestant nationalism in the same period. The long eighteenth
century between 1690 and 1829 is often considered the era of "the
Protestant nation" in Ireland. In this period, Irish Protestants constituted a politically hegemonic class with its own assertive brand of nationalism. Yet between 1650 and 1778, the Irish parliament in Dublin –
the linchpin of Irish Protestant supremacy – had fewer powers than
most of the avowedly colonial assemblies in Britain's North American
colonies (Bartlett 1988: 46). The American struggle for independence,
and its attendant rhetoric of "democracy" and "representation,"
exerted an enormous impact on Irish Protestant nationalism and
Britain's losses in the American war made it uniquely vulnerable to
Irish pressures at that moment. When the American colonies declared

independence, therefore, the Irish Protestant patriots managed to have the constitutional relationship between Ireland and England adjusted and, as Bartlett observes, "succeeded in giving Ireland for the first time something that looked like an independent parliament" (1988: 46). The experiment, however, was short-lived: mounting popular unrest culminated in the 1798 rebellion, which saw the emergence of a radical new republican nationalism determined to sever the link with Britain and to extend civil and religious liberties to Irish Catholics. This rebellion and the dangers of French invasion induced Britain to reassert control over Ireland and persuaded "the Protestant nation" to surrender its long-cherished parliamentary independence rather than to run the risks that full independence might have entailed.

It might be argued, therefore, that while the intellectual stimulus to Irish Protestant nationalism in this conjuncture came from the independence struggles of the North American colonies, this nationalism was actually elaborated in conditions that more closely resembled those in the South American colonies. Like contemporary South American creole nationalism, Irish Protestant nationalism was at its most assertive when domestic conditions were most tractable and the imperial center weakest. But in both instances the demands for independence had to be weighed against the danger of mass insurrection from below. Given the decline of Spanish imperial power, South American creole nationalists ultimately opted, though not without vacillation, for political independence. Confronted by a stronger imperial center closer to hand, as well as by the dangers posed by the threats of a Catholic majority and the new French-inspired republican creed, Irish Protestant nationalism took a different route and opted instead, but not without vacillation either, for complete integration into Britain. It is perhaps a telling sign of the times that it was Daniel O'Connell, the hero of the struggle for Catholic Emancipation in the early nineteenth century, who would come to wear the title "The Liberator" originally invented for Simón Bolívar, the great architect of South American independence (MacDonagh 1991: 171).

The fact that it became part of the British State after 1800 is the main reason why many Irish historians find it difficult to accept that Ireland should be regarded as a colony from this time onwards. It is true that integration into the United Kingdom granted Ireland privileges enjoyed by no other colony. Ireland alone in the Empire sent MPs to Westminster and Irish migrants to the outposts of empire could also profit from what David Roediger (1991) has called "the wages of whiteness." Irish immigrants, that is, could be integrated into the white settler society labor forces or into the colonial bureaucracies in ways not normally open, in an age when social Darwinist and racist ideologies were displacing religion as the major legitimizing discourse of imperialism, to non-European peoples.[6]

Nevertheless, the assumption that Ireland simply ceased to be a colony as a consequence of its legal integration into the United Kingdom runs up against some considerable difficulties – not least the catastrophic dimension to Irish historical development in the century subsequent to the Act of Union. While Irish economic historians seem largely to agree that there was an extended period of modest economic development and prosperity between 1660 and 1815, that economic advance seemed to stall in the nineteenth century. By the 1840s, when Scotland (the other country within the United Kingdom which stood in roughly the same historical relationship to England as Ireland) was becoming an advanced industrial and urban economy, Ireland was still overwhelmingly agricultural and locked into a sustained economic crisis that culminated in the Great Famine, the last great subsistence catastrophe in Western Europe. In the short term, approximately a million people died and a million and a half emigrated as a consequence of this Famine. Over the longer term, a sustained stream of emigration saw more than four million people emigrate permanently between the Famine and World War I. Many European countries experienced high emigration rates in the late nineteenth century, but the Irish outflow was exceptional in its size and duration (Guinnane 1997: 101). The volume of emigration reconstituted the whole structure of Irish class relations: it decimated the rural laboring class and impeded the growth of an Irish urban working class. With the exception of Belfast, the Irish industrial proletariat in this period was mostly concentrated in urban centers outside Ireland. In cities in England, Scotland, and Australia, Irish workers became key constituencies in the emergent Labor parties, but in nineteenth-century Ireland the rural peasantry remained the most revolutionary class. Demographic disaster was accompanied by cultural trauma as English displaced Gaelic as the spoken language of the masses. This lent impetus to a cultural nationalism determined to salvage what it could from the shipwreck of the old civilization and to reverse what was sometimes conceived as a deliberate state-supported policy of cultural assimilation. Many of the long-term social patterns conditioned directly or indirectly by the Famine continued to reverberate across most of the twentieth century in Ireland.

It was this catastrophic dimension to nineteenth-century Irish history that persuaded many Irish nationalists that whatever its constitutional position, Ireland's relationship to England continued to be a colonial one. Economic stagnation, famine and flight, underdevelopment, the collapse of Gaelic culture, the spread of new pseudo-scientific racialist doctrines to legitimate empire all lent force to that conception. Irish nationalists were not alone in drawing such conclusions. On return from a visit to Ireland, Friedrich Engels observed in a letter to Karl Marx in 1856 that "Ireland may be regarded as the first English colony and as one which because of its proximity is still governed in exactly the same old way, and here one can already observe that the so-called liberty of English citizens is based on the oppression of the colonies" (qtd. in Deane 1991: 118–19). Ireland and India were the two key sites for Marx's scattered speculations on colonial capitalist modernization, and it was Ireland that prompted Marx's strongest comments about the regressive (rather than progressive) consequences of colonial rule (Marx and Engels 1971). By the later nineteenth century, moreover, the Indian nationalist movement was taking a keen interest in Irish struggles, and in 1886 complaints were made to Lord Kimberley, the Secretary of State for India, that "all the arts of Irish agitation had come to India" (qtd. in Crotty 1986: 221; on Indian responses to Irish nationalism, see Brasted 1980).

Objections to the idea that nineteenth-century Ireland can be considered a colony usually assume that the country's geographical proximity to or its constitutional merger with the United Kingdom means that its condition was completely different than that of Britain's more distant overseas colonies. Yet in Engels's 1856 observation cited above "Ireland may be regarded as Britain's first colony [which] *because of its proximity* is still governed exactly in the old way." Proximity for Engels is what determines Ireland's colonial status, not what makes Ireland different than other colonies. Following this lead, it is arguable that the Union far from ending Ireland's colonial status served to make the Irish situation in some ways considerably more difficult than that of other colonies. On a political level, the constitutional merger did not undo either the deep ethnoreligious cleavages or the economic dependency hatched in preceding centuries. Irish Protestant nationalism mutated after the Union in different directions, the main line of which saw an erstwhile colonial–settler nationalism with tentative separatist inclinations transmuted into a rearguard imperialist nationalism whose central dogma was that any concession to Irish demands for autonomy was bad for Ireland, Britain, and the Empire.

As the nineteenth century proceeded, Irish nationalism was opposed in Westminster not only because concessions might create a domino effect throughout the Empire, especially in India, but also because they might stimulate the break-up of the British state itself.

Nevertheless, the British position in Ireland became increasingly untenable: because it was formally part of the United Kingdom, Ireland could not consistently be denied British liberal and democratic rights, though these undermined the privileged position of the Protestant Anglo-Irish elite on whose support the Union rested. The northeast of Ulster was the only region where the Protestant population was a demographic majority with a broad-based Protestant working class. Here alone Unionism had a wide populist base and did not simply rest on the monopoly of landed estates or control of command positions in the state apparatus. The uneven development of capitalism on the island had opened up economic cleavages between the more industrialized northeast and the more rural south in ways that had generated compelling economic incentives in this region to maintain the link with Britain. This volatile conjunction of forces created a triangular conflict that would eventually catapult the whole of Ireland into military conflict. Only in the case of Algeria perhaps did another colonial independence movement stimulate such severe political convulsion in the *domestic* politics of a metropolitan European imperial state (Lustick 1993). India was a more important imperial possession than Ireland was and its loss had more far-reaching reverberations for Britain's place in the world. Yet when India was finally "lost" in 1947 there were no army revolts such as the Curragh Mutiny and no internal splits within any of the major British political parties such as the one that shattered the Liberal Party over Irish Home Rule.

V

The development of postcolonial studies in Ireland potentially represents a considerable challenge to Irish Studies as currently constituted. Too often reduced on all sides to a contest between Irish nationalists and revisionists, postcolonial studies' real significance may well lie elsewhere. To determine how Irish social and cultural development was mediated by colonial capitalism must be the goal of any materialist postcolonial studies. From its inception, the colonial process was never simply a matter of the subjugation of this or that territory. It was, rather, an *international* process through which different parts of the globe were differentially integrated into an emergent world capitalist system. Once this premise is accepted, then it follows that the determination of a specific national configuration must be conceived as a product of the global: to borrow Larsen's phrase, the *part* must be thought through the *whole* and not vice versa (1995: 214–15). In contrast to a nationalist conception of Irish Studies obsessed with the discovery of chimerical "national identities," and a liberal area studies alternative that hesitates to look beyond the horizon of the British Isles or Western Europe, postcolonial critique impels Irish Studies in the direction of conjunctural global analysis. From such a perspective, the national arena still remains a crucial site for social struggle, but a true understanding of those struggles can only be grasped contextually within a historically determinate wider global frame.

For the most part, debates about whether Ireland was or was not a colony have rarely got beyond questions of geocultural location and constitutional statute. These are important, but not the decisive issues. If colonialism is conceived as a historical process whereby societies of diverse kind and location are differentially integrated into a world capitalist system, then it is on the basis of a comparatist conjunctural analysis of such processes that debate must ultimately be developed. Cultural analysis has an important role here since this is the decisive area where social conflicts are experienced, articulated and evaluated, but it is ultimately the contradictions of the wider capitalist system that shape those conflicts, whether cultural, political or economic. While it has been suggested here that typologies of colonialism can serve as a useful heuristic device for the analysis of colonial situations, any taxonomy that loses sight of the fact that colonialism is a historically changing process will inevitably be reductive.

As Mulhern (1998: 24) has remarked, Ireland's colonial history, by virtue of its sheer duration, can read like a history of colonialism itself. In the late medieval period the country was, like Scotland and Wales, one of the ragged frontiers of English state expansion and contraction; in the early modern period, a commercial settlement plantation was developed in the same westward thrust as European expansion into the New World. At the moment of the southern state's independence it was constitutionally configured as a white "dominion" like Canada, South Africa, or New Zealand. But this status was conferred against the backdrop of a triangulated military conflict between nationalist, unionist, and metropolitan British forces that split the island into two states. The situation in contemporary Northern Ireland is sometimes compared to that of other ethnic conflicts in Europe, but Northern republicans have also construed their situation in terms of

African-American civil rights campaigns and late anticolonial struggles in South Africa and Palestine. More recently, the Northern "peace process" is repeatedly compared to concurrent processes in the Middle East and South Africa. Even the term "the Celtic Tiger" adopted to describe the current economic boom in the Irish Republic implicitly associates that phenomenon with the East Asian "tiger" economies that have emerged from a colonial history to attain levels of economic development comparable to those in "the West." While the term implies that Ireland has now attained levels of economic development comparable to its Western European neighbors, it also suggests that the historical trajectory of that development finds its closest parallels with other non-European societies. The point, finally, is not to adduce whether Ireland is or is not really "just like" any of these non-European colonial situations since no two colonial sites are ever completely identical. It is, rather, to think the ways in which specific national configurations are always the product of dislocating intersections between local and global processes that are not simply random but part of the internally contradictory structure of the modern capitalist world system.

NOTES

1 David Armitage (1999: 428–29) has argued that "[n]one of the major modes of British historiography in the nineteenth century and most of the twentieth had any place for the imperial enterprise. An insular history of English exceptionalism maintained a willful amnesia about England's outlying dependencies, whether British, Irish, continental European or ultramarine." Empire, he suggests, is a notable absence in the works of several major English historians of the left including Christopher Hill, Lawrence Stone, and E. P. Thompson.

2 For some representative critiques, see Barnard 1990, Bottigheimer 1978, Brady 1989, Ellis 1994, Morgan 1991–92.

3 My reading of Schwarz's article is informed by the commentaries on it by Larsen (1995: 205–16) and Mulhern (1998: 159–60).

4 Important book-length studies on the uses of the language of colonialism in the Irish situation include, as well as those by Canny already cited, Cook 1993; Curtis 1997; Lebow 1979; Leerssen 1996; Ó Buachalla 1996; Robert Williams 1990.

5 Wallerstein 1980 remains the classic analysis of this development, but for a recent alternative account, see Arrighi 1994.

6 The scale of Irish immigration to the US and several British colonies is regularly cited as evidence that Ireland effectively "behaved" as another European imperial center even if it was not formally one. Yet the whole impetus of Roediger's work is quite different. For Roediger, the fact

that Irish in America would often play an extremely reactionary role in that country's race wars is adduced not as evidence that the Irish automatically behaved the same as other imperialist Europeans but, rather, as key to the demonstration of the historical constructedness of "whiteness" as racialized Irish subjects of British colonial rule actively pursued "whiteness" as a means to enter into mainstream American society.

7

Liberation theory: variations on themes of Marxism and modernity

Benita Parry

I

It must initially appear improbable that disciplinary fields constituted around critiques of capitalism and colonialism have given a meager reception to liberation theory. I will return to a tendency among post-colonial critics to disown liberation discourses and practices, and indeed all forms of anticolonialist rhetoric and organization.[1] But first I want to consider why so few of the major Marxist metatheorists in Europe undertook to examine the roads taken by Marxism on colonial terrains. Even if we allow that analyses inspired by Leninist strategies for class and anti-imperialist struggles diverged from the epistemological and aesthetic concerns of Marxisms in the advanced capitalist countries, this indifference takes its place within the wider and longstanding exclusion of non-western knowledge from the canons compiled by metropolitan scholars.[2] In a wide-ranging and provocative essay Göran Therborn acknowledges that Marxism became "the main intellectual culture of two major movements of the dialectics of modernity: the labour movement and the anti-colonial movement" (1996: 74). Yet when considering "Marxism in the New Worlds," he underestimates the creativity and innovations of Latin American and Asian Marxisms, makes remarkably flimsy allusions to its Chinese form, and joins a larger constituency in rejecting Africa as a player in the discourses of Marxism and modernity. Thus while singling out the Martinican Fanon for his capturing of the violent traumata of modernity in the colonial zone, he goes on to assert that most important Marxist intellectuals of Africa tend to be non-black:

Black African culture very different from the Marxist dialectic of modernity, has not (yet) been able to sustain any significant Marxist intelligentsia.

(78)

125

The circumstances overdetermining the inadequate recognition of liberation theory within Western Marxism during the decades preceding and subsequent to the second European war include but are not exhausted by "eurocentrism." As is well known, the main support for anticolonial movements in the imperial homelands came from the political left, while the Marxist perspectives of the Chinese and Cuban revolutions excited considerable interest among many prominent left-wing scholars (Blackburn in Britain; Huberman, Sweezy, Frank, Jameson, Dirlik in North America; Sartre, Althusser and Debray in France). For as long a time-span a small number of Marxist or marxisant social theorists, political economists and historians (Davidson, Worsley, Wallerstein, Saul, Woddis, Hodgkin) greeted the writings and speeches of insurgent intellectuals in Africa as significant analyses of colonialism and imperialism. It seems then that in order to understand why so few of the metropolitan metatheoreticians were aware of and interested in liberation theory, we need to consider both the shift away from the political within the European Marxist discussion, and those rearticulations of philosophy with practice predisposing some thinkers to the serious consideration of alternative Marxisms.

Some decades ago Perry Anderson inadvertently provided some insights into the metropolitan disregard of Third-World Marxisms. Describing the "critical theory" initiated by the Frankfurt School in the 1930s as marking a divorce of revolutionary theory from revolutionary practice within Western Marxism, Anderson attributed the Institute's "overwhelming concentration on study of superstructures" to the failure of mass revolts in Europe (1976: 75). Anderson was to return to this proposition during the 1980s when he found further evidence of Marxism's changing centers of gravity from politics and economics to philosophy and aesthetics, in the virtual disappearance of the "strategic discussion of the roads to a realizable socialism" among Marxists of "Latin Europe" (1983: 16, 7). Where Anderson did detect the reemergence of interest in the operations of contemporary capitalism, he found this "new appetite for the concrete" in the English-speaking worlds of Europe and North America, although he ruefully conceded that his optimism about the "reunification of Marxist theory and popular practice in a mass revolutionary movement signally failed to materialize" (1983: 27). Anderson's overview astutely mapped the circumscribed horizons of European Marxism. At the same time his own field of vision reproduced this truncated view by failing to recognize that anticolonialist insurrections, which at the very moments he examines were expanding exponentially, had indeed joined Marxist theory with revolutionary practice – a blindspot more remarkable in a British Marxist scholar than the myopia of metropolitan theorists in environments where signs of overseas empire were not as ubiquitous.

Anderson's generalized account of the turn from politics within Western Marxism was questioned by Michael Sprinker who recalled Sartre's theoretical concern with the structures and infrastructures of politics and economics, and traced Althusser's move from an earlier and self-confessed "theoreticism," where philosophy was conceived as the "theory of theoretical practice," to an understanding of philosophy as "the class struggle carried forward at the level of theory" (Sprinker 1987: 233). As glossed by Sprinker, the dispute between Althusser and Sartre hinged on the problem of theorizing agency in historical materialist terms: whereas Althusser's theory of historical structures and their transformation through a variety of social practices both retained the primacy of objective conditions in relations of production, and situated the subject as the effect and the bearer of structures, Sartre accommodated voluntarism and intentionality by grounding the intelligibility of history in praxis, an argument which attempted "to capture the essence of all the different social practices . . . in a single philosophical concept of human nature" (Sprinker 1987: 232). Despite these and other fundamental differences between Althusser and Sartre, Sprinker sought for affinities and found that together the two thinkers had reformulated a mode of articulation between philosophy and political practice distinct from the traditional philosophical problematic. This reasoning which refused to counterpose "Sartre's manifest political activity to the supposed mandarinism of Althusser's theoretical project" (Sprinker 1987: 204), was applied by Sprinker to exonerating the theoretical work of both Althusser and Sartre from charges of complicity with Stalinism.

In view of Anderson's observation of the pessimism about metropolitan class struggle which had overtaken so many of the Marxist intelligentsia in Europe, Sprinker's contention also provides an insight into why those who did retain a commitment to the interlocking of philosophy and political practice, should look to the manifest making of revolutions in the non- or nascent capitalist worlds. When it comes to considering the anticolonialism of the two thinkers, Sartre's unequivocal and very public stance is not matched by the dispersed testimony of Althusser, Algerian-born and a long-term Communist Party member. Nevertheless, Gregory Elliott (1987; 1994), has found in Althusser's unpublished papers both criticism of a party leadership for whom anticolonialism was a taboo subject, and strong support for colonial struggles.[3] Elliott also suggests that in logical conformity with the Althusserian revolt against the economism of orthodox historical materialism, and the turn to the historical–materialist concept of social *practice*, Althusser had endorsed the revolutions in Cuba and China, regarding the latter as a "concrete critique" of Stalinism and undertaking to theorize it as such (1987: 252).[4] The obvious place then to seek Althusser's anticolonial concerns is in his Maoism. In a review of Elliott's study, *Althusser: the Detour of Theory*, Joseph McCarney situates Althusser's Maoism in the context of the crisis in Marxism "precipitated by the apparent loss or absence of the historical subject identified by Marx, the revolutionary proletariat of advanced capitalism." Contesting Elliott's critique of this turn, McCarney perceives it as the final phase in Althusser's career as a Marxist philosopher: "Althusser was, at the very least, setting an example to Western Marxist theorists of taking seriously the 'outlying' regions of the world system. In doing so he could be said to be counteracting in some measure one of the weakest features of the tradition, its Eurocentricity and preoccupation with things 'Western' in a provincial sense" (1989: 126–27).

McCarney's remark points to an aspect of Althusser's thinking that has seldom been adequately addressed in the context of European Marxism's restricted horizons. Certainly Althusser paid due regard to Mao's writings, citing his 1937 pamphlet "On Contradiction" as the inspiration for his own essay, "Contradiction and Overdetermination." It was, according to Althusser, Mao's observation that all contradictions are under the sway of the law of unevenness, and his distinction between antagonistic and non-antagonistic contradictions, or principal and secondary contradictions, which generated his own notion of contradiction, not as univocal but as "overdetermined": "complexly-structurally-unevenly-determined" (Althusser 1977b: 210). Althusser went on to observe affinities between Mao's premise on development as necessarily asymmetrical and Lenin's view that the discontinuity of capitalist growth and the gigantic historical contradictions in Russia constituted *the objective conditions* for revolution – the subjective conditions to be forged by a Communist Party. This understanding of combined and uneven development, together with the necessity of a political vanguard, resonates in earlier and concurrent analyses of colonial situations made by liberation theorists who, although probably familiar with Third and in some cases perhaps even Fourth International writings on colonialism and anticolonial struggles, were unlikely to be acquainted with Althusser's work.[5]

An exception was Althusser's pupil and follower Régis Debray, who had collaborated with Guevara and was imprisoned for his participation in the abortive Bolivian uprising. In extensive studies on revolution in Latin America (1970; 1977), Debray challenged the orthodoxy designating Communist Parties as the sole bearers of revolutionary legitimacy, advocating instead that in Latin America, guerrilla *foco* linking an organized military force with a political vanguard were the appropriate vehicles for politicizing the masses and preparing them for insurrection. His essays written between 1967 and 1969 were warmly welcomed by the British New Left's Robin Blackburn, who admired their "relentlessly Leninist focus on making a revolution, as a political, technical and military problem," and was reminded by "their inner unity and unmistakable tone... of burning urgency" of "the insurrectionary debates and manifestos of 1917." Blackburn also commended Debray's move to end the disabling rupture between revolutionary experience and Marxist analysis in Latin America and elsewhere, applauded his linking of revolutionary ethics with technics, and endorsed *foco* theory, which instead of awaiting the maturation of "objectively given social contradictions," prescribed the means for creating the conditions for revolution. "Modern revolutions do not *happen; they are made*" (1970: 11; emphasis in the original). But while defending the essence of Debray's ideas against his detractors, Blackburn did concede "that an aura of adventurism does surround many of his tactical formulae, especially in *Revolution in the Revolution?*" (21).

Because this treatise elevated the military over the political and situated the agrarian struggle as primary, it was repudiated by many on the left, who accused Debray of liquidating the role of Marxist theory, and omitting to analyze the specific class structures and distribution of forces in Latin American societies, where extensive industrialization and urbanization were prevalent (Huberman and Sweezy 1968). It also received comradely criticism from Althusser (1977a): congratulating Debray for providing "negative demonstrations" of wrong political lines by revealing their internal contradictions, Althusser admonished his failure to produce concrete historical analysis specific to Latin America, and essential for determining the appropriate forms of political organization and armed struggle.

If this discussion suggests, as Sprinker argued, that there is no structural incompatibility between Althusserian theory and the pursuit of revolutionary practice, then a very different convergence, this time of Marxist humanism with political praxis, emerges in Sartre's idiosyncratic commentaries on anticolonial discourses and decolonizing struggles. Together these constitute a "poetics" and a politics of colonial revolution. An oftentimes fellow-traveler of a Communist Party which had withheld sanction from the anticolonial wars being fought during the 1950s and 1960s in French Indochina and the Maghreb, Sartre defied the party line by publicly supporting the anticolonial struggles in Algeria, Vietnam, and Sub-Saharan Africa, while also writing polemical articles and including a study of colonialism's ideological practices in his *Critique of Dialectical Reason*. In his 1948 essay "Black Orpheus," prefacing a collection of black poetry, Sartre gave a critical appreciation of Negritude, which he situated as the negative moment of separation and a necessary prelude to internationalism. Such qualified esteem for its finite value in combating racism is exceeded by enthusiasm for Negritude as "a certain affective attitude in regard to the world" (1976a: 41). Using language with the same brio as do his subjects, Sartre hailed the poetry as neither designating nor representing Negritude, but as "making" it (39): "Destruction, auto-da-fé of the language, magical symbolism, ambivalence of concepts, all of modern poetry is there under its negative aspect" (30). In this "sole great revolutionary poetry" (11), Sartre recognized "the old surrealist method" of those Caribbean cultural movements of the thirties such as *Légitime Défense*, which had begun with a Marxist analysis of Caribbean societies and went on to affirm surrealism as "a miraculous weapon" for the struggles of subjugated colonial populations. Thus whereas Sartre did position Negritude as "the subjective, existential, ethnic" stage to be sublated in the formation of a proletariat, he also maintained that it is "not by hazard that the most ardent apostles of Negritude [were] at the same time militant Marxists" (59).

Sartre's essay is both literary criticism which locates the politics in the poetry's vitalizing transgressions of received French language and syntax, and cultural critique sensitive to the dynamics and transience of Negritude. In this last he anticipated Fanon who, having earlier protested at Sartre's relegation of Negritude to a minor term (Fanon 1967a: 132–33), came to acknowledge that the moment of revalorizing native cultures was essential and transitional: "the plunge into the chasm of the past is the condition and source of freedom" (1967b: 43). The affinities between the two thinkers are again apparent in Sartre's introduction to *The Wretched of the Earth*, where he hailed "an ex-native" who bends the French language "to new requirements" so as to speak *to* the colonized, and not, as before, to entreat the colonizer: "In short, the Third World finds *itself* and speaks to *itself* through his voice" (Sartre 1968a: 10). Sartre reiterated Fanon's contempt for the sham, tin-pot native bourgeoisie, and his insistence on the urgency of going beyond national independence. He also confirmed the necessity of combating the violence launched by colonizing powers and settler communities with the violent overthrow of colonial regimes, arguing that this alone would enable the recreation of subjugated peoples and the existential liberation of *all* parties locked in the diseased colonial relationship. What Sartre brings to the critique is a dissident European's understanding of a colonialism which suspends the "universality" of the mother country when pursuing its predatory overseas ventures: "we must face that unexpected revelation, the strip-tease of our humanism. There you can see it quite naked ... It was nothing but an ideology of lies, a perfect justification for pillage" (1968a: 24–25).

In concurring with Fanon's understanding of the rural masses as a "veritable reservoir of a national revolutionary army" (Sartre 1968a: 11), Sartre rehearsed the class analysis of African societies he was to make in a subsequent commentary on Patrice Lumumba's speeches and writings. Although aware of the dilemmas afflicting an assimilated colonial elite, Sartre pointed to those circumstances which had enabled Lumumba's political role in the fight against the colonizing power of the then Belgian Congo. Other separatist organizations had initiated the struggle for independence, but it is Lumumba "who will seize upon revolution as it passes by ... [giving] it direction" (Sartre 1972: 15). Because he knew of life in the bush, in urban settlements, in large provincial cities and the capital; because he had received a Christian education and had gained some knowledge of class struggles in European history, Lumumba was able "to attain universality," to speak "a basic humanism" (15). Access to such concepts placed him above the sectarianism of ethnic and tribal groups, and allowed him "to grasp ... the unity of needs, interests, sufferings." But paradoxically and injuriously this same access doomed a person of purity and integrity, an incorruptible black Robespierre, to be a leader of a nationalist movement dominated by a petty bourgeoisie cut off from their natal community and marginalized by the colonial government they served, a segment who took themselves to be the universal class but discovered only their own class ideology – a use of categories from European history that can no more be faulted than C. L. R. James's similar appropriations in *Black Jacobins*.

Lumumba emerges as a tragic figure in Sartre's narrative, "a revolutionary without a revolution" (34), a leader lacking a liberation army, prohibited by his class affiliations from devising, let alone implementing a radical social and economic program commensurate with the demands of the disaffected masses; a student of colonialism's cunning who could naively proclaim that independence for the Congo was being achieved "through mutual agreement with Belgium, a friendly country with which we are dealing as one equal deals with another" (qtd. 30); a seer with imperfect vision dimly aware that "Congolese independence is not the end but the beginning of a struggle to the death to win national sovereignty" (22), but unable to recognize that the nominal power handed to his own class meant governing so as to secure foreign investments and property and "further colonial interests" (24). Yet for Sartre the incomplete struggle *had* situated the Congo "as a subject of history" (45) and had been *experienced* by participants, in Lumumba's phrase, as an independence won through "a passionate and idealistic fight." It was because Lumumba perceived himself and was perceived by the colonialists as an enemy of colonialism that he was pitilessly fought and ultimately assassinated "by the great capitalists and banks"; and for the same reasons, this "leader of the Congolese National Movement was regarded as a brother-in-arms by Fanon the revolutionary" (5) – a regard etched into Fanon's sober retrospect on Lumumba's grievous defeat: "no one knows the name of the next Lumumba. There is in Africa a certain tendency represented by certain men. It is this tendency, dangerous for imperialism, which is at issue" (Fanon 1967b: 197).

If Sartre's chronicle of Lumumba's downfall laments the inevitable failure of a petty-bourgeois leadership to transform the fight for independence into the overthrow of the colonial state, his critical retrospect is simultaneously a celebration of what an oppressed population, even when handcuffed to a native bourgeoisie, dared to do in the face of international capitalism's remorseless colonialist interventions. Tracing a very different trajectory, his earlier book on the 1959 armed insurrection in Cuba acclaimed "a movement which began in the form of a 'putsch'" and came to surpass its own goals when the insurgents were propelled toward revolution by the demands of the people – an assessment alert to the generative interaction between people and party. Not until embarking on agrarian reform did the rebels come to know the poverty and exploitation of the agricultural workers; but once radicalized by the masses, they went on to expropriate the largely absentee plantation-owners, an attack on the system of property which Sartre welcomed as more significant than any socialist proclamation. This dispassionate view extends to his stark opinion that in Cuba "human abstract problems (honesty, sovereignty) lead to the concrete problems of production and of social structures ... [and] must be solved in terms of production."[6] All the same he is moved by the revolution's "sacred anger" against injustice, and gratified by Castro's description of the new regime as "humanist" (Sartre 1974: 159, 116).

Despite his failure to support the Palestinian cause, Sartre's reflections on colonialism remain a testament to the political, ethical, and affective affiliation of a metropolitan intellectual with the aspirations of the colonial oppressed – a unique achievement acknowledged by Edward Said (2000) in a disappointed and just account of a silence that can be explained, if not justified, by Sartre's anguish over the fate of Jews in Europe. Sprinker has suggested that Sartre's theory of history as possessing "a plot which the actors of the drama suffer and come to know," is best described as a "poetics" of history (1987: 202); and Sartre's respect for liberation struggles where the intelligibility of human agency was manifest (Poster 1979: 112–13) is surely inseparable from an existential Marxism reaffirming subjectivity in the face of its dissolution by structuralism. His *Critique of Dialectical Reason* has been called an historical and phenomenological analysis of the lived realities of both worker and colonial subject (Poster 1975: 269); while Fredric Jameson (1971: 297, 299) observed that it registered "a subjective writing of history reinstating the entire complex of reified relationships in terms of that first and basic reality of human actions and human relations," in this offering "a reworking of the economistic model in that terminology of praxis and overt class conflict which seems now most consistent with the day to day lived experience [of] a new period of revolutionary ferment," evident in the Algerian and Cuban revolutions and the intensification of the war in Vietnam.

The section on "Racism and Colonialism as *Praxis* and Process" in the *Critique* recapitulates in theoretical language the themes Sartre articulated in his polemical anticolonial writings, and by mapping the practices installing and perpetuating the demoralizing embrace into which colonizer and colonialist were locked, Sartre configured a conflictual and debased connection:

the colonialists constantly actualize the practices of extermination, robbery and exploitation which have been established by previous generations and transcend them towards *a system of other values* [racism], entirely governed by alterity ... the colonialist and the native are a couple, produced by an antagonistic situation and by each other ... Thus in their practical, everyday life the exploited experience oppression through all their activities, not as alienation, but as a straightforward deliberate constraint of men by men ... the point of application for counter-violence is

really everywhere *here*...The violence of the rebel *was* the violence of
the colonialist... The struggle between the oppressed and the oppressor
ultimately became the reciprocal interiorisation of a single oppression.
(1976b: 720–33; emphases in original)

Sartre inveighed against the abuse of humanism and universalism
when these ideas were mendaciously invoked to disguise capitalist
exploitation and colonial malpractices, but he did not disown their
ethical potential or abandon their liberatory usages, a stance shared
by theorists in colonized worlds who aspired to realize the *unfulfilled*
enlightenment notions of reason, justice, and egalitarianism. "It is a
question of the Third World starting a new history of Man, a history
which will have regard to the sometimes prodigious theses which
Europe has put forward, but which will also not forget its crimes"
(Fanon 1968: 315). In this and other respects, Sartre's kinship with
another independent Marxist should be observed. C. L. R. James, a
sometime Trotskyist, also recognized the colonial peasantry as a revolutionary force in colonial conditions, acknowledged the significance
of insurgent anticolonialisms sustained by various forms of cultural
nationalism, warned that bourgeois leaderships remained wedded to
retaining the apparatus of the colonial state, and urged the necessity of continuing struggles against a newly installed comprador class
committed to pursuing its own aspirations and protecting foreign
interests.[7] Nor was James averse to the making of an oppositional,
insurgent black identity, arguing that where racism was integral to
capitalism, the category of class must be reexamined. "Negritude,"
he wrote, borrowing Césaire's vocabulary, "is what one race brings to
the common rendezvous where all will strive for the new world of the
poet's vision," a sentiment which he reads as rearticulating Marx's
famous sentence, "The real history of humanity will begin" (1992:
303). It is not therefore surprising that the varieties of post-Marxists
now populating the field of postcolonial studies should look askance –
when they look at all – at anticolonial discourses producing materialist
accounts of class conditions under colonialism, grounded in a Marxist
humanism, seeking to install an ethical universality and a universal
ethic, inspired by communism's grand narrative of emancipation and
signposting utopia on their map of the world.

II

A Marxist presence in the intellectual cultures of the colonized worlds
is ubiquitous and longstanding, having begun just before and during

the 1920s, when communist parties were formed in – to mention only some locations – India, China, Turkey, Thailand, Indonesia, and South Africa, in Latin and Central America (Bolivia, Peru, Chile, Cuba, Nicaragua, and Mexico) where Gramsci's theses on the pursuit of communism in predominantly agrarian societies were a powerful influence. During the 1930s and 1940s, Trotskyist organizations in places as diverse as Ceylon (as it then was), Mexico, and South Africa compiled alternatives to Third International perspectives on colonial struggles. At this time too, and in a quite different register, writers and intellectuals from the Francophone Caribbean – Jacques Stéphen Alexis and René Depestre from Haiti, Césaire and René Menil from Martinique – joined active participation in anticolonial struggles with a heady mixture of surrealism and Marxism in their poetic and polemical writings, a confluence since described as constituting "an important moment in the anti-colonial struggle in the French speaking world" (Richardson 1996: 1). In other contexts, a Marxist vocabulary was adopted, adapted and attenuated in the political discussions and rhetorics of movements pursuing the limited goals of national self-determination and the moderate redistribution of resources.[8]

It has been suggested that there are two Marxisms inherent in the classical tradition, one a science of revolutionary practice, the other a philosophical critique of capitalist modernity written punctually and from within its space. A further breakdown is offered by Therborn, who distinguishes the thinking of the Comintern and Communist Parties affiliated to the Third International, the dissident argumentation of Trotskyism, and the Marxisms of the non-European worlds (1996: 67). Writing in the early 1970s, Jameson remarked that it was "consistent with the spirit of Marxism that there should exist several different Marxisms in the world of today, each answering the special needs and problems of its own socio-economic system." Of these he named "a kind of peasant" Marxism as corresponding to the situations in Cuba, China, and the Third World (1971: xviii), conditions which he subsequently and more appropriately described as structured by the coexistence of non-synchronous historical temporalities.

My discussion here is limited to anticolonial movements in sub-Saharan Africa, and for heuristic purposes, the focus is on those popular struggles distinguished by a commitment to Marxism. Although the writings considered are singularly inflected by their location and moment, they belong with a larger body of materialist analyses of nation, class, and existential conditions distinct from those in advanced capitalist societies.[9] To assume that such situations were common to colonial worlds (and these include the nation-states of Latin America which despite independence from European powers, remained subjected to metropolitan capitalism and their native compradors) is not to overlook that colonial regimes and policies varied, that significant differences existed between territories annexed by an imperial power and states penetrated by foreign capitalism, or between settler and distantly administered societies, etc. Still, it is possible to map the complex structural disjunctures prevalent in the colonies and dependencies: racial domination as an intrinsic although not exclusive component of colonial capitalism; cultural, religious, and linguistic diversity in territories joined by the colonizers for administrative purposes; peripheral economies undergoing a volatile but uneven and incomplete process of modernization; simultaneous but different historical modes of production; the persistence of premodern practices and archaic social forms, discontinuous but coexistent with mechanization, industrialization, and urbanization; class formations distinguished by a vast and unpoliticized peasantry, still influential traditional authorities, a weak native bourgeoisie unable to carry out the revolutionary role performed by that class in Europe, the scarcity of intellectuals and the dearth of a revolutionary intelligentsia and a sizeable proletariat.

Amongst the Bolshevik generation, Lenin and Trotsky had recognized the particular and enormous contradictions within societies undergoing partial conscription into capitalism's world system, and to their analysis of these worlds they brought the theory of permanent revolution. Designating all anti-imperialist struggles, irrespective of their national-democratic agendas and bourgeois leaderships, as revolutionary in the world context, they urged unconditional international support for the right of peoples to self-determination – a right enshrined in *Marxism and the National and Colonial Question*, drafted by Lenin in 1913, but published under Stalin's name (Stalin 1936). Both Lenin and Trotsky recognized the limitations of an independence won through popular alliances, and presupposed that already existing and autonomous political organizations of workers and peasants would proceed to overthrow the colonial state inherited and perpetuated by the native bourgeoisie (Mandel 1995: 91–105). Although not necessarily acknowledged, these perspectives inform the programs of liberation movements.

Writing after his deposition in 1966, his Marxism concentrated by his fall from power, Nkrumah produced a case study of the dire consequences to the arrest of permanent revolution:

the African bourgeoisie, the class which thrived under colonialism, is the same class which is benefiting under the post-independence, neo-colonial period. Its basic interest lies in preserving capitalist social and economic structures ... It is only peasantry and proletariat working together who are able to subscribe to policies of all-out socialism ... It is the task of the African urban proletariat to win the peasantry to revolution by taking the revolution to the countryside.   *(1973: 489–99)*

So too Thomas Sankara considered independence as a transitional phase, and although sympathetic to the masses' perception of national sovereignty in Upper Volta as "a victory of our people over the forces of foreign oppression and exploitation," cautioned that for the imperialists this meant "a change in the forms of domination and exploitation," which now included "the petty-bourgeoisie and the backward forces of traditional society" (1988: 33). Hence he urged that the primary task of the "democratic and popular revolution" (40), which had wrested power from this former class alliance in 1983 and established Burkina Faso, was to construct a new machinery in place of the old colonial state so as to "transform all social and economic and cultural relations in society" (45).[10]

The pursuit of revolutionary goals by liberation movements rested on a conviction in the necessity of vanguard parties. The MPLA (The People's Movement for the Liberation of Angola, formed in 1956) presented itself as *"representing* the Angolan people as a whole ... *fighting for* the realization of the deepest aspirations of the Angolan people and particularly of the most exploited sections of the people, the peasants and workers," and claiming that it derived its strength "from *the support it receives* from the masses of the people" (MPLA 1972: 19, emphasis added). In Mozambique, when "the politics of peoples' power" was confronting that of petty-bourgeoisie nationalism within the ranks of FRELIMO (The Front for the Liberation of Mozambique) and elements within both traditional hierarchies and new comprador elites were ready to reach a compromise with the colonial power, Samora Machel stated: "Today our fight has reached a stage where national unity [essential for combating archaic traditions] is no longer enough, because the fundamental question has now become the triumph of the Revolution and not just national independence" (FRELIMO 1974: 3). "To 'Africanize' colonialist and capitalist power would be to negate the meaning of our struggle" (FRELIMO 1976: 3). Prompted by the impossibility of reconciling "our interests with those of the enemy through any purported 'autonomy' or 'independence' safeguarding the colonial capitalist State," and the recognition that "the conflict between us and the enemy is so antagonistic that only war can resolve it," Machel urged establishing the hegemony of a *new class* distinct from the broad spectrum of nationalists (FRELIMO 1976: 17).

The contemporary critique of written representation as the misrecognition or appropriation of another's consciousness, and political representation as the displacement of the peoples' aspirations by an elite, suggests that the argument for vanguard parties claiming to represent the people, in both senses, must rest on something other than a hermeneutics of representation. And indeed with Amilcar Cabral, an unrepentant advocate of vanguardism, the argument departs from representation as written interpretation or delegated authority, and moves to the category of political practice performed through a symbiosis of party and people. Had Cabral wanted to impress skeptical metropolitan intellectuals (an activity he regarded as a plentiful waste of time) he could have sought validation in Gramsci's "The Modern Prince," written in the 1930s, in which the Italian Marxist proposed a dialectical relationship between the political party and the spontaneous actions of the people, citing those exemplary movements where the leadership had set out to educate and direct spontaneity (Gramsci 1971: 198).

In his many addresses, Cabral, who repeatedly pointed to an ideological deficiency as the greatest weakness of liberation movements, undertook rigorously materialist examinations of colonialism's impact on local economies, social structures, and class formations. He defined the *nationalist* and the *revolutionary* capacity of the indigenous elite, the peasantry, the petty-bourgeoisie, the urban wage-earners and the déclassé, none of whom were situated as homogeneous in their material interests or their relationships to national liberation. The need to forge national anticolonial unity was for Cabral self-evident in a society divided by ethnic, religious, tribal, linguistic and regional differences, and where disjunctive social forms were superimposed, mingled and came into conflict. But he also understood that popular anticolonialism in itself did not constitute revolutionary consciousness, warning that independence attained through alliance politics was an insufficient condition for revolutionary transformation (Cabral n.d.: 437).

Insisting that "*the liberation struggle is a revolution* that does not finish at the moment when the national flag is raised and the national anthem played," and aware that "with rare exceptions the colonial situation neither permits nor needs the existence of a significant vanguard class (a working class conscious of its existence and a rural proletariat)," Cabral argued that "only a revolutionary vanguard, generally an active minority," can distinguish between fictitious political independence, where power passes to a native elite in alliance with imperialism, and the destruction of the capitalist state and colonial social structures (1972: 87–88). For liberation theorists, the necessity of vanguardism was dictated by the strength of the colonial apparatus and the unpropitious distribution of indigenous class forces. Far from excluding or manipulating the people, the party *depended* on their voluntary and autonomous agency: as Basil Davidson has shown, conditions in the Portuguese colonies "demanded absolutely that the peasants, with the few townsmen who joined them, participate out of their own will and understanding" (1992: 299). It was, Davidson continues, this policy of *participação popular*, defined by Cabral as the practice of democracy, criticism, self-criticism, and the responsibility of populations to govern their own lives, that brought the masses into the struggle as armed militants, and gave liberation movements "their true place in history."

The resistance to class analysis and vanguardism in the current postcolonial discussion is evident in Lisa Lowe and David Lloyd's Introduction to *The Politics of Culture in the Shadow of Capital*, which sets out to dethrone class antagonism and political mobilization from their commanding places in the revolutionary canon. Challenging those movements which prescribe political and state-oriented goals, and advocating the dispersal of resistance among the alternative rationalities of cultural, feminist and anti-racial opposition, they circumvent (without confronting) the argument that some structures and social phenomena are more powerful and "determining" than others. Both elite nationalism and anticolonialism are charged with seeking "to absorb subaltern struggles into uniformity with the terms of the political sphere," while struggles fought by Marxists are accused of ignoring "subaltern" rebellions and "different social imaginaries" (Lowe and Lloyd 1997: 6). This agenda situates the so-called subalterns – I prefer the urban and rural working classes of both genders who were doubly dispossessed by native oligarchs and compradors, on the one hand, and modern colonial capitalism, on the other – as a social category fixed in its perceptions, perspectives, and insurrectionary capacities. Yet – and contra Lowe and Lloyd's dictum that under colonialism "class relations . . . are always already predicated upon racialization" (14) – it was with the development of *class consciousness* that the "subalterns" came to understand that their interests and aspirations were incommensurable with those of an elite who had fought foreign domination under the banner of nationalism and "anti-racism" in order to inherit/share the power held by colonial capitalism. With this, in Gramsci's usage, the subalterns ceased to be subalterns. If any claim by a leadership to know the desires and wishes of "the people" requires the closest scrutiny, a compelling case has been made by liberation theorists for the indispensability of "the political" in transforming local, dispersed, and sporadic rebellion animated by disparate goals, into coordinated, participatory, revolutionary activity directed at the overthrow of a coercive state apparatus.

III

Even when patently unacquainted with their writings, some postcolonial critics reproach liberation theorists for inscribing regressive and antimodernist nativisms – a charge only applicable to revivalist tendencies within anticolonialism which were wedded to indurated custom and hostile to socialism. In large, theorists promoted the merging of intelligible, still viable and always mutable indigenous forms with modern cultural practices,[11] although Samora Machel, unusually, focused entirely on the harm of antiquated and negative habits which had been deliberately perpetuated under colonialism:

> Science, and the objective understanding of our country and the world acquired through the practice of class struggle and production are the basis of our thinking ... [and] will be the instrument to liquidate tribalism, regionalism and racism, the mentality inculcated by capitalism, which still make us consider indispensable to our personality all that which is decadent, degrading and outmoded.   *(FRELIMO 1974: 3)*

Nkrumah on the other hand, who rejected Léopold Sédar Senghor's notion of an "African socialism" based on metaphysical notions of the African "as a field of pure sensation" (Hodgkin 1973: 69), and recognized the coexistence of the traditional, the Western and the Islamic in Africa, argued that socialist thought should reassert in a modern context the principles of materialism, communalism, and egalitarianism in which precolonial societies were grounded (Nkrumah 1964). Similarly, Sankara urged the simultaneity of renewal and innovation: "We must be able to take from our past – from our traditions – all that is good, as well as all that is positive in foreign cultures, so as to give a new dimension to our culture. The inexhaustible fountainhead of the masses' creative inspiration lies in the popular masses themselves" (1988: 52).

The value of protean autochthonous cognitive forms in effecting an alternative modernity enters into the discussion of culture's political role.[12] For Mondlane, there was no doubt that the long history of cultural resistance in Mozambique was a precursor to militant anticolonialism; while with the onset of the armed struggle, the new styles of defiance, initiated by peasants and workers in song, dance, and carving expressed a deep-seated hostility to the alien culture, came to influence the art of professionals, and engendered political defiance. In the carvings of the Makonde peoples, "a pieta becomes a study not of sorrow but of revenge, with the mother raising a spear over the body of her dead son" (Mondlane 1983: 104–08). Far from being consigned to the "detritus of history," as has been claimed by participants in the postcolonial discussion (Lowe and Lloyd 1997: 6), liberation writing does indeed invoke different social imaginaries and alternative rationalities – and it is as well to remember that even the bourgeois-led Indian National Congress called on, appropriated, and redirected popular forms of protest and disobedience.

Among the heroes of the Angolan Liberation Front were those intellectuals who at the turn of the nineteenth century, and in protest against the colonizers' attempt to suppress the literate use of native languages, began to use the written word to contest colonialism (MPLA 1972: 7–11). In her Introduction to Agostinho Neto's poems, Margaret Holness observes that writers and musicians contributed significantly to the ferment of rebellion in Angola during the 1940s, when at a time of intensified institutional repression they eschewed assimilation, identified with the people, addressed them in their own idioms, and advocated a restoration of cultural traditions as a means to galvanize a united struggle against foreign occupation (Neto 1974: xviii). For Holness the cultural struggle of the intelligentsia facilitated the growth of a modern national movement, beginning with the *African National League* (1929) and, after 1945, the formation of clandestine political parties.

A more guarded estimate of such cultural interventions was made by Cabral, although he was among those intellectuals and students from the colonies then living in Lisbon, who during the early 1960s had founded a *Center for African Studies* "to rationalize the feelings belonging to a world of oppression and to awaken national consciousness through an analysis of the [African] continent's cultural foundations" (Neto 1974: xviii). If Cabral was later to question the significance of elite cultural resistance, the discriminations of his materialist understanding of culture as inseparable from socioeconomic structures cannot be dismissed as merely instrumental. In "The Role of Culture in the Liberation Struggle," Cabral argued for recognizing the class character of culture within the vertical structure of colonized society, distinguishing between the "masses who preserve their culture" and the restricted phenomenon of "native elites created by the colonizing process," or a colonial diaspora in a metropolis who were "more-or-less assimilated, uprooted and culturally alienated." The desire of this minority to "return to the source" by denying foreign culture its superiority and expressing the discovery of their own identity was dismissed by Cabral as influencing only metropolitan intellectuals and some backward members of their own class, and could not therefore be considered as an act of struggle against foreign rule (1974: 38–45).

In the case of "the people," however, culture was "the dynamic synthesis of the society's material and spiritual reality," serving as a source of physical and psychic energy and enacting indestructible resistance (Cabral 1974: 44). But while emphasizing popular culture as a positive heritage, Cabral also urged the importance of opposing "without violence, all prejudicial customs, the negative aspects of the beliefs and traditions of our people," toward which he all the same shows admirable pedagogic tact: "We are proud of not having forbidden our people to use fetishes, amulets and things of this sort, which we call *mezinhas* . . . We let our people find out for themselves, through the struggle, that their fetishes are of no use" (1972: 71, 129). Cabral's perception of a vibrant people's culture differs from that of Fanon who saw it as irretrievably debased by colonization; yet both converge in proposing that a revolutionary culture can only emerge through the struggle for liberation. Thus in Cabral's view, as the contradictions between the colonial power and the exploited masses sharpened during the prelude to an independence movement, the return recommended by the elite could be "historically important *only* if it involved both a genuine commitment to the fight for independence, and a total, definitive identification with the aspirations of the masses who contested not merely the foreigner's culture, but foreign rule altogether" (1974: 40–42).

For Cabral the negation by imperialist rule of a dominated society's historical process is also a negation of its cultural process, both of which must be repossessed:

A people who free themselves from foreign domination will not be culturally free unless, without underestimating the importance of positive contributions from the oppressor's culture and other cultures, they return to the upward paths of their own culture. The latter is nourished by the living reality of the environment and rejects harmful influences as much as any kind of subjection to foreign cultures. We see therefore, that, if imperialist domination has the vital need to practice cultural oppression, national liberation is necessarily an *act of culture*.   *(1980: 143)*

When Cabral elsewhere speaks of "a return to our history," his advocacy of new directions and expectations of still unimagined futures should not be misconstrued as retrograde (1972: 63).

To observe the arrest of a community's historical trajectory and celebrate its resumption in the context of a burgeoning modernity registers neither a nostalgic infatuation with the past nor mimicry of western notions of progress. As Sankara put it after leading the coup in Upper Volta which overthrew the formal independence earlier granted by France, and resulted in the establishment of Burkina Faso: "You cannot carry out fundamental change without a certain amount of madness. In this case it comes from nonconformity, the courage to turn your back on the old formulas, the courage to invent the future" (1988: 144).

IV

The recuperation of liberation theory as an articulation of a distinctive modernity is urgent in an intellectual climate where there are postcolonial critics who disavow its prior anticolonial critique, traduce its positions, and trivialize its achievements. Consider the preposterous accusation that anticolonialism drew on conceptions of "tradition and cultural anti-modernity" in opposing foreign domination and proposing "alternatives to capitalist development" (Lowe and Lloyd 1997: 9); or Homi Bhabha's censure of anticolonialism as "an anti-imperialist or black nationalist tradition 'in itself' " (Bhabha 1994: 241), an assessment which simply ignores the socialist goals and *internationalism* of Marxist-inspired movements. It was after all an Indian who participated in establishing the Communist Party of Mexico in 1919; from George Padmore, Richard Wright, Langston Hughes, Nkrumah, and Cabral came repeated messages of solidarity with the Black struggles in North America, anticolonial movements in Africa, Cuba, Vietnam, Algeria, Palestine, and Nicaragua; socialist countries were spoken of as allies; Machel and Neto stressed that the Portuguese people were not the enemy, and expressed support for the antifascist struggle in the colonial homeland that had been precipitated by the defeats of the Portuguese armies in the colonies; Sankara declared, "we must define the place of the Voltaic revolution in the world revolutionary process" (1988: 53).

In a different vein, Gayatri Spivak has attributed *all* articulations and practices of anticolonialism to "that class in the colonies" who ignored the subaltern and betrayed the "genuinely disenfranchised," while negotiating with the structures of violence imposed by the colonialists "in order to emerge as the so-called colonial subject" (1995: 146). If this account is true of independence movements controlled by an entrenched and powerful native bourgeoisie who manipulated the insurrectionary energies of the poor in achieving their own, minority ends, it dismisses the experiential transformation of the "subalterns" through their participation, and disregards situations where an organic relationship was forged between masses and leaders sharing the same class interests and revolutionary goals – there is after all no essential and invariable correlation between objective class position and ideological belief or political stance. For Stuart Hall, serenely defying the logic of colonialism's theory and practice, the consequence of the move from difference to *différance* demands that the oppositional form in which the colonial struggle has been represented in anticolonial discourse must be reread in terms of negotiation, "as forms of transculturation, of cultural translation, destined to trouble the here/there cultural binaries for ever" (1996a: 247).

A skeptic has remarked of "reconciliatory postcolonial thought" that it "fuse[s] postcolonialism with postmodernism in [its] rejection of resistance along with any form of binarism, hierarchy or telos" (During 1998: 31–32); and it is now impossible to overlook a strong impulse in the contemporary postcolonial discussion to find a middleground between the terms domination and oppression, to define colonial relationships as generically ambivalent, and to represent colonial locations as always and necessarily the site of dialogue. A tendency to privilege the cultural assimilation sought and achieved by colonial elites over popular resistance to colonial violence[13] is both ahistorical and morally vacant in its detachment from the outrages visited on the dispossessed. A more fitting recognition of the adversities they endured and the courage they displayed can be found in Fanon's pledge: "As for we who have decided to break the back of colonialism, our historic mission is to sanction all revolts, all desperate actions, all those abortive attempts drowned in rivers of blood" (1968: 207); while Davidson's remembrance of the insult delivered by colonialism brings a necessary ethical dimension to its critique: "This has been the missing factor in all European-centred histories of Africa; the deep and lasting sense of injury, that colonial dispossession was felt to have done to the way that people had lived and should live. It is the factor of moral legitimacy" (1992: 297).

The inadequate reasons advanced by the postcolonialist critics cited above cannot account for the devastating retreats from the revolutions inaugurated by liberation struggles. Among the more persuasive if still insufficient explanations for the reversals are the impossibility of building socialism in one country and the "basic contradiction... between an economic strategy of modernisation and industrialisation, and a political strategy of popular mobilisation and democracy" (Bertil Egerö, qtd. in Davidson 1992: 305). Others factors adduced by Davidson are social and economic emergencies arising from pre-existing and disastrous colonial policies and the consequent halting of revolutionary momentum, the adoption of a command economy on Soviet lines and advice, the assassination of politically competent literates, and the fostering of destructive factions by hostile states. At the heart of Davidson's interpretation, as glossed by Lazarus, is colonialism's legacy: what the newly independent nation-states inherited from the colonial powers "were states of a particular kind, scored and configured both 'internally' and 'externally' by their specific history as colonial dependencies in the capitalist world system... occup[ying] dependent and cruelly circumscribed positions as peripheral formations in the global economy" (Lazarus 1999a: 106). But these bleak accounts neither disparage the revolutionary energies and ethical impulses of those who made national liberation possible, nor do they preempt the possibilities of renewed mass participation in a political process that has been arrested but not defeated: where the conditions making for anticapitalist colonial struggles have not disappeared, the conditions making for guerrilla insurgencies remain, as is evident in Africa, South Asia, the Philippines, and Latin America.

A very different and negative assessment of the inevitable, because structural, setbacks to national liberation has been made by Arif Dirlik when examining the contradictions of a modernist Marxism "brought face to face with the premodern cultures of agrarian societies," where "unprecedented historical forces" have displaced societies from earlier historical conditions and relocated them "irretrievably within a new global economic, political, and ideological process" (1997b: 71, 69). The *problems* identified by Dirlik in his writings on Chinese Marxism (1997a, 1997b) are relevant to other national or cultural spaces where disjunctive social forms and modes of production were in the process of transformation by global capitalist forces. However the *consequences* Dirlik extrapolates from these historical encounters, namely the impossibility of translating Marxism into another idiom or implementing an alternative modernity, are less certain. His focus on a contradiction between the anticapitalist aspirations of national liberation movements and their commitment "to the developmentalism of EuroAmerican modernity" is premised on interpreting Marxism as a theory informed "by the spatial and temporal assumptions of a Eurocentric capitalism" (1994a: 64–65), whose "particular historical trajectory" assisted by the complicity of Marxism, "end[ed] up as a teleology world-wide in marking time" (1993: 142). But did not liberation thinkers, reassured by the alternative systems still standing in the way of capitalism's accelerating global reach, anticipate the immanent possibility of harnessing "development" to the construction of socialist societies, where modernity would mean the fostering of an anticapitalist ethos and the implementation of anticapitalist policies? And is censure of Marxism's collusion with this or any other teleology sustainable, given a theory of continuing sublation and a worldview where the supersession of capitalism signals the beginning of "real history" and not its closure?

An argument which situates contradiction as intrinsically disabling and dooms overdetermined projects to certain failure forecloses on the originality and autonomy of differently articulated projects of modernity. In Dirlik's view, colonial societies were "compelled into modernity not as its subject but as its object," because of which Third World modernity, "irrevocably alienated from its origins in Europe," has been "experienced not as an internal development but as an alien hegemony" (1997b: 68, 70). Yet on the evidence of liberation writings, modernity was apprehended as neither imposed by a foreign power, nor the gift of a predatory colonialism which had institutionalized retardation in pursuit of its own immediate interests, and in a vain attempt to deny the colonial people the status of modern subjects. Where the discontinuities in structural, cultural, and existential conditions were egregious, as in sub-Saharan Africa, those few with access to a larger cognitive field afforded by a secular education, and aware of living in chronologically simultaneous but non-synchronous moments, transcribed the experience of modernity as ontological dilemma, political problem and promise of emancipation.

Fredric Jameson has proposed that if "modernization is something that happens to the base, and modernism the form the superstructure takes in reaction to that ambivalent development, then perhaps modernity characterizes the attempt to make something coherent out of their relationships" (1991: 310). Because the alterations to "base" and the innovations in "superstructure" were uneven and unfinished in colonial worlds, the modes of cognition and structures of feeling inscribed by those conscious of inhabiting multiple locations and temporalities do not duplicate the turbulent European articulations of modernity, suffused as these were with the seismic effects of accelerated capitalist transformation, graphically invoked in the *Communist Manifesto*: "Constant revolutionizing of production, uninterrupted disturbance of all social relations, everlasting uncertainty and agitation distinguish the bourgeois epoch from all earlier ones. All fixed, fast-frozen relations, with their train of ancient prejudices and opinions are swept aside, all new-formed ones become antiquated before they can ossify" (Marx and Engels 1988: 36–37). Rather, the utterances of the small but not insignificant revolutionary intelligentsia of sub-Saharan Africa register an affection for *and* a dislocation from tradition, a propulsion toward but not an integration into the modern as received via colonialist intervention. If colonialism was the messenger of modernity's transformative capacities and emancipatory potential in colonial spaces, its message installing exploitation, inequalities, and injustice was refused. These disjunctions suggest a particular sensibility to modernity on colonial terrains, its intellectual and imaginative horizons extending from indigenous cultural and cognitive forms, to premonitions, not blueprints, of the *post-capitalist*.

Curiously it is Dirlik who, having asserted that "[t]he rewriting of history after the Eurocentric teleology of capitalist modernity, ruled out the possibility of looking into the past as a source of possible future alternatives to this teleology" (1999: 20), elsewhere provides an eloquent counter-argument to this indictment:

the goal of socialist revolution for the last two centuries has been to transcend capitalist modernity to create an alternative modernity closer in its constitution to the Enlightenment vision of human liberation. It is noteworthy that socialism, and not just "utopian socialism," retained in its vision of the future memories of the premodern community, but only in the form reworked by reason and the subjective goals of modernity; the contradiction endowed socialism with a revolutionary dynamism.

(1997b: 62)

This I read as implying that narratives of modernity's expectations are not predestined to reiterate capitalism's inspiration or aspiration.[14] Nor were modernity's pasts wholly entrapped by capitalism's ideology, its aesthetic including jazz, the Harlem Renaissance, the avant-garde of the Russian Revolution, and the florescence of art and writing in the Caribbean. It was after all in pursuit of a condition which colonialism sought to withhold from subjugated peoples, and which capitalism was generically incapable of fulfilling, that liberation movements initiated struggles invoking resilient and constantly reinvented indigenous traditions in envisaging alternatives to the existing social order, not as ends but as beginnings. When the urbane narrator of Alejo Carpentier's novel, *The Lost Steps*, recalls a tavern on the edge of the South American jungle called Memories of the Future, he delivers an epithet appropriate to liberation theory's variations on modernity.

NOTES

My thanks to Arif Dirlik, Gregory Elliott, Robert Fine, and Peter Gutkind.

1 Exceptions include Brennan 1997, Chrisman 1995, Lazarus 1999a, Said 1993, San Juan 1997, and Young 1998.

2 Those troubled by the refusal of continental philosophy to engage with other cognitive traditions include Bernasconi 1997, 1998. Discussion on the omissions from philosophical discourse has thus far centered on the status, or rather the dismissal of African philosophy. See Outlaw 1996, Serequeberhan 1996, 1997.

3 Personal communication with the author.

4 In print is an essay on Wilfredo Lam, the surrealist Cuban painter and anti-imperialist radical (Althusser 1995).

5 For a critique of Mao's Stalinism, see Deutscher 1977.

6 This assessment is in line with Sartre's notion of scarcity as a negative force defining human relationships: "The origin of struggle always lies ... in some concrete antagonism whose material condition is scarcity" (1976b: 113).

7 Despite which he wrote as sympathetically of Nkrumah's achievements and downfall as Sartre had done about the detours of Lumumba's radicalism. See Bogues 1997, Buhle 1986, James 1977.

8 In his early writings, Nehru traces the genesis of nineteenth-century imperialism to capitalism, and writing in 1939, considered that the "great world crisis and slump seemed to justify Marxist analysis" (1965: I. 278, 625). Julius Nyerere defined "African socialism" as following Christian precepts, rooted in the communal values of traditional society, and committed to destroying exploitation and injustice, hence making it impossible to interpret "Africanization" as the replacement of non-African landlords, employers and capitalists with their African counterparts (1968). A more robust appropriation of Marxism was made by a now unrecognizable Robert Mugabe: "The Party [ZANU, Zimbabwe African National Union] has accepted scientific socialism as its guiding philosophy ... We ... have a duty to read and understand what the fathers of that theory actually said. We also have to examine that theory in the light of our history and the environment of our country" (1983: 38).

9 For some examples, on South Africa see Alexander 1979 and Tabata 1974; on Filipino liberation movements see San Juan 1998; on Latin America, see Brennan 1997; on Guyana, Rodney 1990; on India, Sarkar 1989. See also Césaire 1972; Miller and Aya 1971.

10 Similarly, Agostinho Neto regarded the armed rebellion in Angola as "a school... the means whereby the people will continue the struggle in the future" (MPLA 1972: 7).

11 As Eqbal Ahmad has observed, a revolution must not only "promise a new vision of society," but must also "be congruent with the old culture [since] the symbols of revolution and styles of leadership derive heavily from the local culture and constitute the creative links between the old and the new" (1971: 63–64).

12 Fanon's writing on this has been extensively examined and glossed by Lazarus 1990, 1993, 1997.

13 Between the late 1950s and the 1980s the prominent politico-intellectuals assassinated by agents of colonial powers included the following: Lumumba (Congo/Zaire), Cabral (Guinea-Bissau), Walter Rodney (Guyana), Jacques Stéphen Alexis (Haiti), Mondlane and Machel (Mozambique), Ruth First (South Africa), and Sankara (Burkina Faso).

14 Samir Amin has proposed that we should think of modernity as an unfinished project in which human beings make their own history, its failures the results of capitalism, but its manifestations not restricted to its capitalist forms, and its furtherance possible only by going beyond capitalism (1997: 103).

8

Sex, space, and modernity in the work of Rashid Jahan, "Angareywali"

Priyamvada Gopal

> It is not possible for the colonized society and the colonizing
> society to agree to pay tribute, at the same time and in the same
> place, to a single value... The truth objectively expressed is
> constantly vitiated by the lie of the colonial situation.
>
> *(Frantz Fanon, "Medicine and Colonialism")*

Some five decades before the Rushdie affair, Rashid Jahan, a young
Muslim woman in India, was warned by newspaper announcements
to retract the two stories she had contributed to a collection in Urdu
called *Angarey* (Live Coals). She was also threatened with kidnapping and disfigurement; community leaders denounced her and her
three male collaborators. Friends urged her to employ a bodyguard;
she did not do so, saying that it would interfere with her work as a
doctor in poor areas. *Angarey* came out in 1932. Within months, the
British government had banned it, citing section 295A of the Indian
Penal Code which targets any person who, "with deliberate and ma-
licious intention," attempts to "outrag[e] ... the religious feelings of
any class of His Majesty's subjects, by words either spoken or written,
or by visible representations" (104). As a woman, and one who had
chosen to write about sexual harassment, birth control, pregnancy,
abortion, and women's health, Rashid Jahan (called "Angareywali"
or "The 'Angarey' Woman" by some) became the symbol of the cultural violence allegedly perpetrated by the collection of stories. The
Angarey volume itself is widely understood to have inaugurated a
long phase in literary radicalism on the Indian subcontinent during
its transition from colony to nations between the 1930s and 1950s.
The highlight of this epoch was the formation of the influential Indian Progressive Writers Association (PWA) and the Indian People's
Theatre Association (IPTA). Rashid Jahan, who was active in both

organizations, later became a member of the Communist Party of India; she and other communists were even arrested and jailed briefly in 1949 by the new government of free India. In addition to organizing PWA conferences and writing plays for IPTA, she edited a political monthly called *Chingari* and published in other magazines: one of her stories was translated in the American left journal, *New Masses*. While her writings seem to have received little attention in the decades following her death in 1952, her influence has been gratefully acknowledged by such Urdu literary luminaries as Ismat Chughtai and Faiz Ahmad Faiz.

Rashida (as she was known) had also trained as a doctor at Lady Hardinge Medical College in Delhi, which had been established in 1916 with the express purpose of educating native women in Western medical practice. Her experiences as a doctor were central to her work as a writer. As part of a relatively early cadre of female Indian professionals and, certainly, of Muslim women doctors, she found herself thinking about the relationship between the modern breed of "new woman" to which she belonged and the constituency in whose name she had been created. As David Arnold (1983: 265) has remarked, the training of Indian women in colonial medical institutions itself came about as a result of the "fervent politicization" of colonized women's bodies. Medicine and technology were, of course, central to polemical debates about modernity and colonialism. "Western" (allopathic) medicine was particularly susceptible to accusations of invasiveness since it could not "be meaningfully abstracted from the broader character of the colonial order" (Arnold 1983: 8). Given their simultaneous investments in science, women's health, anticolonialism and social justice, feminists like Rashid Jahan had to develop critical apparatuses that would enable them to resist the violence of colonial projects without at the same time conceding ground to the self-appointed guardians of "traditions" within and without their natal communities. If "postcolonial feminism" has been appropriated, in the name of anticolonialism, to legitimate a largely post-representational politics which seeks a thoroughgoing repudiation of concepts like reason and progress (figured purely as the bequest of Western Enlightenment), the work of earlier feminists like Rashid Jahan offers a richer legacy that serves to reconfigure this prevailing ethos in less reductive and more productive directions.

It is now something of a critical commonplace that Marxist political and literary traditions inevitably subordinate gender to class. This assumption, as Paula Rabinowitz (1991: 6) has pointed out, results in the elision of certain types of women's writing (such as that inspired by the American Popular Front in the 1930s) from literary histories like the *Norton Anthology of Women's Literature*. For contemporary feminist studies, one of the more deleterious and paradoxical results of the assumption that Marxist thought is *constitutively* incapable of engaging gender or sexuality has been a narrowing of what is considered feminist: "Women's literature, like woman's place is viewed as private and extrahistorical, providing a particularistic vision in contrast to the universalized stance of masculine discourse" (Rabinowitz 1991: 7). As Rabinowitz suggests, we need to understand how women's lives, however private, "nevertheless construct political history and how women's writings engage in debates that extend into the so-called public arena." To write such "regendered" histories of literary radicalism in South Asian colonial and postcolonial contexts is to return to the work of feminists like Rashid Jahan, Razia Sajjad Zaheer and Ismat Chughtai (among others) to try and understand the ways in which they engaged not only issues of gender, sexuality, and domesticity, but also modernity, colonialism, nation-formation, state, community, and social justice. Regendered literary histories would also examine the *intersectional* nature of their thinking rather than rely on recycled political and critical axioms about writing on the left. Susie Tharu's and K. Lalita's claims – such as that PWA-inspired work relegated gender issues to attitudes that would be resolved after the overthrow of capitalism – are not only caricatures, verifiably inadequate with regard to the work of several different writers, but actually obscure necessary analysis of more challenging problems thrown up by this body of work.

Rashid Jahan, "lady doctor," for instance, wrestled specifically with issues of scientific and secular thought in relation to the female body. The kinds of questions she investigated remain relevant to contemporary feminist engagements with science, technology, and culture. What is the relationship of the body to the ideologies and institutions that seek to shape it? How does this relationship affect the way we seek to liberate the body from suffering? How might we recuperate scientific and medical knowledge from the power relations in which they are imbricated while understanding that knowledge is never politically unmarked? Rashid Jahan's work is, at one level, an early feminist attempt to deal with the conundra of modernity in a colonial context in which, as Frantz Fanon suggests: "The truth objectively expressed is constantly vitiated by the lie of the colonial situation" (1967c: 128). As her dialectical understanding of "modernity" and "tradition," and bodies and discourses deepens, Rashid Jahan's work progresses from relatively simplistic documentary-style depictions of the female body to offering nuanced insights about female bodies and subjectivities in relation to colonial, modern, traditional, and national institutions. In particular, her work shows an evolving critical understanding of gendered bodies and identities in relation to modernizing urban spaces. As the development and reconstitution of these spaces entailed new kinds of mobility for women like her, Rashid Jahan found herself returning to questions of representation in complicated ways that both resonate with and challenge the tortured post-representational ethos that dominates feminist and postcolonial studies today.

A story like "Voh" or "That One," for instance, focuses on the figure of the middle-class female professional in relation to gendered modern institutions such as the girls' school and the clinic – and the classed Other woman whom she encounters here (Jahan 1988; English translation 1993). The story, which is remarkably sparse, quite explicitly foregrounds the politics of speaking for or even *about* the "other." It concerns the chance encounter of the narrator, who is a teacher in a girls' school, with a grotesquely disfigured woman at a clinic. After an exchange of "smiles" with this literally faceless woman, the narrator finds out from the pharmacist that the woman, only referred to as "That One" (which might well be translated as "The Other") is a prostitute suffering from a venereal disease. Later she is visited by this woman during her lunch hour at the girls' school where she works. To the discomfort of the narrator and her colleagues, the visits continue on a daily basis, until a woman sweeper at the school picks a fight with the unappealing visitor and beats her out of the premises.

"I first met her at the hospital. She had come there for treatment and so had I" (Jahan 1993: 119). The opening lines of the story lay out the new spatial and institutional configurations that enable this encounter between the two women whose paths, only a few years previously, might not have crossed so easily. The narrator belongs to the emergent class of the professional middle-class woman who works outside the home; her interlocutor is a working-class woman, the public exploitation of whose labor and sexuality has long been institutionalized. At first, it is only in terms of her own being that this encounter has significance for the narrator – as a kind of inverted romance with her own emotional existence at the center:

I was working at a girls school. I was still fresh from college. The future was a garden where no flower fell short of a rose or a jasmine blossom and the world lay stretched out at my feet. Life was a stream in a moonlit

night, rippling gently here, cascading into a waterfall there. I was happy.
I had no idea what the wrench of pain might be. (119)

There is only a hint of irony here as the narrative draws on the high
sentimental rhetoric of the "afsana" or romantic short story that was
especially popular with a female readership. The narrative even takes
this rhetoric seriously, using it to set up a contrast between what it sees
as the privileged world of the narrator and the wretchedness of That
One. Indeed, in describing her own coming to political consciousness
through Rashid Jahan's influence, Ismat Chughtai would use a similar
distinction: "The handsome heroes and pretty heroines of my stories,
the candle-like fingers, the lime blossoms and crimson outfits all vanished into thin air. The earthy Rasheed [sic] Jahan simply shattered all
my ivory idols to pieces ... Life, stark naked, stood before me" (qtd.
in Tharu and Lalita 1993: 118).

At first, the stakes in "That One" seem mainly to be the narrator's
unlearning of her own privilege. Accordingly, her initiation into the
"real world" is one where her sheltered senses are now subject to
strain:

I felt repulsed too, but somehow managed to look straight at her and
smile. She smiled back, or at least I thought she tried to – *it was difficult
to tell*. She had no nose. Two raw, gaping holes stood in its place. She had
also lost one of her eyes. To see with the other she had to turn her whole
neck around. (119; *my emphasis*)

The physical otherness of this woman is crucial to the narrative of encounter and (failed) attempts at empathy and solidarity. If the claims
of professional feminist organizations like the All-India Women's
Congress (AIWC) to speak for all women were based on an unexamined premise of shared biological being as sufficient common cause,
it is a premise that is all too easily disrupted by this decaying and
grotesque physique that not only evades conventional modes of communication but also makes "knowing" difficult. At the same time, the
rejection of her (common) humanity by the pharmacist is problematic:
"That one is a scoundrel, a filthy whore. She's been rotting to death,
that one, bit by bit. And now she thinks of treatment." For the pharmacist, it is outrageous that the clinic treats this woman as a body that is
deserving of treatment like any other: "The doctor has no sense either.
Just hands a prescription over. Ought to be thrown out, she ought,
that slut!" (119). As histories of hospitals and medicine in colonial
India suggest, these institutions themselves were initially associated
with the lower echelons of society; efforts were later made to court the

patronage of the higher castes and classes, especially women considered "respectable" (Arnold 1983: 258). Given this context, "That One"
is an account, not only of the emergence of middle- and upper-class
women into these public institutional spaces, but also of how these
spaces and their erstwhile denizens were themselves altered and affected by the entry of the former. If the narrator sees That One as the
embodiment of a reality she has been hitherto sheltered from, it is also
true that the narrator's presence is part of a transformation of That
One's reality and not necessarily in salutary ways.

As the bamboo curtain of the school's staff room rises day after day
to admit That One, her forays into the narrator's "respectable" space
become a journey in the reverse direction with the proverbial curtain now raised by the Other. Not surprisingly, this unexpected move
brings the apparently modern and egalitarian foundations of institutions like the girls' school and the hospital to crisis: "The principal
was annoyed too . . . 'Must you invite her into the school? I'm sure
our parents will take exception to a loose woman like her entering our
premises'" (120). As That One seemingly takes silent charge of their
encounters, the narrator herself feels a deep sense of passivity, even
helplessness: "Every day I would decide to put a stop to it all . . . All
the same when she came the next day I would offer a chair and mutter,
'Please sit down.'" This unexpected loss of agency – and the return of
her own romanticizing gaze – forces the narrator to move the focus
from herself, her emotions and her encounters with another reality,
to That One: "There she sat, just gazing at me with that crooked eye
and that ghastly nose-less face. Sometimes I thought I saw her eye fill.
What was passing through her mind? I wondered" (120). The educated woman here has information, but not insight. A stray moment
of identification also inspires the narrator to think about who this
woman really is as another human being: "What was she staring at?
What was she thinking about? Had she once been like me? I shivered
at the thought."

As it turns out, it is That One's belief that the narrator, Safia, "knew
nothing about her" that has sustained this curious romance with its
daily offering of a jasmine flower from the former to the latter. After being attacked by the sweeper, Naseeban, who calls her a whore,
a devastated That One weeps, not for the blood trickling down her
temple but because "[n]ow you know everything" (122). Her dramatic
last words suggest that her only stake in this relationship was the hope
that the narrator was ignorant about her past, allowing her to live in
a make-believe world of purity and romance. But it is not implausible

to imagine that a woman used to being the object of curiosity, revulsion, pity, or fear might enjoy an empowering sense of subjectivity in a relationship where none of these emotions seem to be overtly at work. What she sees as a fresh beginning also gives her some control over how she is perceived. For one who has been also an object of sexual exploitation, this relationship of apparent mutual respect with another woman may also be an opportunity to imagine and experience reciprocal desire. The quasi-romantic overtures that That One makes toward Safia invert the gaze directed at the prostitute in reform discourse: "I was being made into an object of ridicule in the school. Still, whenever she placed a flower before me, I would tuck it into my hair and her face would once again crease into that horrifying smile" (121). Inasmuch as it deflects the epistemic violence of the objectifying gaze from center to margin, this mutuality, however tenuous, opens up possibilities for non-hierarchical, collaborative, and transformative sorts of knowledge. Of course, within the parameters of the story, these remain just that – possibilities – that may or may not come to fruition.

The emerging liberal-modern fiction of mutuality is one that the narrative, in fact, maintains even as it recognizes its impossibility under the circumstances. It is noteworthy that the decisive act of repudiation comes neither from the doubtful narrator nor her sneering colleagues but another working-class woman. When That One blows her nose and wipes her fingers on the wall, the old sweeper, Naseeban, apparently forgetting "all the good breeding culled from twenty years of working in the school" hits her hard in the back with a slate (121). By placing the actual burden of rejection on Naseeban's "old back-alley self," the narrative absolves the narrator and her colleagues from any direct participation in class hostility. Yet we know that Naseeban only articulates their own suppressed instincts, Safia's included: "Nobody would sit in the chair she used. I don't blame them. It wasn't their fault. She looked so revolting. I couldn't bring myself to touch the chair either" (120). Indeed, the othering of That One is so complete, that an older teacher does not regard her as a woman at all: "Tut, tut. You ought to observe purdah before that one." The veil in this instance is intended to reinforce gendered class distinctions to the point where only upper-class, sexually "pure" females count as "women." Once again, the narrative subjects the concept of shared womanhood to scrutiny, suggesting that gender is inflected by other coordinates, most saliently, class and community. "That One" problematizes the universalizing assumptions of the category "woman," without, however, dissolving biological specificity or human commonalities into the purely discursive.

The split in the narrator's consciousness with regard to That One is worth commenting on: on the one hand, she shares the revulsion of those around her; on the other, she finds herself responding to That One's overtures of friendship. Part of her insists on a profound moral difference between them that is also a rejection of the other's claims to a humanity in common: "Doesn't she have a mirror? Doesn't she know she's reaping the fruit of a sinful life? Why doesn't anyone tell her ... Does she really believe that I consider her only *another* sick *person*?" (121, my emphasis). But, at the same time, she cannot help wanting to know more, to go beyond the apparent and plumb the depths of this stranger: "Does she have a family? Where does she live? Where does she come from?" This bifurcation in the narrator's consciousness, the veil, as it were, between her impulse not to recognize That One as another human being and her need to know more is integral to the kind of realism that the story attempts to evolve. The will to ignorance, to refuse to probe reality, is problematic even as coming to knowledge is never a simple process. In this regard, That One's sad parting remark is important – for it too is preceded by a momentary act of veiling: "She hid her face in her hands and a moment later said: 'Now you know everything,' and left" (122). It is certainly plausible to read this moment in terms of the subaltern's fundamental desire to remain inscrutable to reading. Her actions would then indicate a deliberate veiling that speaks to her need to evade appropriation as the subject of understanding or knowledge. To respect inscrutability is, presumably, a way to avoid epistemic violence.

But there would be something lacking in such a reading even as it cautions us against a naive humanism that enjoins us to "only connect," to use E. M. Forster's famous phrase. To repeatedly emphasize the ineluctability of subaltern consciousness and the intractability of the subaltern's subjectivity to understanding is, paradoxically, to refuse her the subjectivity that she herself reveals glimpses of. Like the narrator in this story, it is important to ask: "Why does she come here?" What motivates her to repeatedly seek out the company of the woman she has made eye contact with just once, if what she wishes is to remain ineffable? On the face of it, the narrative itself offers no real insights since the only explicit suggestion it makes is that That One seeks a romantic relationship where she can fantasize living a different, more "pure" existence. But is it really only the loss of that make-believe persona that That One laments in her parting words? For it is also possible that her comment is a reference to what she sees as a lost struggle to solicit an understanding from the narrator that will not partake of the conventional "knowledge" that typically determines readings of her diseased body. In other words, hers could also be a quest for a more genuine, reciprocal understanding that would enable her to develop new kinds of relationships, as opposed to the lack of knowledge that equates disease with moral decay and grotesque bodies with inhuman-ness. "What does she feel when she comes to the school," the narrator wonders. One possibility is that "she" sees this space, so crucial to the emancipation of one class of women, as one that will allow her too to resist the degradation and determinism that she is subject to elsewhere. Naseeban's hostile words insist that this will not be possible: "You bastard, you whore, who do you think you are? Yesterday you were loitering at the street corner, and today as your flesh falls rotting apart, you parade here like a lady" (121). Vicious as they are, the sweeper's words may actually serve as an honest insight into the egalitarian pretensions of the place where she herself has worked in a menial capacity and which has, in fact, brought little emancipation or transformation to her own life.

In their introduction to the second volume of their anthology, *Women Writing in India*, which includes "That One," Tharu and Lalita raise an important question for feminist scholarship: "What are the dimensions in which the working-class woman is imagined in stories such as Rasheed [sic] Jahan's ...? " (1993: 82). Their own reading is categorical: "It is the nameless middle-class woman, the story implies, who must lift the veil of her consciousness and find the resources to look this figure from the real world straight in the eye." The "other woman" in a story like this, "the prostitute, the working-class woman is a figure cut to the measure of this middle-class woman's requirement that is also, we must not forget, the requirement of the nation" (83). This cautionary claim is one that must be taken seriously. It is often the case that stories about those at the margins, including histories of the subaltern are, at one level, "stories of the center, told by the center" (83). In the case of written literature, literacy and access to the means of intellectual and literary production themselves make this hierarchy inevitable. Even as we keep this caveat in mind, however, it seems necessary to read a story like "That One" more carefully, as much for what it does not say explicitly as for its narrative claims. One of the more dynamic uses of veiling and unveiling which Tharu and Lalita's reading overlooks is the way in which the veil also becomes That One's means of shaping her identity. By literally crossing bamboo-curtained borders to claim institutional space for herself, That One attempts to draw a curtain over the history of her interpellation as "whore." To say that this is a subaltern imagined by the center is indisputable at the most literal level of authorial biography; but to use this biographical fact to flatten the range of possible understandings and insist on an inevitable ideological "pandering" is questionable.

Moreover, given how contested a category "nation" itself was at this point, it is unclear what it would mean to simply "pander" to its requirements. While the account that "That One" offers is made possible by the institutional spaces of the modern nation-in-the-making, what actually takes place in these spaces is determined by more than a set of "requirements." In fact, Rashid Jahan's story tells us something about how interactions within these spaces exceed, subvert, or even simply evade the expectations that precede them. (Indeed, That One's very presence in these spaces brings them and their "respectable" citizen-denizens to crisis.) As such, "That One" is also an account of the meanings of nation and national modernity – as defined by institutions and the spaces they create – for those outside the center. Sociologist Kalpana Ram has suggested that

[w]hile it is important to register the kinds of conceptual/social exclusions that may be at work in the hegemonic intellectual paradigm, it would be a mistake to assume from this that the hegemonic paradigm has not also exercised considerable influence over marginalized social groups, or that very sense of exclusion has not been operative as a point of mobilization for them. (1996: 315)

My argument is less that hegemonic paradigms and institutions exercise influence over the margins than that we need to pay attention to how those margins approached, appropriated, and consequently altered those hegemonies themselves. This work – which need not entail romanticizing subaltern capabilities or ignoring the power dynamics that make "appropriation" difficult – is especially important given the contemporary theoretical emphasis on problematizing "modernity" and "reason" in the name of this very subaltern.[1]

In some ways, Rashid Jahan's concerns with regard to modernity and tradition were similar to and can be amplified by those of another famous doctor-intellectual working in a colonial context. In an essay entitled "Medicine and Colonialism," Frantz Fanon wrote:

Introduced into Algeria at the same time as racialism and humiliation, Western medical science, being part of the oppressive system, has always provoked in the native an ambivalent attitude . . . [T]he colonial situation is precisely such that it drives the colonized to appraise all the colonizer's contributions in a pejorative and absolute way. *(1967c: 121)*

Unlike primary colonization ("military conquest and the police system"), technological and scientific advances can offer objectively identifiable benefits, but in a colonial situation they are either perceived as intrinsically linked to other acts of violence or are actually put to bad use by those in power. The wheat becomes inseparable from the chaff in a situation that is "vitiated by the lie of the colonial situation." For Fanon, this state of affairs is intrinsically tragic, for though he empathizes deeply with the suspicion of the colonizer's apparatuses and intentions, he also identifies with a pull, felt by the native himself, to act "from a strictly rational point of view, in a positive way" (126). (He offers a medical example here: "my son has meningitis and it really has to be treated as a meningitis ought to be treated" [126].)

The dominant group arrives with its values and imposes them with such violence that the very life of the colonized can manifest itself only defensively, in a more or less clandestine way. Under these conditions, colonial domination distorts the very relations that the colonized maintains with his own culture. In a great number of cases, the practice of tradition is a disturbed practice. *(130)*

In emphasizing that the practice of tradition is "disturbed," Fanon is less invested in debunking "tradition" than in suggesting that the natural logic of culture is never simply about conserving or consolidating notions of the "self" or the "indigenous." On the contrary, under normal circumstances cultural processes are transformative. The practice of tradition is "disturbed" inasmuch as it can entail a refusal to engage, reflect, learn, and strategically appropriate the unfamiliar; this kind of ossification, in certain situations, requires the psychic violence of going against one's better judgment.

Rashid Jahan's work also suggests a less dyadic understanding of cultural dynamics in colonial situations. Writers like her had come to see themselves and their cultures as capable of radical change through self-critique in ways that would neither simply accede to nor blindly counter the colonizer. For the questions raised by a story like "That One" are not only: "What do I think of That One?" but also: "How is she imagining herself?", "What is her relation to these new spaces" (hospital and school) and, equally important, "How is she imagining me (the narrator, the educated middle-class woman)?" Despite the ostensibly revelatory nature of its closing lines, the story is less invested in claiming access to the subaltern's consciousness than in suggesting that her relation to the institutions and ideologies of the modern must figure in our histories and programs. What does it mean, for instance, that the sick woman does insistently, in the contemptuous words of the pharmacist, "think about treatment"? Or that she feels empowered to come to the school to gain a new sense of self? In her investigation of the gendering of the flâneur in Western modernism, Susan Buck-Morss has pointed out that there is a "close connection between the debasement of women sexually and their presence in public space" (1986: 118). The insistent, "offensive" presence of That One, so "awkward" and "humiliating" for the narrator, cannot but be subversive in a very similar context which associated the sexual debasement of women with their entry into public spaces. (It is the narrator, interestingly enough, who experiences a sense of debasement which That One refuses to feel.) In that sense, the story poses compelling questions: beyond "uplift" and "progress," which we do well to problematize, what did colonial/postcolonial modernity and its institutions mean to the gendered subaltern? And how might a knowledge of her responses and her engagements affect, not only the way we think about modernity or progress, but the very setting into place of new communities and institutions?

Given these possibilities, it seems entirely reductive to claim that a story like "That One" is not really different from those more conservative ones that "raise few threats to a patriarchal order," and that it "manages the shift into the modern while maintaining the authority of the old order" (Tharu and Lalita 1993: 83). Such a critical framework is limited by the assumption that any and all indigenous attempts at social change and reform are ineluctably subsumed within colonialist and nationalist projects ("derivative," as Partha Chatterjee [1989] suggests). Rashid Jahan's work, by contrast, shows an increasing interest in subject formation and social transformation as intersectional and dynamic processes where coordinates such as class, gender, caste, and race inflect each other. Her work examines the dialectic of self and structure, and a dynamic, ongoing engagement of bodies, psyches, institutions, and ideologies. Foregrounding the ways in which women's relationships to their bodies and to space shift in response to historical and social exigencies, even early stories like "A Tour of Delhi" and, later, "One of My Journeys" explore questions of habitus (broadly defined as the organization of the senses and cognitive capabilities into different ways of being, knowing, and acting) as opposed to "identity" or "subjectivity" alone.

In the reform narratives that Tharu and Lalita allude to, bringing women out of seclusion into the public is figured as a charitable act that focuses on the object being moved rather than on a dialogic reconstitution of spaces and spatial divisions themselves. Rashid Jahan's work, in contrast, repeatedly posits the still rarely discussed and importantly feminist question of women's *responsibility* in relation to the structuring of new spaces and communities. "One of My Journeys," for instance, sharply critiques the reenactment of religious–sectarian ("communal") hostilities between two groups of women sharing an all-female space. The encounter here in a modern, technologized, and nationalizing space takes place in the portable seclusion of a woman's compartment in a train and as in "That One," gender becomes an insufficient marker of commonality as various other coordinates of identity – caste and religion in particular – emerge to generate animosities. Rather than write it out of the equation, the story suggests that gender must be seen both in its complexity and in its capacity as a critical political force that will question the ways in which other identities operate. There is an insistence in Rashid Jahan's work on seeing women as political subjects and actors who bear civic and social responsibilities with regard to emancipation and democratization. New spaces need to be defamiliarizing in a way that allows for a radical unlearning of old political habits. If in Fanon's famous narrative of the unveiling of Algerian women, the reconstitution of women's being-in-space gets unproblematically mapped on to the aims and achievements of the national revolution itself, for Rashid Jahan, this relearning, re-establishing, and distorting of "corporal patterns" must be a thoughtful process where women learn to be accountable political actors who must critique and refashion the ways in which national spaces constitute themselves (Fanon, 1967c: 59).

Elizabeth Wilson has pointed out that in the European context, the fragmentariness of urban life in distinction to rural life means that "we observe bits of the 'stories' men and women carry with them, but never learn their conclusions" (1992: 107). Rashid Jahan suggests that these "brushings against strangers" are also the stuff of which stories are made and relationships forged; the happy endings can be worked out, at least in the realm of possibility. Wilson also points out usefully that "we cannot automatically accept the nineteenth-century ideological division between private and public spheres on its own terms" (98). In many ways, the work of Rashid Jahan on women's experience of space in a colonial, urbanizing context works similarly to challenge such assumptions. It is also, of course, an investigation of utopian possibilities for reconfiguring spatial relations. The author's insistence on women's political agency warns against reducing the scope of women's actions by reading them as only signs or objects of reform.

As such, Rashid Jahan's work brings to crisis certain canonical readings of gendered modernity in the colonial context. The most well-known cartography of cultural modernity in India has been developed by Partha Chatterjee whose insightful work maps a spatial dichotomy of home and world which "resolves" the paradoxes of Indian nationalism. Chatterjee suggests that Indian nationalists who found themselves drawn to the very Western and modern idea of the nation-state realized that to adopt this framework wholesale would be to concede superiority to the colonizer. Yet the nation was a powerful and attractive framework for self-assertion. The "resolution" of this paradox came in the form of a separation of private and public, inner and outer, spiritual and material which then mapped on to the division between the spheres of the national and the familial:

The world is the external, the domain of the material; the home represents one's inner spiritual self, one's true identity ... It is also typically the domain of the male. The home in its essence must remain unaffected by the profane activities of the material world – and woman is its representative.
(Chatterjee 1993: 120)

If the West had superiority in the sphere of the world and subjugated non-European peoples on these grounds, for the nationalists "it had failed to colonize the inner, essential, identity of the East," which resided in the feminized sphere of the home.

Chatterjee's account has a certain intuitive resonance for students of both nationalism and women's history in its attempts to offer a nuanced account of the paradoxes of modernity and nation-formation in (post)colonial contexts. Yet, there are serious limitations to his account, the most significant of which is the slippage whereby what purports to be an analysis of "the women question" becomes principally an account of male nationalist anxieties around cultural identity and colonial subjection. Chatterjee's characterization of the home–world dichotomy is that it is the answer to the problem of how to retain "the self-identity of national culture." That it then becomes the "ideological framework within which nationalism answered the women's question" seems incidental (1993: 120–21). Chatterjee's picture of *how* the nationalist "resolution" entailed a gendered division of space does not really explain *why* this solution was gendered in this way. While he concedes that his conclusion looks little different from "the typical conception of gender roles in traditional patriarchy," he insists that the rationale at this point in history is intimately bound up with specific nationalist crises of identity (120).

Ironically, in the process of elaborating the *symbolic* role played by gender in nationalist crises of modernity and self-identity, Chatterjee winds up giving short shrift to the "women question" itself. As Wilson has suggested in the context of European modernism, the study of "'woman as sign' too often ends with *reduction* of woman to sign" (1992: 104, Wilson's emphasis). The symbolic gendering of space was to have obvious material consequences in women's lives, but what precisely was the "women question" – as opposed to the tradition–modernity question? And why did the resolution play itself out on the bodies of women? There is also something problematic about the assumption that "the nationalist mind" was always already male and "self-identity" vis-à-vis modernization was fundamentally a crisis of masculinity. This limitation stems partly from the attempt to generalize about nationalism from the written works of a few select male writers and to theorize about practice from the standpoint of intellectual history alone. But beyond that, Chatterjee also seems unwilling to read women's relationship to cultural processes as anything other than reactive. As she emerges in his account, the Bengali middle-class "new woman" writes about her relationship to the dichotomies that structure nationalist thought, and perhaps her occasional subversions and appropriations, but never finds herself in a dynamic and dialectical and *lived* relationship with cultural processes. Even when he makes a self-conscious move from discussing discourse *about* women to emphasizing women's speech, Chatterjee is unable to conceptualize such a dialogism. Instead, he claims, women's "autonomous subjectivity" is to be found in the domestic archives of home rather than "the external domain of political conflict" (1993: 137).

Rashid Jahan's stories problematize this picture. She writes in a historical period that directly follows the nineteenth-century context that Chatterjee discusses, but her treatment of very similar spatial divisions is strikingly different. Modernity cannot be successfully sutured and contained in the "world" and, even so, women do not necessarily adhere to these divisions. They cross boundaries, not as assertions of "autonomous subjectivity" but as participants in historical processes of change. Of course, the very existence of male and female enclosed spaces within larger public spaces makes evident the efforts to control the gendering of public spaces, precisely to avoid an imagined sexual chaos and the real possibilities of violence. The attempts to replicate the spatial divisions of middle- and upper-class homes in public spaces would seem to buttress Chatterjee's argument that women and tradition were both contained through seclusion, but clearly, such replication and suturing is impossible. Portable seclusion can only be a moment within a larger movement of encounter and spatial reconstitution. Moreover, the seclusion of women in spaces such as the "ladies compartment" in trains, brings to the fore a different problem: gender may function as a lowest common denominator of identity, but it is thrown into crisis at precisely the moment in which it is deployed in all-female public spaces. In the women's clinic, the girls' college, or the crowded protection of the ladies compartment, the category "woman" seems entirely inadequate to capturing identity: class, religion, community, marital status, and educational levels all inflect gender to produce a range of gendered identities. A feminist understanding of the "personal as political" must necessarily, therefore, be broadened to include considerations of transforming relations between women in the context of the reconstitution of civic spaces and institutions.

If the driving force of Chatterjee's analysis is a desire to prove that modernity itself is inimical to postcolonial cultures and needs be sutured in order to be contained, Rashid Jahan and Fanon embrace – cautiously and critically – a certain dialogism of everyday life in the modern world. This dialogism is inherent in culture-as-process. The dynamism of this process, Fanon suggests, is arrested under conditions of colonization where "colonial domination distorts the very relations that the colonized maintains with his own culture"(1967c: 130). Under such conditions, what gets entrenched is "an attitude of counter-assimilation, of the maintenance of a cultural, hence national, originality" (1967c: 42). For Fanon, as for Rashid Jahan, this tendency to counter-assimilation, while understandable, cannot be allowed to destroy a culture's capacity "to re-evaluate its deepest values, its most stable models" (42). For Rashid Jahan, modernity in the colonial context cannot be reduced to a pedagogical project that inflicted violence on a colonial subject. On the contrary, as some of her stories, like "Will the Accused Please Stand," suggest, the violence and racism of the colonial project often relies, *not* on a ruthless universalism, but on an unfair and inequitable relativism which works to justify its hierarchical existence. While Fanon himself displays some ambiguity about whether reason is a Western concept, one to which non-European cultures must be open, Rashid Jahan's work seems to suggest that critical and rational faculties are fundamental to and recuperable within any cultural context.

In the final instance, what emerges in Rashid Jahan's work, are reflections on the possibility of an anticolonial, feminist and socially engaged habitus that would actively engage the challenges and contradictions of the transitional period. Such a habitus would not necessarily develop through the somewhat mechanistic (and voluntaristic) "processes of ideological selection" that, according to Chatterjee, were deployed by male nationalist reformers (1993: 121). Rather, it would be necessarily negotiated and developed through the exigencies of daily existence at the intersections of the colonial, the modern, the feudal, the industrial, the familial, the public, the traditional, the private, the communitarian, and the national. This framework of dynamic transformation, where the gendered subject engages critically with historical circumstances even as she is shaped by them, opens up possibilities outside the dyad of determinism and voluntarism. Postcolonial studies and feminist theory have much to gain from such frameworks. Marxist feminists in the Third World and feminists of color in the US, for instance, have long dealt with situations where their critique of their own communities and indigenous patriarchies are seen as betrayals and sometimes appear, even to their own watchful eyes, uncomfortably close to racist perceptions of these communities. For us today – as for Rashid Jahan yesterday – there is a continued urgency to the project of critiquing imperialism and negotiating cultural difference, without giving up on the possibility of self-critique and social transformation altogether.

NOTE

1 While this trend crosses cultural and scholarly contexts, I refer here primarily to the recent work of scholars affiliated to the Subaltern Studies Collective including, most prominently, Dipesh Chakrabarty, Sudipta Kaviraj, and Partha Chatterjee. For a trenchant critique of the disappearance of the subaltern from this project, see Sarkar (2000).

9

Was there a time before race? Capitalist modernity and the origins of racism

Helen Scott

Some of the most comprehensive recent histories of race confirm the link between racism – the systematic oppression of groups on the basis of supposedly biological, inherent qualities readable in external characteristics – and capitalism. Robin Blackburn's *The Making of New World Slavery* uses extensive, detailed research to reveal that racism is modern and traceable to a specific phase in capitalism's development: the institutionalization of racial slavery in the colonial Americas. Blackburn provides an important key to understanding the character of the link between capitalism, slavery and racism when he places the concept of modernity at the heart of his analysis. He writes of the plantation slavery of the New World:

> Its development was associated with several of those processes which have been held to define modernity: the growth of instrumental rationality, the rise of national sentiment and the nation-state, racialized perceptions of identity, the spread of market relations and wage labor, the development of administrative bureaucracies and modern tax systems, the growing sophistication of commerce and communication, the birth of consumer societies, the publication of newspapers and the beginnings of press advertising, "action at a distance" and an individualist sensibility.
>
> (1997: 4)

These "processes" develop over several centuries and only reach maturity with capitalism's hegemony. Because of its transitional nature – no longer clearly feudal, not yet fully capitalist – the early modern period provides particularly rich fodder for investigating the emergence of structures and ideologies associated with capitalist modernity.

"Postcolonial Shakespeare" has been an increasingly visible area of study within the field over the last two decades. From the 1980s interesting and challenging critical studies have interrogated the racist and imperialist uses of Shakespeare's drama, particularly *Othello* and *The Tempest*, drawing on anti-imperialist literature such as the revisions of *The Tempest* by Caribbean writers George Lamming and Aimé Césaire (Brown 1985, Griffiths 1983, Hulme 1981, Newman 1987, Nixon 1987). Subsequent critics have shifted attention to the moment of the plays' production, scrutinizing the cultural and literary products of the early modern period for evidence of emergent racist and colonialist discourses or their precursors. Some of this work explicitly disconnects racism from capitalism, often pointing instead to an assumed tradition of ancient and biblical racism, while other studies seek to trace the development of "modern" ideologies in the period which saw the gradual coming into being of modernity.

The risk of "presentism" – the habit of projecting contemporary assumptions back into periods before their inception – is an obvious one for such ventures. Racism itself tends to create its own pseudohistory of universal racial hostility, and the idea of race is so pervasive in our times that it is a challenge to conceptualize a time that was otherwise. Recent studies in postcolonial Shakespeare have explicitly questioned many of the assumptions behind racialized readings of Shakespeare.[1] The 1998 collection, *Post-colonial Shakespeares*, edited by Ania Loomba and Martin Orkin, consciously interrogates the notion that modern, racist, colonialist ideology was hegemonic in the early modern period. The introduction observes that English colonialism was barely in its infancy, and suggests that the New World context of Shakespeare's plays has been inappropriately overemphasized. The editors highlight recent claims that "present-day meanings of 'race' and 'colonialism' cannot be applied to the past. It is possible, for example, that blackness may not have been the most outstanding marker of race in early modern Europe" (5).

Yet more often than not the contributors to Loomba and Orkin's volume emphasize the discursive continuities rather than the breaks. So Jonathan Burton refers to the "eurocentric principles" (44) and "eurocentric travelers' accounts" (46) of that period. Similarly, he describes Othello as "racial other" (56) and argues that Leo Africanus subverts the dominant racist discourses about Africa. Kim Hall employs Omi and Winant's concept of "racial formations" in order to show that Shakespeare's poems display "the ideology of white beauty" (1998: 66). And Margo Hendricks sees Shakespeare's *Rape of Lucrece* as an "encounter with the ideology of race" and the "ideology of racial identity" (1998: 88). While many of these critics point to ideological "precursors," "rehearsals" or "precedents" for racism proper, some argue explicitly that racism preceded capitalism. For example, Ania Loomba herself disconnects slavery and racism: "... well before the actual enslavement and colonial plunder of Africans began, racist stereotypes which were obsessed with color and nakedness were well in place. In fact in several colonial situations these stereotypes provided an ideological justification for different kinds of exploitation" (1998b: 149).

At times evident anti-Marxism accompanies the separation of capitalism and racism. David Brion Davis's introduction to the *William and Mary Quarterly* special issue, "Constructing Race," rejects the Marxist connection between racism and plantation slavery and suggests that such debates about the relation between economic and ideological systems are no longer useful (1997: 8). Similarly James Sweet reverses Eric Williams's assertion that "slavery was not born of racism: rather, racism was the consequence of slavery" (Williams 1966: 7) and argues that "the origins of racism preceded the emergence of capitalism by centuries" (Sweet 1997: 166). While claiming some continuity with Williams, Sweet in fact jettisons the central thesis of *Capitalism and Slavery*: that racism is inextricable from capitalism.

In what follows I draw instead on Marxist accounts of the origin of racism, and focus on the ideological *differences* between the early modern and our own era. A crude materialist explanation of racism may expect to see modern ideologies arise simultaneously with the first economic signs of capitalism: agricultural and mercantile capitalist exchange; the "primitive accumulation" of capital in the colonies of the New World and so on. But a more dialectical materialist understanding sees the ideological as well as the economic roots of racism: the argument that I recount here locates modern racism as the result of a collision between a new system of production – the plantation slavery which Marx termed "primitive accumulation of capital" – and a new ideology – possessive individualism – which was consolidated by the bourgeois revolutions of the late seventeenth and eighteenth centuries. Hence, what follows should be seen not as an attempt to establish the exact beginning of modern racism, but rather to suggest that aspects of early modern culture that some have understood as contiguous to racism could also be seen as decisively distinct. Perhaps such attention to the *breaks* may assist in the project of looking beyond the dominant ideas of our time and help us to conceptualize entirely different ways of understanding the world. As Lerone Bennett (1975: 10) has insisted, speaking of English colonialists in North America:

[M]ost important, if hardest for us to understand, race did not have the same meaning in 1619 that it has today. The first white settlers were organized around concepts of class, religion, and nationality, and they apparently had little or no understanding of the concepts of race and slavery.

Drawing on the rich tradition of materialist investigation, in this chapter I first outline the particular character of the link between capitalism and racism before suggesting an interpretation of Hakluyt's collected travel narratives. My understanding of this early modern text departs from the influential reading by Winthrop Jordan, who highlights its racial connotations, and instead emphasizes those aspects of Hakluyt's collection that hark back to a premodern world view.

Capitalism, Slavery, and Racism

One of the primary questions concerning the roots of racism is why Africans were incorporated as slaves in to the plantation economies of the Americas.[2] Winthrop Jordan, in his 1968 study *White over Black*, holds that Africans and not Europeans were exploited because of extant white prejudices linking blacks to slavery. And yet initially whites *were* used as forced labor. Ancient slavery, we know, was not racialized, and nor was the slavery that still existed in parts of Europe in the early modern period (Smedley 1993). The African slavery that Queen Elizabeth invested in is more appropriately placed with the older variety. There is considerable historical evidence that the idea of white slavery was tolerated in Elizabethan England, and when the plantations of the Americas needed a labor force, the owners looked to the European laboring class before they systematically enslaved Africans. As Eric Williams summarizes: "[u]nfree labor in the New World was brown, white, black and yellow" (1966: 7). Most Africans were kidnapped or bought, transported in inhuman conditions and sold into servitude from 1619 onwards. But, as Bennett points out "most of the first white settlers came the same way, and most of them were sold, as the first blacks were sold, by the captains of ships or the agents of captains of ships" (1975: 10). When tobacco first became a significant and potentially profitable crop, white laborers outnumbered blacks on the plantations:

The first boom in what would eventually become the United States took place during the 1620s, and it rested primarily on the backs of English indentured servants, not African slaves. Not until late in the century, after the boom had passed, did landowners begin buying slaves in large numbers, first from the West Indies and, after 1680, from Africa itself.

(Fields 1990: 101–02)

These indentured servants were not considered chattels, and they were (at least theoretically) able to work off their indenture and become free; the children of these servants were not bound by their parents' servitude. This was true for whites and blacks.

The colonial ruling class faced a crisis as the large plantations increasingly required a massive, cheap, and controllable labor force. First they extended the terms of servitude for indentured servants, then they looked for alternative sources of conscripted labor. Vagrant English children were considered as an involuntary work force for Virginia plantations between 1618 and 1622.[3] John Locke's *Fundamental Constitution of Carolina* "declared boldly for a hereditary aristocracy based on a permanent system of forced labor – black and white" (Bennett 1975: 57). Kidnapping became a common practice in major cities such as Bristol and London; transportation of convicts was another method of supplying a flow of bodies.

These historical facts contest the idea that negative connotations associated with blacks created the necessary preconditions for their enslavement: it seems that the plantation owners were ecumenical in their brutality and were more than willing to enslave the English lower orders. However, there were pragmatic and ideological problems associated with this project. For one, mass emigration to the colonies from England ran counter to the needs of the mercantilists back home, who were embarking on an industrialization program that required its own large, cheap labor force. Furthermore, any increase in the levels of exploitation would have exacerbated already high levels of rebellion.[4] In the emerging capitalist nations of Europe the oppressed and exploited were engaged in their own struggles, and had fought for and won some crucial measures of protection. The colonial ruling classes had to face the consequences of resistance from below not only in the colonies but also in Europe. In contrast, Africans removed from their home countries were severed from their fellows still there, and the colonial rulers did not have to concern themselves with the impact of their actions in Africa: "Africans and Afro-West Indians were thus available for perpetual slavery in a way that English servants were not" (Fields 1990: 104).

This goes some way to explaining why Africans became the source for slave labor. It is not that Africans didn't resist enslavement – the powerful record of consistent slave rebellions throughout the Americas in the eighteenth and nineteenth centuries alone would refute any such idea. Nor is it the case that European ruling classes – feudal or bourgeois – have ever been squeamish about crushing the rebellions of the European working classes. But the turn to African slaves avoided both the recurrent problem of labor shortages, and ultimately circumvented the increasingly obvious contradiction between the growing ideology of "free labor" and the reality of mass permanent enslavement.

To fully understand the consolidation of distinct racial slavery and ideology, one thus has to consider more than "purely" economic factors. Feudalism allowed for no concept of natural liberty. As Fields writes, "Whatever truths may have appeared self-evident in those days, neither an inalienable right to life and liberty nor the founding of government on the consent of the governed was among them" (1990: 102). There had been a tension, but no *de facto* contradiction between being human and unfree; this was consistent with the feudal system and its concomitant notions of peoples' natural position in a social order ordained by God, entailing specific ties to the land, kinship networks, manorial lords, and so forth. This is Bennett's point when he contends that European settlers in the New World of 1619 "had no concept of race and slavery": racism was not necessary to legitimize the removal of a laborer's "freedom," because no such freedom existed in fact or theory.

But the development of mercantile, agricultural, and then industrial capitalism broke down the old feudal systems and worldviews, transforming all social institutions and bringing new conceptualizations of individuals, natural and civil rights. By the late seventeenth century the fundamental features of capitalism were well underway in England: the rise of "free" wage labor; the separation of this labor from the land and the means of production; and the transformation of labor and land into commodities. These new social relationships brought with them radically different value systems: individualism, valorization of absolute private property and the accumulation of wealth. Central to this was "possessive individualism" – the notion that individuals are free and human due to their sole proprietorship of their own person (McNally 1993).

Most importantly the English Revolution gave birth to a vestigial form of the radical new concept of the Rights of Man which would be extended and broadened in the American and French Revolutions of 1776 and 1789 and the American Civil war of 1865. The coming to power of the bourgeoisie ushered in this revolutionary new idea of individual freedom. Bourgeois ideology thus advanced human rights, yet also masked actual inequality with the idea of natural liberty. Ownership and appropriation of land and resources by a minority were justified by the "right" to accumulate wealth and the sacrosanct status of private property. Thus the philosopher John Locke "made a positive value out of the unequal appropriation of most of the wealth (capital) by a few individuals, reasoning that such accumulation was a 'natural right'" (Smedley 1993: 48). Furthermore, the separation of labor from the land and means of subsistence forced workers to sell their labor in order to survive, yet this was euphemized by the rhetoric of "free" labor and the notion that labor power is a commodity equivalent to other goods sold on the market.

The emergence of this ideology of the individual, personal liberty and freedom coincided with the intensification of slavery at the end of the seventeenth century. The ruling class increasingly defined slaves as property, rather than as people, and placed the property rights of the planter above the individual rights of the slave. There was an obvious and intractable contradiction between the idea of inalienable individual rights and the actuality of mass enslavement. If humans have the right to liberty in their persons, then enslavement removes humanity. Or, conversely, only nonhumans can be enslaved. The ideology of race served to justify the denial of rights to slaves: defenders of slavery categorized blacks as a "subhuman" group consequently undeserving of bourgeois rights. Thus developed a new criterion of status, located in natural differences, readable in external characteristics. From this moment on, differences in skin color, once regarded in much the same way as other human differences such as size and hair color, and certainly as far less important than religion or status, acquired terrifying significance.[5] From now on blackness and whiteness were taken to be absolute indicators of identity: to be white was to be "free" and to be black a "slave."

Any conspiracy theory would be woefully inadequate to account for the development of racism. To paraphrase Marx, the plantocracy existed under conditions not of their own choosing. Nonetheless it is possible to see in the last decades of the seventeenth and first decades of the eighteenth centuries something that looks very much like a campaign of separation and subordination which was supported by the entire state infrastructure. The first goal was to ensure black subordination. The state passed laws removing legal, property, and civil rights from nonwhites between 1670 and the 1750s; this involved revoking previous laws and rewriting others. Virginia colony's gradual shift away from a categorization based on religion to one based on race exemplifies this process: the possibility of converting to achieve free status was denied by a 1667 decree stating that "Baptisme doth not alter the condition of the person as to his bondage or freedom" (qtd. in Bennett 1975: 67). In 1670 the question of who could be enslaved in the first place was answered: "All servants not being Christians imported into this country by shipping shal be slaves for life." This law did not exempt blacks who had been baptized in Africa, Europe, the West Indies or other colonies, but a further act in 1682 eliminated all confusion by declaring that

all servants except Turks and Moores which shall be brought or imported into this country, either by sea or land, whether Negroes . . . Mullattoes or Indians, who and whose parentage and native country are not christian at the time of their first purchase of such servant by some christian, although afterwards, and before such their importation . . . they shall be converted to the christian faith . . . shall be judged, deemed and taken to be slaves.
(qtd. in Bennett 1975: 67)

Thus Virginia inextricably linked status to hereditary membership of specific groups.

Clearly these laws and statutes had the aim of incontrovertibly associating all blacks with slavery. The other dynamic of the campaign was racial segregation. For this whites had to be taught to be white, and blacks taught to be black, and the two groups separated. To this end an unequivocal punitive system was created to ensure and maintain absolute racial division. Laws against miscegenation, intermarriage, and association were passed throughout the colonies in the last decade of the seventeenth and first of the eighteenth centuries. The former interracial coexistence among laborers was ruthlessly dismantled.[6]

The system of permanent racial slavery required an ideology of race based on the idea that "whites" and "blacks" are absolutely different. This set in motion a history of racial oppression and racist ideas that did not end with slavery but has continued to be central to modernity. The next major phase of imperialist expansion in the nineteenth century added new depth and complexity to racism, and exploitation of immigrant labor in the twentieth century further expanded the scope of racist differentiation and scapegoating. Racism has assumed different forms in its history, but it has been a constant feature of capitalist society.

Premodern prejudices of all sorts clearly existed prior to the consolidation of capitalism. But such prejudices were fundamentally different from modern racism. [While Spanish attitudes to Moors and Jews from the fifteenth century on are sometimes presented as evidence of premodern racism, this hostility, based on the desire of the Spanish state to consolidate its rule by homogenizing the population, lacked the biological foundation that is fundamental to racism. Oppression on the basis of cultural or religious criteria allows for the possibility of change, whereas biological determinism falsely posits essential and unchangeable differences between groups (Smedley 1993: 65–70). Such earlier hostility is better categorized as heterophobia, or fear of difference, and xenophobia, fear of strangeness, which were certainly features of premodern and early modern societies. Religious chauvinism was assuredly a feature of precapitalist Europe (or, more precisely, the area that would become Europe). Zygmunt Bauman (1991) uses this distinction when he differentiates between premodern persecution of Jews and modern, racially based, anti-Semitism. The former was based on either religious oppression (which allowed the possibility of conversion to Christianity) or suspicion of Jews as travelers and strangers in the Diaspora. The latter, in contrast, insists on the absolute, inherent, genetic, and moral inferiority of Jews *as Jews* and allows for no possible transformation or conversion to "human" status. Abram Leon's Marxist analysis (1970) goes one step further to show that the religious and national "roles" of Jews in fact have distinct social roots. He uses the concept of "people-class" to discuss the "specific economic function" of Jews historically and to debunk the notion of transhistorical "racism" against Jews. In some instances early modern culture is more aptly located in the context of such heterophobia and xenophobia than against the trajectory of modern racism.

Winthrop Jordan and Hakluyt's voyages

That cultural products look very different when seen through the lens of an earlier nonracial world view becomes clear when considering the travel writings catalogued and published by Richard Hakluyt (1552?–1616), British geographer and publicist for expansion. Winthrop Jordan's influential reading locates the collection in the emergent structure of modern racism.[7] But the significance of the narratives is radically altered when they are placed against the backdrop of an earlier consciousness.

Benjamin Braude, I think rightly, observes that Hakluyt's large and diverse anthology resists summary or generalization, but posits, *contra* Jordan, that the "concluding index, by virtue of what it selects and how it characterizes the volume's contents, conveys a neutral and almost respectful attitude" towards the black inhabitants of Africa (1997: 135). Michael Neill also recognizes that the collection displays "a certain ethnographic objectivity" (1998: 366). Perhaps the first thing to note about Jordan's reading is that it tends to emphasize those narratives, such as that by George Best, that lend themselves to a racial reading, while overlooking those that resist incorporation into a racist schema.[8]

Jordan's position is that the narratives of Africa collectively construct two distinct and incompatible groups, "Negro" and "English," whose differences emanate from their identities rather than their actions.[9] He endows skin color with overarching significance in this system of absolute differentiation and discerns obsessive reference to Africans' "blackness" which are indicative of the English construction of Africans as a species apart and inferior. He writes: "Travelers rarely failed to comment upon" skin color (4). Certainly there are a number of references to skin color in Hakluyt's collection – though it is fair to say that not only "black," but also "olive," "tawny," "yellow" and other hues are mentioned. Furthermore, where skin color is referred to, as in this example quoted by Jordan, it is often comparable to other factors of at least equal import: "These people are all blacke, and are called Negros, without any apparel, saving before their privies" (Jordan 1969: 4). Seldom is skin color mentioned in isolation, but one could select numerous passages that omit mention of skin color while retaining other observations.

Jordan comments that "the most arresting characteristic of the newly discovered African was his color" (4), but for at least some of the travelers, skin color is far less "arresting" than singular *cultural* features. Towerson's description in "The first voyage to the coast of Guinea" gives some indication of this:

There are neere to the Sea upon this River divers inhabitants, which are mighty bigge men and go al naked except some thing before their privie parts, which is like a clout about a quarter of a yard long made of the barke of trees, and yet it is like a cloth . . . Some of them also weare the like upon their heades being painted with divers colours, but the most part of them go bare headed, and their heads are clipped and shorne of divers sorts, and the most part of them have their skin of their bodies raced with divers workes, in maner of a leather Jerkin.   (*Hzkluyt 1903–5, v. 6: 184*)

Towerson is strikingly contemptuous of the people he observes (most aggressively so a few lines later when he compares women's breasts to the udders of goats), but also admires specific artifacts and social habits. Usually the features he sees as most strange and *different* are

forms of decoration, materials (such as the curious bark) and craftwork that are unfamiliar to him. The example of the "raced" skin is
mentioned in other accounts, and is seemingly more interesting and
curious than complexion, which, as in this description, is frequently
not referred to at all.

Most importantly, skin color, even when labeled "black," seems not
to have the same significance as within a racist system. Jordan obscures
this dissimilarity when he quotes a "Spanish chronicle translated into
English in 1555":[10]

One of the marveylous thynges that god useth in the composition of man,
is colour: which doubtlesse can not bee consydered withowte great admi-
ration in beholding one to be white and an other blacke, beinge coloures
utterlye contrary. Sum lykewyse to be yelowe which is betwene blacke
and white: and other of other colours as it were of dyvers liveres.

(Jordan 1969: 7)

Jordan observes that "the juxtaposition of black and white was the
most striking marvel of all." But the text leaves open the possibility
that the "most striking marvel" is the *range* of skin colors. Even more
significantly, this chronicler remarks that "[o]ne of the marveylous
thynges that god useth in the composition of man, is colour . . ."
This reflects a religious worldview that assumes people of all colors
share a common humanity derived from god, while modern racism,
in contrast, denies the fact that humans of all colors form one species.

Jordan sees in the English travelers a sense of shared identity against
which Africans are absolutely other: "No matter how great the actual
and observed differences among Negroes, though, none of these black
men seemed to live like Englishmen" (25). But frequently these narra-
tors exhibit a decidedly nonracial logic in that they judge not according to who the people are but by what they do. Africans are not all
equally unlike the travelers: they variously exhibit cultural traits that
are similar and dissimilar to English social practices. The factors most
frequently judged are trade, religion, literacy, clothing, food, and housing. These accounts contain rigid and value-laden assumptions about
appropriate cultural and social practices, and often do find specific
African societies lacking and even despicable. But these judgments
seem more consistent with the cultural mores of the old rather than
the new.

Most frequently Africans are seen as "inferior" when they live in
tents or huts, do not wear clothes or engage in trade, have no identifiable religion, art, or legal system, and are illiterate. This description

from the second voyage to Guinea is typical of negative accounts: "a people of beastly living, without a God, lawe, religion, or common wealth" (Hakluyt 1903–05, v. 6: 167). So too is the scornful account of the "people of Libya called Garamantes, whose women are common: for they contract no matrimonie, neither have respect to chastitie" (168). However, when Africans engage in practices valued by the English traders and explorers, the descriptions are no longer derogatory. William Towerson's account of his voyage to Guinea includes favorable as well as critical descriptions:

we went into their Townes, which were like to twentie small hovels, all covered over with great leaves and baggage, and all the sides open, and a scaffolde under the house about a yard high, where they worke many pretie things of the barkes of trees.   *(Hakluyt 1903–05, v. 6: 185)*

The houses are compared to "hovels" but the craftwork is "pretie" and esteemed. Towerson proceeds with a detailed and appreciative account of the town's handiwork – "yron worke they can make very fine . . . Their golde also they worke very well" (197). Here we see cultural attributes determining evaluation. These Africans are admirable for their trade, crafts, and social order; elsewhere we are given favorable descriptions of Africans' trading habits, kings and emperors, defense strategies, towns, hospitality and loyalty (145, 149, 168). Unlike in racist ideology, the differences between the English travelers and some African people are cultural and variable, not permanent and absolute.

As the repeated references to status indicate, these narratives often notice distinctions of class over and above those of "race." The kings, emperors, chiefs, captains – more generally the rulers – are distinct, often, from the commoners. Towerson's account of a "Negroe" "Captaine" conveys respect and awe:

the Captaine of the Towne came downe being a grave man . . . Wee saluted him, and put off our caps, and bowed our selves, and hee like one that thought well of himselfe, did not moove his cap nor scant bowed his body, and sate him downe very solemnly upon his stoole: but all his men put off their caps to us, and bowed downe themselves.   *(196)*

This leader is perceived as powerful and superior (the English acknowledge this by removing their caps and bowing) he has good trade skills and keeps his people under control. Strong rulers and obedient loyal subjects draw respect from the English travelers.

When considered against the backdrop of broader depictions of other cultures, and indeed of different classes of Englishmen, derogatory descriptions of Africans acquire a changed significance. Taken alone, the assertion that a settlement of Africans are "a people of beastly living, without a God, lawe, religion, or common wealth" (167) could indicate generalized English scorn of Africans *as Africans*. But when compared to accounts of non-Africans, this becomes less likely. This narrative of the search for a route to China and "the East" describes various "uncivilized" cultures: the Samoyeds "have no houses...but only tents made of deers' skins...their knowledge is very base, for they know no letter" (David 1981: 48); and the

Scrick Finns are a wild people which neither know God nor yet good order; and these people live in tents made of deers' skins, and they have no certain habitations but continue in herds and companies . . . And they are a people of small stature, and are clothed in deers' skins, and drink nothing but water and eat no bread but flesh all raw.   *(David 1981: 52)*

The first two volumes of Hakluyt's voyages contain numerous derogatory descriptions: the Tartars are "barbarians" and "cannibals" (Hakluyt 1903–05, v. 1: 51); the Muscovites are idolatrous (v. 2: 269); the Samoeds have strange bloody idols and don't live in houses (v. 2: 338–39); and the Lappians have no clothes, no art, no homes, strange eating habits, and unacceptable matrimonial practices (v. 2: 417). Just as various African peoples are denigrated for their clothing, housing, eating habits, literacy, and religion, so the inhabitants of these Northern regions are found to be similarly wanting; in both cases cultural traits are definitive.

Perhaps the most significant indicator of the nonracial character of Hakluyt's collection is that the idea of a "white" identity is apparently absent. While isolated uses of "European" or "white" as categories of people may be found earlier, neither was commonplace until the second half of the seventeenth century. Nor were the geographical distinctions that we take for granted today. As Braude observes, "the notion of the division of the world into three and more continents, according to the *Oxford English Dictionary*, did not exist before the seventeenth century" (1997: 109). It is likely that the modern concept of a shared English identity against which Africans are "other" lagged even further behind.

A wider survey of literature of this time suggests that the English travelers did not think of "English" people as civilized. Just as literacy, religiosity, housing, clothing, industry, and cultural practices determine the civility or savagery of Africans and other peoples, so did the literate English hold their "fellow countrymen" to such bench marks of civility, and find the majority to be impaired. Hakluyt's "Discourse of Western Planting" of 1584 subjects the English lower orders to exactly the kind of chauvinistic abuse used against "foreigners" in the travelogues. His description of the burgeoning population of England illustrates this:

> Nowe there are of every arte and science so many, that they can hardly lyve one by another, nay rather they are readie to eate upp one another: yea many thousands of idle persons are wthin this Realm, wch having no way to be sett to worke be either mutinous and seeke alteration in the state, or at leaset very burdensome to the common wealthe, and often fal to pilferinge and thevinge and other lewdnes. *(qtd. in Hadfield 1998: 103)*

Even the trope of cannibalism, which becomes central to racist discourse, is applied here to the English lower orders. This suggests that Hakluyt and other early modern travelers, merchants, and rulers saw the world first and foremost in terms of class and status rather than race and nation.

These examples have a direct bearing on whether or not we see Shakespeare's plays in terms of a racialized consciousness. Is *Othello*, as so many people have differently argued, a play about race? Does it bear the seeds of modern racial discourse? The frequent references to blackness and whiteness seem to indicate that it is and does. But these references are always combined with other factors, such as age and background. Rather than seeing color as the paramount point of identification, Othello sees his blackness as one possible factor, along with his manner of speech, age and so on, which distinguishes him from Desdemona. Most importantly, he is an outsider to the enclosed world of Venice's nobility. In Cinthio's novella, the source for Shakespeare's *Othello*, the moral of the story is that Desdemona made a mistake in marrying someone so different – so "unsuitable by reason of race, creed and education," as Frank Kermode (1974: 1198) summarizes. "Race" here, as Shakespeare would have understood the word, refers to "bloodline" or "inheritance"; it is very different from the spurious biological divide between "blacks" and "whites."[11]

If cultural difference is placed at the center of the plot, we can see that *Othello* is motivated by prejudice against strangers, rivalry for careers, greed, and suspicion of greed. Othello is defined not in terms of an eternal essence or genetic makeup readable in his skin color and physical features, but by social categories and roles: gullible outsider, valiant soldier, exotic traveler, suspicious husband, and so forth.

Subsequent critics have *found* what to modern eyes and ears are racial slurs, but it is probable that they had no such significance in the first decade of the seventeenth century.[12] C. L. R. James acknowledges this in his sketched reading of *Othello*:

I say with the fullest confidence that you could strike out every single reference to (Othello's) black skin and the play would be essentially the same. Othello's trouble is that he is an outsider. He is not a Venetian. He is a military bureaucrat, a technician, hired to fight for Venice, a foreign country. The Senate has no consciousness whatever of his color. That is a startling fact but true. They haven't to make allowances for it. It simply has no place in their minds. *(James 1960: 141)*

As James maintained, there is considerable reason to place literary representations of Africans and blackness – whether negative or positive – in an early modern conceptual framework that is prejudiced and intolerant but not yet racist. Recognizing and drawing attention to the chasm between the worldview of the earlier period and that of our own enables us to envisage a time before race, which in turn may assist in the struggle to build a future without racism.

NOTES

1 Bartels 1997 provides a useful counter to the racialized reading of *Othello* and stresses that racist and imperialist ideologies were not yet fixed. See also Neill 1998.
2 The focus of this chapter is on North American racism, and I shall be considering the English slave system rather than those of the Spanish and Portuguese in the Latin American colonies. These systems exhibited many dissimilarities and unique features which are beyond the scope of this short piece. Yet it is also the case that "[a]ll forms of colonial slavery bore numerous institutional similarities in the use and treatment of Africans as slaves" (Smedley 1993: 136).
3 On the deportation of children, see Allen 1994.
4 As Fields explains, "to have degraded the servants into slaves *en masse* would have driven the continuing struggle up several notches, a dangerous undertaking considering that servants were well armed, that they outnumbered their masters, and that the Indians could easily take advantage of the inevitably resulting warfare among the enemy. Moreover, the enslavement of already arrived immigrants, once news of it reached England, would have threatened the sources of future immigration" (1990: 103).
5 Skin color was not the only racial marker. The oppression of the Irish also came to be justified in racist terms, and other physical traits were selected as evidence of their inferiority.
6 There were high levels of interracial sexual, domestic, social, and political relationships in the American colonies of the seventeenth century.

Nicholas Canny tells us that "[t]here are … many references in the local records to the existence of cordial, and even sexual relationships between black and white servants in seventeenth century Virginia, and … whites even combined with blacks against their masters"(1979: 35). See also Bennett 1975: 19.

7 *White over Black* is cited by many critics who read the literature of the Renaissance racially. See Barthelemy 1987: 3, 5, 121–23; Boose 1994: 41; Hall 1995: 2, 1998: 66; Leininger 1980: 290; Vaughan and Vaughan 1997: 29. For an important critique of *White over Black* on the grounds of anachronism see Braude 1997: 129.

8 Hall cites George Best to illustrate her claim that "[c]learly what interests Best, Browne, and the many writers who participated in this debate, even indirectly, is the problem that dark skin and certain physical features posed for a culture that believed that God made man in his own image" (1995: 13). Burton interestingly argues that Africanus's *Geographical Historie* is distinct from other accounts because it gives "generous treatment of African accomplishments and interest in Islam" (1998: 46). While I concur with his reading of the *Historie*, I would argue that the fluid, contradictory, unfixed representations of Africa and Africans found within are typical of the range of travel narratives of the period, rather than the exception. See Hannaford 1996.

9 Jordan writes "the African's different culture – for Englishmen, his 'savagery' – operated to make Negroes seem to Englishmen a radically different kind of men" (1969: 28); "from the first, Englishmen tended to set Negroes over against themselves, to stress what they conceived to be radically contrasting qualities of color, religion, and style of life, as well as animality and a peculiarly potent sexuality" (15; see also 5, 6, 19, 21, 26). The Vaughans use language similar to Jordan when discussing Hakluyt in their study of Elizabethan attitudes to Africans (1997: 33).

10 The passage is from Francisco Lopez de Gomara. The Vaughans, departing from Jordan on this occasion, say "[n]otable throughout Gomara's lengthy paragraph on pigmentation is the absence of value judgments; his discussion of various human colors privileged none." They see this as the exception for the genre, however, and turn to other accounts that display "an English fixation on the Africans' blackness" (1997: 28).

11 This is the way 'race' is used in *The Tempest*, also – for example when Miranda speaks to Caliban of "thy vile race" (I ii 359).

12 Neill (1998) emphasizes the nonracist dynamics of *Othello*, pointing to contextual evidence that suggests that the definitive distinctions of the period are "cultural and religious rather than racial." He concludes that the play itself displays "progressive racialization."

Part III

Marxism, postcolonial studies, and "theory"

10

Postcolonial studies between the European wars: an intellectual history

Timothy Brennan

I

Postcolonial studies entered the academy in the mid-1980s as a form of theory, when theory was still an embattled enclave on its way to becoming a large and dominant space. To the profession at large, postcolonial studies simply *was* literary theory in one of its specialized institutional forms, and (more to the point) this was also how scholars wanting to break into the field saw it (Hulme 1989, Spivak 1988, Marrouchi 1997).[1] To speak of the conflation of postcolonial studies and literary or cultural theory in this way is, of course, to speak phenomenologically – that is, to speak of a perception that acquires the status of truth within a bracketed reality. For seen in retrospect, postcolonial studies obviously offered any number of archival, or polemical, or expository projects from the very beginning, not only theoretical ones – especially in the disciplines of history and anthropology where ideational discourse has always arrived rather late and tentatively.

And yet, from the mid-1980s onwards, academic audiences took postcolonial studies to be an adjunct of the same intellectual concerns that had rudely entered their domains only a handful of years earlier in the form of genealogical displacements, psychoanalytic treatments of the subject, analyses of discursive power, and programmatic demands for decentering. These are the array of meanings I am alluding to by the blanketing term "theory," which not only *can* be used, but really must be used in this reductive way because of the phenomenological existence these practices acquired – ones that were both widely evident and immediately understandable to audiences in precisely these terms. Over time, this array of meanings amounted to a virtual ethics of poststructuralism, freely applied to diverse situations and investigative contexts with a rigorous conformity.

The routines and customs of professionalization, in other words, gave postcolonial studies a meaning that was separable from its ostensible project of exposing Western dominance or giving a voice to non-Western forms of knowledge. At the same time, its institutional life made this project appear inseparable from the practice of a highly selective and largely Continental theory. When revisiting the intellectual history of the interwar period, one is retrospectively struck by the role played by certain of its lineages in later consecrating Europe *within* postcolonial studies, extending sacral European clichés of value into other spheres in new, more appealing, more apparently self-critical forms. We have not really begun to ask hard questions of the *prehistory* of theory found in the interwar period, nor the role that this prehistory played in the emergence of postcolonial studies.

Let me begin by recounting a revisionist history – the revision of a revision, if you will – that I attempt to fill out in the passages that follow. The Nietzschean traditions that had been developed in the interwar period by, among others, Georges Bataille, Oswald Spengler, Georges Sorel and (less obviously) Martin Heidegger are Eurocentric in a special sense – a sense that the contemporary critic, fearful of the charge of oversimplification, has been reluctant to broach. Postwar theory emerged in a recoil from the fearful openings of the interwar period in the colonial sphere, and these openings were themselves inflected by popular-front sensibilities that had made inroads through the work of communist theorists into the life of high theory and the official arts. While enhancing the repressed Other, postwar appropriations of this interwar Nietzsche set about crafting a style of ambiguity that reclaimed for Europe the subterranean, heterodox, and lonely language of revalued value.

The theoretical landscape that postcolonial studies entered, then, represented above all a dialectical completion of a process that developed in the heart of empire, and that set out systematically to cover the tracks of its own history. Purportedly driven by the desire to combat Eurocentrism, the field emerged speaking a language that was Eurocentric reflexively and automatically, one in which Europe existed speaking the language of "difference." The tendencies, moods, and aesthetic idealisms jumbling together to form the supposedly heterogeneous and decentering impulses of theory confounded themselves. What writers like Emmanuel Levinas or Jacques Derrida left out of their parochial fixations on the Graeco-German West constructed by

Romanticism (the object tirelessly exposed in their writing) is much less pertinent than their vigorous prolongment of European superiority in the guise of an anti-Eurocentric critique that has rarely been called by its rightful name (Bernasconi 1998, Critchley 1995).

If theory has insistently sought to make us reject origins and be suspicious of sources – which in geopolitical terms are usually seen as being culpably related to mythical projects of nation-forming – it is because the recourse to ur-communities and earlier peoples is usually intended to authenticate attempts to consolidate actual governments, a problem that bears on the interwar period's foundational attempts to establish forms of third-world sovereignty. We might recall that Michel Foucault, for example, translated Nietzsche's original concept of *genealogy* in the specific context of being a member of a repressed sexual minority and a devoted (one might even say obsessive) anti-Hegelian. The germ, however, of the original concept in Nietzsche remains at the core of his fundamentally duplicitous operation of practicing history while not practicing it. Nietzsche's intention had been to claim rights for aristocratic privilege and the frankly recidivist and racialist principle of *Rangordnung*.[2] Genealogy was a decisive methodological invention because it was about family. It connoted not agency or transformation but the genetic inevitabilities of paternity. At the same time, it apotheosized etymology and therefore neatly fit itself into the larger principles of postwar theory's linguistic turn, which Nietzsche had been among the first to forecast. At the same time, it was about the creation of a truth-by-design embedded in a linguistic trace. The genealogical method so valuable to the Foucauldian lineage in postcolonial studies conceals a source-specific elitism and racialist filiation that it wants very much to supersede, and feels utterly uncompelled to explain or distance itself from.

A similar set of troubling problems await us as we pass from Nietzsche's legacy-in-blood and aristocracy of merit to the intellectuals who drew on Nietzsche to get past Marx. What do we make, for instance, of Derrida's borrowings from Edmund Husserl given the latter's frank interventions against non-European cultures as myth-ridden and unself-reflexive? For his part, Heidegger's writing is filled with emphatic third-worldist echoes – his idealization of the peasant, his concept of thought as a path through the woods (*Holzwege*), his caricatures of the mystificatory cult of the soil and of a village craftsman's ideal of counter-technology, all of them joining his orientalist borrowings from Eastern philosophy late in his career. Derrida's foundational anti-foundationalism, moreover, offers a critique of logocentrism and orality by casting the latter as naive, superstitious, nostalgic, and authentically inauthentic. We have been unable to ask what such theories imply for non-European peoples overburdened, not by the "metaphysics of presence," but by the repressive technologies of writing that deconstruction itself mercilessly extends.

We begin to see in these examples the establishment of debt. Although negatively, the interwar scenes of theory found expression in the confluence of the interwar avant-gardes and Marxism, particularly the organizational Marxism of the Third International, which prompted a reconsideration of the colonial question, and provided a novel, more radical, formulation of it. Postcolonial studies has therefore been caught in a double-bind comprising incompatible intellectual traditions. Under the forces of the conservative public climate in which it came into being in the 1980s, theory's obsession with the topic of Marxism in contemporary theory has certainly been paradoxical. If in the postcolonial discussion an undifferentiated Marxism has played a frequent role, it has done so usually as an example of how a certain brand of Eurocentrism promoted technological or disciplinary modernity, and therefore, by definition, was antagonistic to non-Western forms of emergence (Bourdieu 1990: 113–21; Nandy 1995: 82; Prakash 1992: 8–9).

But there is irony in this claim. Postcolonial studies descended in altered form from the anticolonial liberation movements whose most intense interval stretched from 1947 to 1979 (the years in which theory came to prominence) and whose links to interwar Marxism are obvious and overdetermined. The confusions underlying postcolonial studies' self-image (and the fight over theory within it) lie in the fact that the tendency derived from a parentage it sought to suppress. I would like to consider one aspect of that parentage here.

II

Between World Wars I and II, European consciousness of the colonies changed sharply and, to some, threateningly. From 1880 to 1939, European artists and social theorists came to focus on the non-Western world as a world populated by articulate and angry *colonials* rising in arms and speaking more loudly and clearly than ever before. Public figures and intellectuals began mixing deliberate protests against colonial policy with more cultural allusions to race, modernity, and metropolitan value, often in highly coded or unconscious ways. As distinct from the colonial discourse of earlier centuries – the writing of

Montaigne on cannibals, say, or the orientalist paintings of Delacroix –
intellectuals were working for the first time within a structure of inter-
active, crosscultural contacts that combined an aesthetic of "primitive
art," on the one hand, with political uneasiness toward a colonial
system, on the other. My intention below is to distinguish between
these two forces (which in much recent criticism are not so much confused with, as substituted for, one another) while showing how they
merged in the creation of the theory whose mantle postcolonial studies
later assumed.

The conventional intellectual histories tell us that non-Western motifs were particularly strong among the interwar avant-gardes – the
African, Brazilian and Polynesian motifs of Expressionism and early
Cubism, for example – although of course it was not only the artistic
avant-gardes but psychoanalysis with its studies of totemism and religion, early sociology, Sir James Fraser's studies of mythology, Andre
Gide's and Victor Segalen's travel narratives, and other intellectual
movements that were overtaken, in various degrees of subtlety, by an
obsession with the world beyond Europe's borders in the early part
of the century (Bongie 1991).

The common view within postcolonial studies is importantly at
odds with this casual assessment. The reigning view has been expressed well by Edward Said in *Culture and Imperialism*, where he
argues strongly that until recent decades Europeans saw "India and
North Africa with a combination of familiarity and distance, but never
with a sense of their separate sovereignty." Only very recently, he
stresses, has one witnessed "the massive intellectual, moral, and imaginative overhaul and deconstruction of Western representation of the
non-Western world" (Said 1993: xix–xxi). The point is well taken –
since the newness of this sort of penetrating anti-imperialist ethos
alluded to by Said is obviously relative – but the point is nevertheless
untrue.

A book still needs to be written on the development of anticolonial sentiment launched by modernity. Such a study would undoubtedly begin with the anticolonial writings of Bartolomé de las
Casas and Bernard de Sahagun in the early sixteenth century or with
the Enlightenment declarations of outrage against colonial injustices
found in such varied places as Abbé Raynal, Immanuel Kant and
Johann Gottfried Herder, as well as the self-serving, mercantile anticolonialism of the late eighteenth century in the writings of Jeremy
Bentham (*Emancipate Your Colonies*, 1783) and Adam Smith – all of
which make the *process* of anticolonial theory more multidimensional,

more radically based in the dissident wings of European thought than they do in our current renderings. It is true that such positions, partial as they are, only mitigate Said's point without eliminating it. However, the argument collapses when one looks at the last decades of the nineteenth century and the period before the first World War when a small but important movement of moral revulsion against imperial practices found expression among the Little Englanders, a group working in concert with a wing of the English Liberals and Radicals (and eventually Labour), whose most eloquent and prolific exponents included H. R. Fox Bourne, E. D. Morel, Edward Carpenter, and J. A. Hobson, who later became famous for writing *Imperialism: A Study* (1902) because Lenin borrowed from it, even though it was only one of Hobson's many books against imperialism (Porter 1968).

The need to argue that true anti-imperialist theory only arises in the post-World War II period is hard to understand when there is so much counter-evidence. But then again, to see the world as a dialectical process of punctuated discovery requires a strategic orientation that theory has more or less destroyed, for it would mean giving support to an intellectual and political lineage that goes by a variety of non-identical but related terms – left Hegelianism, the labor movement, social democracy, Marxism. Said intimates the elusiveness of this lineage for contemporary theory when he mentions some of the architects of that welcome overhaul of imperial value that he raises in his quotation – the ones, he posits, who represent the true breakthroughs missing in earlier eras. Elusiveness is intimated because, while giving us their names – Amilcar Cabral, Frantz Fanon, C. L. R. James, Walter Rodney – we are given no sense of the traditions that made them, as though their contributions were divorced from this same unnameable lineage, or as though they were products of colonial insight forged in countless acts of racial slighting or European outrages on foreign soil, erupting of themselves in what is now commonly thought of as an "epistemic break." On the contrary, each of these theorists and activists was the direct product of interwar Marxism as a matter of sentiment, impulse, and conscious intellectual alliance.

It was, however, especially (and significantly) the Marxism of the Eastern periphery of Europe that played the largest role in nudging intellectuals into a liberatory view of non-Western societies between 1905 and 1939. But one must also make a distinction here. It was not the Frankfurt School but cultural Bolshevism and the larger network of fellow travelers it spawned that made possible the early twentieth-century sensitivities towards colonial oppression, distinct forms of peripheral cultural value, social theories of uneven and combined development, and many of the other preoccupations (often by other names) that inform and substantiate what we today call postcolonial studies, even if this is the sort of statement that is not so much denied, as not allowed to be true.

This different mapping of influences and conceptual novelties from the interwar period eventually leads us to the forbidding subject of the Russian Revolution. The revolution – present everywhere and nowhere in our intellectual lives, and crowding analysis like a vulgar intrusion or a fearful threat – created a full-blown *culture* of anti-imperialism for the first time, and it is striking and deeply revealing that the topic has been so carefully avoided in the postcolonial discussion. Among the characteristic sponsors of this new anti-imperialist culture were journals like *Le Paria*, the organ of the Union Intercoloniale – the branch of the French Communist Party founded in the early 1920s to support insurgency in the colonies (Ho Chi Minh and Hadj Ali were among those involved) (Cassou 1935: 257; Georges 1923: 469–70; Edwards 1999: 121–22; L'Association des écrivains progressifs 1935: 462). Added to this was Leopold Senghor's *Comité de defense de la race nègre*. Overviews of the communist press in France will find PCF leader Maurice Thorez writing "Sur les problèmes coloniaux," supporting the independence of Algeria while theorizing the color line in strikingly contemporary ways. With an insight advanced for his time, he declared: "France, like Algeria, is but a melange of twenty races" (Schram and Carrère d'Encausse 1965: 350; Racine and Bodin, 1982: 110).

In England, varied networks with their own publications brought anticolonial sentiment into places the Little Englanders never reached. A partial listing of the relevant organizations include the League Against Imperialism, the Negro Welfare Association, the League of Coloured Peoples, and the India League, all sponsored by the Communist Party of Great Britain. CPGB journals such as *Inprecor*, *Communist International*, and *Labour Monthly* were read not only in England but in the colonies, carrying essays by the likes of Caribbean activist, George Padmore and future independence leader, Jomo Kenyatta on "The Revolt in Haiti," "Forced Labour in Africa," and "Labour Imperialism in East Africa" (Callaghan 1997–98: 518, 522). For the German case, one found rich material in the Congress of Oppressed Nationalities, which met in Brussels in 1927 under the direction of Willi Munzenberg, and played its own part in extending anti-imperial sentiments in unprecedented ways.

The new culture of anticolonialism thrived in the art columns of left newspapers, cabarets of the political underground, mainstream radio, the cultural groups of the Popular Front, Bolshevik theater troupes, and the responses to, and borrowings from, all of these in the various avant-garde arts and in the insurgent disciplines of sociology, psychoanalysis, and ethnography, as well as in phenomenology – none of which could fail to take stock of the revolution's implications for the idea of the West. Through many mediations and appropriations, the new sciences of these years formed the core thinking of Derrida, Foucault, and Lacan by way of a return to Heidegger, Freud, and Bataille. These precursors were the continental thinkers from the interwar period who worked within a tradition consciously at war with Marx – a war that took place in an act of modernizing and updating Nietzsche for interwar conditions, when that still relatively obscure German thinker was catapulted into prominence as *the* riposte to Marxism's history, its human perfectability, and its mob.[3]

The Russian Revolution, to put it plainly, was an anticolonial revolution; its sponsorship of anticolonial rhetoric and practice was self-definitional.[4] It created a massive repertoire of images, tropes, and vocabularies that hovered over everyone's thinking – from right to left – throughout the post-1905 period. "Russia," Rolf Wiggershaus reminds us, was to interwar intellectuals not merely a place where the Left had seized governmental control, but "the land . . . promising and embodying 'community': this was Lukács's mystical and radical answer to 'western Europe', which was stagnating both in relation to the objective spirit and to the problem of the individual . . . 'Russia' was to represent the 'coming light' for 'western Europe'" (1994: 78). The revolution delivered Europe into a radical non-Western curiosity and sympathy that had not existed in quite this way before, and this had its effects on the questions scholars posed, the sourcework artists used, and the news intellectuals followed.

It is at least arguable, for example, that the African nonsense verse of Dada, the grand civilizational comparisons of Oswald Spengler's *Decline of the West*, the Afro-Caribbean record collections of Paul Derain, Freud's venture into totemism, Bertolt Brecht's reliance on Chinese theatrical forms, Louis Aragon's Parisian "peasants," and the ethnographic surrealism of René Ménil, Michel Leiris, and Marcel Griaule were all affected deeply by the anticolonial energies of the Soviet idea.[5]

In the first half of the twentieth century, Marxism produced a particular constellation of thought that achieved mass density in regard to its colonial object, became a source of inspiration on a continental

basis, knit together systematic investigations in several disciplines simultaneously, and lay behind the compulsive turning toward colonial
motifs – often highly mediated ones – in writers who never consciously
adduced Marxism, who were hostile to it, or who flirted with it briefly
before heading off in new directions. One sees this even in those places
where connections between interwar Europe and anticolonialism actually *have* been analyzed as an adjunct of the avant-gardes and of
the prehistory of contemporary theory: namely, in Surrealism. We
have largely forgotten such events as the counter-exhibit to the 1931
Colonial Exhibition in Paris titled "The Truth about the Colonies,"
a collaboration between the Surrealists and the French Communist
Party, although some interesting recent research is reminding us of
them (Edwards 1998, Richardson 1996). Not since the early 1970s have
critics felt the obligation of acquainting themselves with the quite
overwhelming evidence of anticolonialism's communist currents.

Although not typically seen this way, the Third International (or
"Comintern") disseminated Marxist ideas outside of European circles to ordinary people on a mass basis for the first time. But its
significance was not merely organizational. It was also theoretical.
It altered European agendas and tastes by situating the European in
a global relationship that was previously unimaginable. The Third
International brought emissaries from throughout the colonies, who
now formed a single, unified front meeting European intellectuals
on a formally equal footing.[6] This was unique in European history.
This new relationship between First- and Third-World intellectuals
departed sharply from the one established by the jobbers, journalist
explorers, missionaries and anthropologists through whom views of
the world had previously passed.[7] The International also undoubtedly entered Eastern and Western Europe in the guise of a threat from
the colonial periphery (Datta Gupta 1980: 1–4, 238–39), and may be
said to have carried on, for example, Leon Trotsky's and L. Parvus's
theorization (following the failed revolution of 1905) of "uneven and
combined development," a concept taken up in theory repeatedly
since (Trotsky 1969; Smith 1984). The same can be said of Trotsky's
thesis of "permanent revolution" where, dwelling on the discrepancies of trade and imperial law, he stipulates that developing nations
cannot achieve democracy by modeling their countries on Western
European forms – a proposition the International (it must be said) did
not consistently follow, but it is a theory often repeated without attribution. A symptomatic manifestation of the International's decisive
break with European norms can be seen in the Baku Congress – the

so-called meeting of the peoples – held in Soviet Azerbaijan in 1920. It was the first non-Western congress with the explicit purpose of denouncing Western imperial expansion, and of uniting peoples of vastly different languages and religious affinities (Riddell 1993, Roy 1964, Lazitch and Drachkovitch 1972).[8]

A good deal has been written about the disdain for local and national needs and desires that took place within the International over time – its transformation from Comintern to Cominform as Fernando Claudin put it – and some of the most active non-European intellectuals in the International eventually turned against it (George Padmore, for example). This is true and meaningful, but one is still forced to remark on the telescoping of the process, which fails to appreciate the conceptual breakthrough of the International alluded to, for example, by the noted Indian historian K. M. Panikkar when he points out that the revolution "create[d] doubts in the minds of thinking people about the validity of many things which they had accepted without question from the West...quicken[ing] the pulse of the peoples of Asia" (1959: 192).

Despite the social setting the revolution created, its epistemological contributions were limited by activism's draining of time from contemplative thought. It was left to the fellow-travelers and to communist intellectuals from the colonies to explore the implications of contrasting cultural values first embodied in the social transformations of the 1920s. If we are familiar with the extensive work of C. L. R. James in this respect, of Mao, of George Lamming or René Depestre – and it only takes mentioning these names to recognize how often they are treated as being either irrelevant to theory or beyond communism – there is no real sense of how widespread this culture of anti-imperialism was (James 1992: 331–46). The recent rediscovery of Langston Hughes's journey through the Soviet provinces of Turkmenistan and Uzbekistan in the 1930s – *A Negro Looks at Soviet Central Asia* (1934) – is only one of many such examples (Moore 1998). In a humorous, brisk prose, Hughes unsentimentally expresses a view widely held at the time – that the Soviet Union was the only power on earth that understood the right of nations to self-determination, and that materially aided anticolonial movements.[9]

While it is often argued that postcolonial studies departed from the Marxist-inflected anticolonial movements by locating resistance within *discourse* (and *Orientalism* as a foundational text is often cited as having effected just this transformation), the argument is based on an unsustainable reading of Said and a failure to appreciate his sources, as I have argued elsewhere; and this view also selectively excludes those thinkers like Frantz Fanon, Mahasweta Devi, Edouard Glissant and others who play such formative roles in the discourse of postcolonial studies, and yet whose apprenticeship occurred precisely in the excitements generated by the traditions I am revisiting here (Young 1995: 57).[10]

III

By stressing the non-Western influences on high theory in the periods before and after World War I, I am emphasizing how tenuous and yet defining they became for people with vastly different sympathies at roughly the same time. These gesturings towards the non-Western tended to enter European art and thought osmotically, at times even ironically, and they did so forcefully (if not uniquely) via the Bolshevik revolution. The non-West was simultaneously an imaginative resource and an uncomfortable impression, or at another extreme, an uncomfortably ecstatic one. Indeed, this confusion implicit in the interwar period provides the opportunity for a skillful conflation of the two tendencies of avant-garde primitivism, on the one hand, and anticolonial protest, on the other, in current postcolonial theory.

Raymond Williams, for example, notes in his posthumous collection, *The Politics of Modernism*, that between the two World Wars the enabling condition of avant-garde cultural practice was the sudden proximity of intellectuals from distinct national traditions speaking different languages on foreign territory. This cultural disjunction, he argues, had become uniquely productive, finding its basis not only in the new European colloquy produced by the imperial-nationalist hysterias of World War I, but also in a distant, instinctive reaction to the colonies, which began to assert themselves following the pressures and distractions of the War. This was the historical moment that witnessed a more concentrated outbreak of independence movements in the global periphery than had occurred in earlier periods (in the Philippines, Cuba, and Puerto Rico between 1900–03; in China in 1928; or in Libya and Ethiopia in the 1930s). Williams interestingly suggested, in other words, that the avant-gardes were in part a response to the colonies (1989: 43–47).

The process was actually more nationally and politically specific than Williams implies. The European avant-gardes arrived overwhelmed by the crises that in a few years would create the Soviet Union, borrowing the revolution's genres (the manifesto); adopting its anti-bourgeois rhetoric; shunting the elitist culture of museum and gallery into an impractical, but denunciatory "life"; and angrily repudiating Western urbanity. Like the revolution which looked to Germany for assistance, the avant-gardes looked West from the East (Tzara hailed from Romania; Kandinsky from Russia; both emigrating later to Paris, although with very dissimilar politics). While not setting out to aestheticize politics, artists like these were acutely aware of how close the relationship between Russia and the colonies was (Tzara 1977: 51, 57–58). Just as it is often forgotten that Tzara moved left as he moved West – eventually joining the Communist Party after arriving in Paris – similar passages are lost in translation. It is usually glossed over, for example, that Nancy Cunard's groundbreaking compilation, *Negro: An Anthology* (first published in 1934) – an unprecedented documentary record of African influence in society and the arts as well as an anticolonial compendium, gathering together essays by George Padmore, Zora Neale Hurston, Arthur Schomburg, Josephine Herbst, and others – was not a *surrealist tract* as some have called it (Cunard 1970). It grew out of an organizational and interventionist emphasis that Cunard exhibited both before and after the book's appearance while working on the Scottsboro case, on the protests against the invasion of Ethiopia and in support of the Spanish Republic. She ends one of her own essays in the book with the exclamation: "Up with an all-Communist Harlem in an all-Communist United States" (55).

When one scours the writing of scholars whose commentary on the interwar avant-gardes is already justly famous, accounts of the participation by avant-garde intellectuals and artists from Latin America, Africa and Asia is almost nonexistent (Bürger 1984, Clark 1995, Crane 1987, Foster 1996, Paz 1974, Poggioli 1968). The national and ethnic evasions of an earlier critical practice, if not the political, have of course been directly addressed by postcolonial studies (Kesteloot 1991, Unruh 1994). But the trajectory from avant-garde art to cultural *theory*; or from either to the political cultures of opposition in Europe to colonial rule, is rarely drawn in a careful, historical way. Conventionally, there are numerous allusions to jazz in such studies, to African design in Cubist paintings, to the various Parisian International Expositions, to "montage," and to the effects of Polynesian form on the Musée de l'homme. In more than a few, even recent, contributions to modernist art history, we have once again been brought to visit the problem of the primitive (Hiller 1991, Krauss 1994, Rubin 1984). But they seem uninterested in the available documentary evidence opening out the inquiry to a broader culture of anti-imperialism. To do that, one would have to resist seeing the period from a familiar angle: the one focusing on the uses of African or Polynesian art for types of European disenchantment; dwelling on the power of that art to offer an organic, unmediated relationship between producer and product, or delivering a subjective, spiritual unity (in Tzara's assessment, "simple rich numinous naivety" in place of "this dark grinding whiteness") (J. Lloyd 1991: 92, 100; Tzara 1977: 57–58). By contrast, it would have to theorize the avant-garde itself as a *creolized* formation in the manner of Williams.

The relative theoretical sophistication of Williams here is related to the socialist traditions of his training, and his willingness to recognize the lineage I called, in a general way above, social democratic (in its pre-World War I senses). By contrast, scholars have usually approached this period of colonial obsession by compacting the *colonial* or by reducing it to the creative gestures of a theoretical anti-Marxism that was also anti-bourgeois. The political danger of independence in the periphery as well as the eventual relativization of European thought itself implied by this shift in anticolonial consciousness is foreshortened in what is usually called in such studies "the primitive," a term that the critic both disapproves of and indulges in at the same time: a guilty pleasure (Kuper 1988, Miller 1991, Torgovnick 1990). This approach is insufficient, I have been arguing, for many reasons but especially because sentiment follows structure. In other words, the lust for primitive art was part of a longer process in which the colonies imaginatively invaded the European Continent, and under assumed identities, achieved a clarity whose contexts were decidedly geopolitical, although not always understood that way. If the Boer War, the Spanish–American War, and the massacres of the Belgian Congo inflamed sentiment before World War I, it was primarily the outrages in Abyssinia (Ethiopia), Morocco and Algeria that electrified opinion between the Wars, although the structure of resistance was far greater and more articulate because of the Russian Revolution, whose networks of terms and meanings allowed disparate outbreaks to acquire coherence. As a political unconscious, the view to the colonies had been inspired by the revolution's expanding influences.

IV

The links between the theoretical, not necessarily organizational, Marxisms of interwar Europe, and the anticolonial intellectuals who anticipated postcolonial studies as we now understand it, were also close and sustained, in part because of the anticolonial heart of the Soviet idea. One could turn, for example, to Ernst Bloch's famous coinage, *Ungleichzeitigkeit* (temporal incommensurability) from *Heritage of Our Times*, which carries on in a German context the concept of uneven and combined development coined by Trotsky and Parvus, and which echoes the ongoing Marxist theorization of the metropolis at war with the countryside – a paradigm drawn from the *Communist Manifesto*, elaborated by Antonio Gramsci in his political writings and in the *Quaderni*, and succinctly phrased in the title of one of Williams's books: *The Country and the City*. Gramsci may be more widely read than his contemporaries today, but he was not at all unique by Third International standards when he cast anticolonial agitation in post-ethnocentric terms. "The indigenous peoples [of Algeria] were not even left their eyes for weeping," wrote Gramsci in 1919. "For several years we Europeans have lived at the expense of the death of the coloured peoples: unconscious vampires that we are, we have fed off their innocent blood" (1990: 59). The saliency of Gramsci's work to the entire postcolonial problematic is, of course, known. But he was not a renegade from the Third International. He represented its collective wisdom.

There will not be the space required to develop these observations here, but a few further sketches might indicate direction. The conceptual tools of Marxist theory have for the most part been taken up by critics from the colonies rather than metropolitan intellectuals, even while it is the latter who insist – paradoxically – on the Eurocentrism of Marxism. In many respects it is *this* juncture above all that I have been tentatively exploring here. Marxism is confronted by a theory that borrows from it while disavowing the debt, inverting positions, or bungling their original contexts until anticolonial meanings blur. Let me give two quick examples. They are merely meant to stand for the kind of circuits that linked avant-garde primitivism, postwar theory, and the world of the Third International.

In an article from the 1950s on the Dadaist filmmaker and painter, Francis Picabia, the famous Cuban novelist and musicologist Alejo Carpentier recalled the uneasy relationship of both Surrealism and Dada with the cosmopolitan circles of Zurich and the revolution itself (Carpentier 1985: IX. 383–89). As a Cuban novelist who spent a decade in Paris between the wars as critic and radio producer on the fringes of Surrealism, Carpentier here casually reveals the attractions of the Soviet arts to Continental intellectuals, which contributed to his later understanding of the "marvelous" not only because of their technical innovation, but their holding in suspension the agrarian and the urban, the West and the East, drawing on an ambiguity that was, even before 1917, precisely Russia (VIII, 354).

Carpentier is interesting when placed alongside Bataille for showing, in interwar terms, the two strains that re-emerge (and conflict) in postcolonial studies. It took Surrealism and its latter-day offshoot, the Collège de Sociologie, to articulate separately the strains that communism had already partly united. Carpentier and Bataille worked together on Bataille's journal *Documents*, and Carpentier translated Bataille's early plays into Spanish before arriving in Paris in 1928 (Warehime 1986). Although each bore witness to the political unconscious of the Russian revolution, the Collège was in a way the avant-garde's *answer* to the threatening Third World conjured by the Bolsheviks.

In Bataille's *La Part maudite* (*The Accursed Share*) – whose first volume was published in 1967 – one can see culminating this exchange between Marxism and the colonial obsession, one that had been gnawing at Bataille from the interwar period onwards. The remarkable book fits itself within the familiar genre of attempts to work one's way out of Marxism by revizing its fundamental economic concepts – by destroying their capacity to attract, which might be said to be one of postwar theory's explicit intentions (Eribon 1991: 52, 137). In Bataille's case, this entailed a by-no-means arbitrary recourse to ethnographic exempla drawn from a variety of sources, but based on the interwar emphasis on the colonial primitive: Aztec sacrifice, Mexican potlatch, Islam and Lamaism (Bataille 1991). In his analysis, these individual studies lead up to and punctuate his later chapters on Weberian Protestant capitalist ethics and (not unexpected in the pattern we have set up here) a final chapter on Soviet Industrialization, which organically grows out of his concern with the non-Western earlier in the book, and which is explicitly linked by him to it.

I have chosen Bataille here as much for his departures from a pattern of influence as for his paradigmatic status. A perfect synthesis of interwar Marxism and the avant-garde primitive, and an obvious precursor of postwar theory (Foucault took more from Bataille, perhaps, than he took from any other French source), Bataille pays homage to communism while attempting to supervene it, supplanting productivity with excess, production with consumption, and the sovereignty of states with the sovereignty of subjects (Bataille 1993: 368). Nurtured in an interwar political milieu intensely aware of the colonies, and drawing on the resources of the antibourgeois shock of the primitive,

Bataille set out in the 1960s – at the highpoint of anticolonial independence movements, when over two thirds of the world was nominally
communist – to unite both strains. The marvel for today's postcolonial
critic is not that Bataille rejects communism, but that he concedes so
much: "communism," he writes in *The Accursed Share*, "is the basic
problem that is posed to each one of us, whether we welcome it or reject it: communism asks us a life-and-death question" (366). Bataille's
own quirky Marxism of the 1930s is usually glossed over in accounts
of his work, in much the way that Weberian and Simmelian sociology (or, indeed, Freud's writing on civilization) are studied without
reference to the attempt of each to outmaneuver Marxist initiatives
and dampen Marxism's extensive support networks and intellectual
enthusiasts as *the* grand philosophy of the social.[11]

Bataille here wrestles with his own acknowledgment that the
Bolsheviks had gone beyond the theoretical breakthroughs of sociology which posited (in the work of Simmel, for example) an objective
culture that lived in self-sustaining forms; or that cultural practices
like religious belief had veiled political consequences (the project of
the Young Hegelians in general, but especially Ludwig Feuerbach).
They took the view that objective cultures could be changed by an
act of conscious, collective will through the institution of policies,
and that by so doing, the relationship between the cultural and the
material could be clarified even as it was strengthened. The arts became politically conscious in a new way following the avant-gardes
because of the strong links of this new sociological view of "culture" to the distancing and counter-European thrust of anticolonial
knowledge.

Bolshevism sought to escape the everyday – a concept they all but
invented in their cultural organizations as *byt* – through policies of
cultural uplift. The Collège – in a frankly reactive gesture – did so
through extremes of experience outside reason: explorations of per-
versity, pain, waste, jouissance, all of them conferring legitimacy on
a body past utility, morality, sense, or meaning. It sought models for
this transgression by looking at Medievalism and at anthropology's
primitive which foregrounded cultural differences that questioned the
self-evidence of present practices (the ecstasy of Christian mystics, for
example). All of these are conceived as taking place outside of history
in a double sense (the invisible at home, and the foreign abroad). The
attempt of Hegelian man is here seen as a futility: the attempt to fill
a negativity or void with action, productive work, discourse, power.
Seen in this very unHegelian way, negativity ceases to be a process, a

communal "coming to self-understanding," and instead takes on the form of a thing or a place within which to dwell, in all honesty: to express the nothingness that Man is. What is affirmed is the ultimate limit, which is death.

There is no question that Bataille's universe of terminology and affective responses are highly derivative ones. He extols interwar communist legacies in the very act of repudiating them, drawing all of his questions from those first laid out by the revolution he sought to learn from while fleeing. What one sees in late Bataille is a rejection of an interwar obsession with sublating Marxism and of simply replacing it with Marxism's *other*. His more modulated response considered sovereignty the paramount question ("sovereignty" as a pun, however, shifting the term's meaning from polity to self). Bataille, unlike much of postcolonial studies, borrows without concealing his debts. At war with itself, postcolonial studies cannot get beyond Bataille's quandary, and opts to go less far in drawing conclusions about a "general economy" whose Marxist inspirations are undeniable. In this sense at least, theory's apotheosis of the present deranged from its enabling past leaves postcolonial studies an orphan.

NOTES

1 Peter Hulme argues that postcolonial theory arose as a critique of continental traditions. One has to concede the ambiguity of the term "tradition," certainly, and the concession would make any judgment of this claim difficult. But in spite of certain theorists declaring themselves enemies of "Western metaphysics" (the kind of critique Hulme undoubtedly has in mind), Gayatri Chakravorty Spivak has already pointed out in "Can the Subaltern Speak?" that postcolonial studies has been very *uncritically* critical in regard to its French sources. One would want to look more closely at individual careers, for instance; Foucault and Derrida both played the official role of French cultural ambassadors, pronouncing without any embarrassment whatsoever the glories of the French language and its civilization. For some tentative moves in the direction of this critique of poststructuralist Eurocentrism, see Marrouchi 1997: 9; Said 1983a: 222; Stoler 1995.
2 I am aware, of course, that the doctrines of the current critical canon on Nietzsche – codified first, perhaps, by Walter Kaufmann in the 1950s – takes it to be common sense that Nietzsche was no racialist, no German nationalist, no politico. This doctrinaire truth, however, is abundantly disproved by the Nietzschean corpus which continually rallies its readers under the sign of an embattled and surrounded Europe: "We Europeans." Expanding on this point will have to wait for another essay.

3 Heidegger's uses of Nietzsche, although far from open in the manner of Bataille, is not as controversial as that of Freud, who nevertheless acknowledges in a rather condescending way in *An Autobiographical Study* (1924) that Nietzsche and he agreed "in the most astonishing way" (1952: 67).

4 It is this sort of geographic understanding of Russia's ambiguous identity in colonial terms that prompts Samir Amin, for example, to draw a distinction between the peripheral countries as such, and the "semi-peripheries" among which he counts the Austro-Hungarian and Russian empires. Like China, the Ottoman Empire, and Persia – Russia was a semi-colony, albeit with its own colonizing past (1990: 45–46).

5 As I have argued elsewhere, the most influential current accounts of this group of writers have ignored the communist element entirely. See Clifford 1988.

6 In a number of postmortems, even committed communists once involved in the International excoriated it for its "defective understanding of the situation in other countries," and for "projecting Russian problems into other countries" (Roy 1943: 42–43). Similarly, it is the case that revolution in China and in India was actually hampered by the International's closed models. It is often forgotten, though, that while these facts are true, the International created networks, goals, and governmental assistance through which communists from the colonies themselves arose.

7 Of course, the same could be said of the postwar period as well. Kwame Nkrumah, Jawaharlal Nehru, Julius Nyerere, Frantz Fanon, Ho Chi Minh, C. L. R. James – the entire foundation, theoretically and practically, for the discourse of an emergent and angry colonial resistance was the result of explicitly Marxist legacies. The patterns of affiliation, intellectual contact, and joint policy laid down by the International were to various degrees behind each of them.

8 The congress took place under the horrified gaze of H. G. Wells and several secret informers who covered the event for British newspapers. Wells ridiculed – while feeling uneasy about – the Baku Congress's denunciations of the British empire. The congress prompted swift counter-actions by Parliament, which signed a trade agreement with the Soviets in order to end their "anti-British" agitation in the East (White 1974: 492–93). The Baku Congress, alternately portrayed as a brilliant opening and as a cynical act of consolidating Soviet power in the oil-rich Muslim provinces, helped the young republic win the initial confidence of its domestic minorities; however, it was at the same time an attempt to project an idea beyond Soviet borders: the revolution in a specific form – what Teodor Shanin has called the world's first anti-imperial movement, although obviously not the first anticolonial one (Löwy 1993: 127; Roy 1964). The effectiveness of Baku has been disputed. M. N. Roy, for instance – the Bengali activist who collaborated with Lenin personally in the drafting of the latter's "Theses on the National and Colonial Questions" – called the Congress "Zinoviev's Circus," an act of frivolous agitation at a time when parties were barely organized in Asia. It however brought

together over two thousand delegates, mostly from Turkey and Persia and some from China and India. Others have claimed its propaganda value immeasurable, and it was widely reported on in the West (White 1974: 513–14). Roy, like Padmore, would later severely criticize the practical "stupidity" of many of the International's leaders while praising its accomplishments (Roy 1943: 42–48).

9 Another interesting source in this regard – one to my knowledge unexamined in this context – is the *Revista de Avance*, an art and philosophical journal published in Cuba in the early 1920s by some of the future founders of the Cuban Communist Party. Its articles remind one of the early Gramsci of *Il Grido del Popolo* and *Avanti*, turning with flair, for example, to a variety of subjects, including critiques of cosmopolitanism, protests against Southern lynch-law justice, declarations of independence for Puerto Rico, endorsements of femininism, analyses of Bertrand Russell's theories of language, and a study of Vanguardism in the light of race.

10 The Comintern's actual *writing* on imperialism was unprecedented for its grasp of the racial dynamic, of Western arrogance, and of the liberatory desires of people largely consigned by its European contemporaries to ogling intrigue, artistic raw material, or irrelevance (Eudin and North 1957: 45–46, 199, 267–68).

11 Freud's negative preoccupation with socialism, for example, can be found throughout his writing – from *Group Psychology and the Analysis of the Ego* (1921) where he turns political identities into narcissistic identifications or cults of leadership, to his loaded remarks in *Beyond the Pleasure Principle* (1920) on the "superstitious 'instinct towards perfection'" that is always ignorant of the "economic situation." Flagging his droll meaning with quotation marks, he alludes to the labor movement in *An Autobiographical Study*: "The World War, which broke up so many other organizations, could do nothing against our 'International'" (Freud 1952: 34; Freud 1961: 616).

11

Marxism, postcolonialism, and
The Eighteenth Brumaire

Neil Larsen

I. Points of departure

What is nowadays perceived as the mutual antagonism of Marxism and postcolonialism rests, in fact, on a rather more intimate and disparate relationship than may be supposed, even by a well-meaning intention to mediate between the two. Although postcolonialism in its presently domestic/institutionalized form has no doubt contributed to the fashionable dismissal of Marxism as a "discourse" reducible to its "Western" and/or "modern(ist)" origins, postcolonialism's own genealogy as an instance of "theory" or even just as a strategy of "reading" can, in a roundabout way, be traced back to Marxism itself. Of course, there is a sense in which all contemporary "theory" with social implications can be shown to bear a necessary, if tensile relationship to the thought of Marx, at least if one accepts the view expressed by Sartre in *Search for a Method* that a "going beyond Marxism" will be "at best, only the rediscovery of a thought already contained in the philosophy which one believes he has gone beyond" (1968b: 7).

But what I refer to here is something more discreet: the sense, which postcolonialism inherits directly from poststructuralism, that Marxism can be purged of its 'Hegelian' birthmarks and incorporated successfully within the same critical spirit that animates the poststructuralist critique of the sign. Althusser, Deleuze and Guattari, Laclau and Mouffe's *Hegemony and Socialist Strategy*, even the latter-day Derridean "Marxism" of *Specters of Marx* are all as much the forebears and tutors of postcolonialism as are DuBois, Gandhi, Fanon, Antonius or other "third world," anti-colonial avatars. One is sometimes inclined to believe that, in fact, postcolonialism as currently practiced has a great deal more to do with the reception of French "theory" in places like the United States, Britain, Canada, and Australia than it does with the realities of cultural decolonization or the international division of labor. Like poststructuralism, postcolonialism as a theoretical and critical project is non-Marxist, but it does not frame itself *directly* as an anti-Marxism. Rather, it erects itself on a Marx *as already read* – by Althusser, above all, and then subsequently by a Laclau or a Stuart Hall, etc. At a minimum, postcolonialism bears an archeological relation to a Marx that, to follow Foucault's familiar thesis, hovers, along with Freud, over all "theory" itself as a "discursive practice . . . heterogeneous to its subsequent transformations" (Foucault 1984: 115). If one is to pose even the theoretical possibility that a Marxist criticism might, in Jamesonian fashion, make room for the putatively valid insights or discoveries of postcolonial studies within its mediated totality, postcolonialism will first have to be traced back to the point in its own intellectual genesis at which the thought of Marx *in its unity* appears to it as a "point of departure," to be either embraced or refused. Not Marx as "text," or even as "discursive practice," but Marx as *method*, as a *necessary* relation of theory and practice, must first be so positioned as to be able to 'speak' to the postcolonial critic.

In the last analysis, such a genealogical encounter would require a working back out and beyond the older, arch-debates occasioned by the structuralist and poststructuralist claims to (post-)marxisms of their own, beginning with the problem of Althusserianism itself. This obviously can't be fully rehearsed or even sketched in here, but I want to attempt a short cut by way of an unusually discreet textual constellation: the explicit citation and subsequent exegesis of a particular phrase from Marx's *The Eighteenth Brumaire of Louis Bonaparte* in one of the ur-texts of postcolonialism: Gayatri Chakravorty Spivak's "Can the Subaltern Speak?" What this particular moment of citation itself discloses is a common metaphoric and conceptual node within which both Marxism and postcolonialism encounter each other as, in principle, commensurable "theories": namely, representation itself as a subject/object relation in which epistemology and history, "knowledge" and "power," appear to become fused.[1] I refer, of course, to the well-known phrase from the concluding section of *The Eighteenth Brumaire*, written in reference to the French "small peasant proprietors" ("*Parzellenbauern*") who were, in Marx's view, the social class *politically* "represented" by the dictatorship of Napoleon III: "They cannot represent themselves; they must be represented" (Marx 1972: 239).

II. "They can be represented; they must not represent themselves."

The occasion for "Can the Subaltern Speak?," as its readers will recall,[2] is a taking of issue with "Intellectuals and Power," a 1970s "conversation" between Foucault and Deleuze in which all pretensions of radical intellectuals to "represent" the workers' struggle are abjured, and a "diffuse," de-centered strategy, clearly *sans* party or "revolutionary vanguard," is proclaimed. In short, emancipation, theorized in a manner consistent with Foucault's well-known "power/knowledge" formula for a "microphysics of power" and "specific intellectuals," can and must take place independently of "representation."

Spivak rebukes such a neo-spontaneism for failing – in its Deleuzian collapsing of interest and desire – to problematize its own metropolitan outlook, and thus of leaving what she terms the "epistemic violence" of imperialism essentially intact, despite overt gestures of anti-elitism. Have not Foucault and Deleuze too conveniently forgotten a history of Western victories for the oppressed that have left a non-Western, super-oppressed "Other" in chains? What can a politics freed of representation mean for this – "subaltern" – Other, if in fact it had *already* been relegated to the status of something non-representable?

Marx's phrase comes back into play here for its greater caution in observing something like this gap within "representation" itself. *The Eighteenth Brumaire's* word for the "political," seemingly subjectless and unfree "representation" of the *Parzellenbauern* is *"Vertretung"* (implying a "rhetoric-as-persuasion") and not the "economic," as well as epistemological *"Darstellung"* ("rhetoric-as-trope"). By now Spivak's argument – political, exegetical, and philological all at once – has taken on a density and an indirectness that has confounded many a reading. But the detectable inference here is that the Western intellectual or "S/subject" has been positioned in relation to the "subaltern" much as, in Marx's estimation, Louis Bonaparte had positioned himself in relation to the *Parzellenbauern*: the "S/subject's" power to "represent" (*vertreten*), resting on the powerlessness of the "Other" to self-represent in this sense, is cloaked in a philosopheme of representation (*Darstellung*) that is, in principle, free, unaffected by power-relations. The "freedom" of the *Parzellenbauer*/subaltern to "represent itself" (*sich darstellen*) in, say, an "idée napoleonienne" or a Foucauldian program for "micropolitics" is the ideology, the unfreedom of its *Vertretung*, its being-represented in subjection to an intransitive "executive power."

Taking, perhaps, some liberty with the intertextuality set in place by Spivak's citation of the *The Eighteenth Brumaire*, one might read "Can the Subaltern Speak?" as a catachrestic rewriting of the latter in the following, precise way:

They cannot represent themselves; they must be represented [*Sie können sich nicht vertreten, sie müssen vertreten werden*] *(Marx 1984: 131)*

becomes:

A. **from the standpoint of the Western imperial "S/subject":**
They can represent themselves [*Sie können sich **darstellen***];
[but] they must be represented [[*aber*] *sie müssen **vertreten werden***];
B. while, **from the standpoint of the "subaltern"** it is rewritten as:
[Since] we can be represented [[*Denn*] *wir können **vertreten werden***];
[therefore] we must not represent ourselves. [[*So*] *müssen wir uns nicht **darstellen**.*]

   The intellectual, even if "sympathetic" a la Foucault and Deleuze, "dissimulates" his or her own complicity in the continuous "constitut[ion] of the colonial subject as Other" (Spivak 1988: 280–81) by "conflating" the two senses of representation, disguising the "epistemic violence" wreaked on the Other as something remediable on the level of *Darstellung*. This remains so even, and perhaps especially *when* such conflation is followed by a quasi-anarchist disavowal of all representational mediations as unnecessary impediments to emancipation. For this Other as "subaltern," it becomes vital, then, to refuse the *Darstellung*, the "staging of the world in representation" (279) in which its Otherness for "power" is constituted, if the reality of its own colonial/imperial *Vertretung* is not itself to be concealed. And, argues Spivak, we owe this insight into the "complicity of *vertreten* and *darstellen*, their identity-in-difference as the place of practice" (277) not to Heidegger or Derrida, nor, even, to Althusser, but to Marx himself, a Marx "obliged to construct models of a divided and dislocated subject" (276); a Marx with "cautious respect for the nascent critique of individual and collective subjective agency"; a Marx for whom "the projects of class consciousness and the transformation of consciousness are discontinuous . . ." (278).

III. *Parzellenbauern* of the world, unite!

But to even a moderately circumspect reader of *The Eighteenth Brumaire*, Spivak's extrapolations from this phrase will quickly come to seem doubtful. While of some philological interest, the *Vertretung/Darstellung* distinction cannot be cited as evidence, one way or the other, for a Marx "obliged to construct models of a divided and dislocated subject whose parts are not continuous or coherent with each other" (Spivak 1988: 276). From the standpoint of the *unity* of Marx's thinking in the *The Eighteenth Brumaire* – the standpoint to which I aspire throughout – this is to commit the fallacy of collapsing the text's theoretical content onto the level of a purely lexical set of distinctions. Moreover, it implies the unlikely notion that Marx might have construed, in the relation of the *Parzellenbauern* to their representative/*Vertreter*, Napoleon III, a *generalized* relation of class *per se* to its political forms or modes of representation. In fact, not even the peasants themselves as a class are held to this rule. "The point should be clearly understood," states *The Eighteenth Brumaire* not even a page after its disparaging diagnosis of the *Parzellenbauern*, that

the Bonaparte dynasty represents the conservative, not the revolutionary peasant: the peasant who wants to consolidate the condition of his social existence, the smallholding, not the peasant who strikes out beyond it. It does not represent the country people who want to overthrow the old order by their own energies, in alliance with the towns, but the precise opposite, those who are gloomily enclosed within this old order and want to see themselves and their smallholdings saved and given preferential treatment by the Empire. It represents the peasant's superstition, not his enlightenment; his prejudice, not his judgement; his past, not his future; his modern Vendée, not his modern Cevennes.   *(Marx 1972: 240)*

True, Marx's word for "represent" here is not *vertreten* but *repräsentieren*, but "Can the Subaltern Speak?," sensibly, thinks better of arguing here that yet another mode of representation, distinct from *Vertretung*, is brought into play. Louis Bonaparte's power to represent (*vertreten/repräsentieren*) the *Parzellenbauern* does not, as "Can the Subaltern Speak?" infers, rest on a nonidentity of "desire and interest," or a crisis of subjective/collective agency as something intrinsic to all class difference but on something specific to *this* class – the *Parzellenbauern* – under given historical conditions. These are historical conditions that, in an earlier conjuncture, when the first Napoleon had completed the anti-feudal revolution that had given them their *Parzellen*, determined a *relative* identity of interest and desire, of *Vertreter* and *vertreten*, and that, in a possible future, might again allow for a conscious class agency as the peasants "find their natural ally and leader in the *urban proletariat*, whose task is to overthrow the bourgeois order" (Marx 1972: 242).

It is telling, indeed, that "Can the Subaltern Speak?" in its haste to make of Marx a precursor for the deconstruction of the subject-as-agent, excludes entirely from consideration *The Eighteenth Brumaire's* richly elaborated, differential analysis of class agency in the case of the two hegemonic, *socially* representative classes, bourgeoisie and proletariat. No faithful reader of *The Eighteenth Brumaire*, Spivak included, could speculate as to its "critique of the subjectivity of a collective agency" without calling to mind the passage in the opening section of the text in which Marx contrasts "bourgeois revolutions, such as those of the eighteenth century" to "proletarian revolutions, such as those of the nineteenth." The former "outdo each other in dramatic effects" but are "short-lived" and followed by a "long period of regret" in which past heroics are reduced to the everyday drudgery of bourgeois existence. The latter, by contrast "constantly engage in self-criticism and in repeated interruptions of their own course," retreating before their Antaeus-likened opponent "until the situation is created in which any retreat is impossible, and the conditions themselves cry out: "Hic Rhodus, hic salta! . . ."" (Marx 1972: 150). And here, too, a single chiasmus – from an immediately preceding and equally memorable passage of *The Eighteenth Brumaire* – crystallizes the dialectic in question: "Previously the phrase transcended the content; here the content transcends the phrase." ["*Dort ging die Phrase über den Inhalt, hier geht der Inhalt über die Phrase hinaus*" (Marx 1988: 22).]

None of *The Eighteenth Brumaire's* various lexemes for "representation" are present here on the surface of the text, but the concept itself is surely at work. Unlike the *Parzellenbauern*, both bourgeoisie and proletariat *can*, it seems, "represent themselves." For *both* an "identity of interests" clearly *does* "produce a feeling of community, national links" and "a political organization." For the bourgeoisie as collective subject/agent, however, self-representation is only accidentally – "ecstatically" – a real self-knowledge and self-activity. The self-representation "works" in the sense that it enables a momentary, accidental identity of class subject and class agent. But this identity – this "*sich vertreten*" which is also a "*sich darstellen*"– disintegrates as soon as its (historical) work is accomplished. The "phrase transcended the content" here denotes a surplus of representation that is perfectly compatible with a form of class agency, but that has its reverse side in a *deficit of consciousness* in relation to "content."

Here I essentially follow Lukács's thinking in his essay on "Class Consciousness" in *History and Class Consciousness*. A still unsurpassed reader of Marx, Lukács argues for a fundamental difference in *structure* between the class consciousness of the bourgeoisie and that of the proletariat. Whereas, for the former, the immanent contradictions of capitalist society constitute the outward, formal limits of consciousness, for the latter the same contradictions become the potential *content* of consciousness. For the proletariat such contradictions are expressed as an "antagonism between momentary interest and ultimate goal" (Lukács 1997: 73). Yet for *History and Class Consciousness* this precisely does *not* imply any belief in a "true," proletarian, in place of a "false," bourgeois, class consciousness but rather a consciousness in which "the objective aspiration towards the truth" is "immanent" (72). And even here "the mere aspiration towards truth can only strip off the veils of falseness and mature into historically significant and socially-revolutionary knowledge by the potentiating of consciousness, by conscious action and conscious self-criticism" (72–73). Plainly one cannot read all of that into "the content transcends the phrase," but Lukács's structural analysis captures and develops here, as neither Althusser nor (post-)Althusserian theory ever could, the grounding philosophical concepts and method that elicit the words themselves.

Thus the proletariat – to develop this same reasoning in terms of representation – would not be seen to resolve the bourgeois surplus of representation in favor of a merger or identity of "phrase and content." Rather it would *subsume* within its own *self*-representation the contingent, seemingly irrational and "ecstatic" quality of "bourgeois revolution." Representation would now no longer stand between class subject and class agency, screening the first from the second; it would disclose itself as simply the objective *self*-mediation of a class consciousness in whose formal make-up consciousness and agency, desire and interest, *Vertretung* and *Darstellung* can now potentially coincide. "Content," in "transcending" the "phrase," would reveal the phrase itself as merely a *moment* of content, inseparable from the latter's dialectical law of development. Representation itself would no longer appear as an unmediated cleavage or "discontinuity" of subject and object leaving history to one side or the other, but as a process consubstantial with history as a unified, yet contradictory process of ceaseless self-mediation.

The fundamental point of all this, against Spivak's reading of Marx, is that the divergence of *Vertretung* and *Darstellung* is not constitutive, nor even "symptomatic" of class but is *itself* relative to class difference as Marx theorizes it. It can only appear to mark a "discontinuity of class consciousness and the transformation of consciousness" if we read the *Parzellenbauern* as a metonymy for class as such, or, in more general terms, if we abstract representation from consciousness, enforcing an initial separation between the two to which neither *The Eighteenth Brumaire* nor Marx's thinking as a whole conforms – and which it has arguably already superseded. Both *Vertretung* and *Darstellung* as distinct, opposing moments of representation become, in Marx, sublated moments within the more concrete category of consciousness as both class-determined and as, in Lukács's words, "immanent in history" (1997: 77).

IV. The (postcolonial) desire called . . . Marx?

Still there is, it is true, nothing sacrosanct about the literal and integral text of Marx, nor even about the conceptual system it reflects – and nothing to prove, a priori, that "Can the Subaltern Speak?" might not be right about the inherent "discontinuity" of class self-interest and consciousness that it, in my view, falsely reads into this text. The downright strange thing about Spivak's essay – made even stranger by the fact of its own rapid elevation to near-legendary, "textual" status – is that it would think of advancing a theory of class consciousness infused by the aporias of "representation" (as understood in, say, Derrida) in deference to the authority of a work that can rather easily be shown to resist, if not refute such a notion. What could motivate such a reading? What "desire" – now perhaps genealogically carried over into postcolonialism as an established trend – could be at work here? It would only beg this question, in the end, to point to Spivak's debt, however critical, to Althusser, or to liken "Can the Subaltern Speak?" to kindred, post-Althusserian and "secular poststructuralist" exegeses of Marx, among them the *Anti-Oedipus* and even Derrida's *Specters of Marx*, which owes something of its own citational, Heideggerian/hermeneuticized relation to Marx as "text" to Spivak's earlier foray into this shadowy territory. In a sense Foucault was right about Marxism as discursive practice, at least rhetorically: a citation from Marx can be found – or "spun" – so as to prove virtually anything, from history as the "spectral" to the need to divide Poland. And protesting, "orthodox" counter-exegeses – of the sort in which I myself have just indulged – may ultimately be rather futile gestures. To answer, here, the question of "desire" (or "interest") we need to think more carefully not just about the current rhetorical uses and abuses of Marx, but about what precise sorts of cross-passages and subterfuges historical actuality has itself opened up to radical "desire" in Marx's text. If postcolonialism can be shown, after "Can the Subaltern Speak?" to rest on a discernible misreading of Marx, this genealogical result will only retain its interest – and the opportunity of a commensuration be preserved – if it can be further shown how the thought, or system of Marxism, as subject to the same desire, might come to reread, or rewrite itself.

Let us, to simplify matters, consider yet again the passage from *The Eighteenth Brumaire* – "...now the content transcends the phrase" – written over, as it were, by Spivak's citation – "They cannot represent themselves ..." (In the spirit of "Can the Subaltern Speak?" we might, clumsily, rewrite it too as "then the representations transcended what was represented; now what is to be represented transcends the representations.") Here, to reiterate, Marx formulates a dialectical inversion in which the aporetic, 'discontinuous' movement of representation, its constantly renewed surplus or deficit, reappears as subsumed in a historical relation of *internalized* difference (eighteenth century vs. nineteenth century, past vs. present) that is, moreover, determined as a class (conscious) difference: bourgeois vs. proletarian, or, even better, bourgeois vs. "social" revolution. The nonidentity of representation, once concretized socially and historically, no longer posits a pure identity as its "other" but rather a dialectical reversal, or *Aufhebung*. Representation as proper to a consciousness in-itself (a "false consciousness") becomes representation as proper to a consciousness raised to the level of the "in and for itself." One understands nothing of *The Eighteenth Brumaire* – and, in essence, nothing of Marx – if this dialectic of the *"an und für sich,"* straight out of Marx's own sublating, critical embrace of Hegel, is missed or obfuscated.

But one's "reading" of Marx on this point must also concede the extreme vulnerability of the theory of a *class* – that is, a *historicized* – consciousness "in and for itself" (Lukács's proletariat as "identical subject/object of history") to its own historicity when history-as-present itself appears, perversely, to withhold its promise. "The content transcends the phrase": Marx writes these words, putting the verb *"hinausgehen"* in the present tense, in 1851 or so. Revolution – a "revolution of the nineteenth century" – is understood to be imminent. A century and a half later, after the close of a twentieth century that at various moments imagined Marx's prophecy fulfilled, the words are still electrifying, but they cannot shake the ironic reading that would question whether they too have not become a mere "phrase," and the deeds of the (perhaps false) prophets who uttered them a new "nightmare weighing on the brains of the living." Perhaps, in fact, the "situation" in which "any retreat is impossible" has not yet been – or is only now being – "created." But, even if so, must not we, as the twenty-first century readers of a nineteenth-century call to arms, inexorably come to think of a "content going beyond the phrase," of a class "in and for itself," as a prophecy turned wishful thinking, as a revolutionary perlocution reduced to no more really than a constantly resurfacing "desire"? And if such is, for better or worse, the "desire" animating *The Eighteenth Brumaire*, must we not allow that, all else aside, it is a desire shared by "Can the Subaltern Speak?" – and perhaps by postcolonialism as a whole?

Read in this light, Spivak's pseudo-exegesis – in fact, a move to reverse the thrust of Marx's reasoning by collapsing history back into a textualized "representation" – begins to seem almost a gesture of orthodoxy, at least in the sense of a reader's loyalty to a literal text. The desire for the "content" to "transcend" the "phrase" need not relent simply because history gives the appearance – to Marxists and postcolonialists alike – of having fallen back once and for all "behind its point of departure," back into an eternal re-enactment of "bourgeois revolution" as surplus of representation. One has only to read the second half of the dialectical chiasmus differently – to interpret the present-ness of "hinausgehen" (Dort ging . . . hier geht . . . hinaus) not as denoting imminence but as a sign of Eternal Return, as the present-ness of the "always already" – and the desire for transcendence will appear to *itself* as realized. In this way, Marx's verdict on the *Parzellenbauern* as, so to speak, beneath self-representation does more than write over, palimpsest-like, the remainder of *The Eighteenth Brumaire*, including its opening invocations of a revolutionary eschatology. The reverse subsumption of "content" back into representation, of the prophetic and perlocutionary back into the aporia of *Vertretung/Darstellung*, obeys the urge to rescue, at least as *affect*, the possibility of a *hinausgehen*, a "transcendence." What if, in "transcending the phrase," "content" were disclosed not as immanent to history as a rational-dialectical unfolding, but as immanent to representation, to the "phrase" itself – as a "content" existing not on the outer, historical circumference of subject/object nonidentity but on its inner, infra-representational threshold, in that "inaccessible blankness circumscribed by an interpretable text" (Spivak 1988: 294)? One wouldn't need to cast off Marx, as urged by a Foucauldian poststructuralism or postcolonialism, but simply to read a text like *The Eighteenth*

Brumaire from back to front, from representational "discontinuity" *back* to class-consciousness, from *Parzellenbauern back* to bourgeoisie and proletariat.

Very much in the manner of Althusser, "Can the Subaltern Speak?" shows how the desire that Marxism come true compensates for an abandonment of its *method* – historical, dialectical and, in this, anathema to Spivak's deconstructionism – by clinging even more doggedly and with an almost obsessive philologism to its "text." This latter is not simply "misread" – as if a second, more careful reading would be enough to restore dialectical method and "discourse" to at least a relative unity. The "text" is read, as it were, *against* its own methodological content, as if the purportedly failed prophecy contained, hidden somewhere in its explicit wording, another, inadvertent prophecy, audible only in a gap between text and method, "phrase" and "content." The wider this gap the more closely one must scan and the more "theoretical" significance one must purport to find in the words themselves – at the level of the sentence or even of the lexeme. In the interstices of *Vertretung/Darstellung*, Spivak discovers the secret passage into a Marxism through the looking glass, a passage into what is almost an alter-history, a secularized and teleological "textuality" in which "content" can "transcend the phrase" because content was always itself only a phrase too.

In all of this "Can the Subaltern Speak?" conforms to a broader ideological/literary affiliation to Marx initiated by Althusser and refined in secular poststructuralisms and post-Marxisms from Laclau, Hall, and Butler to much of today's standard-issue Cultural Studies. Marx's systematic placement of class difference at the center of all seemingly transcendent questions (aesthetics, ethics, etc.) makes him, one now finds, a philosopher of "différance" as well – so long as one can drain all historical and dialectical substance out of "class" itself. Spivak's unique contribution to this effort was, of course, to equate the abstract, textualist notion of deconstruction with a principle of anti-colonial/anti-imperial subversion, to lift, via "representation," the textual out of the historical and re-map it onto the "postcolonial." The post-*historical* desire deposited in the text of *The Eighteenth Brumaire*, by means of an exegetical feint, here became the new form for an older, "third-worldist" and "essentialist" desire (for the *nation* as prior to the social revolution) likewise conscious of having been betrayed by its own eschatology. The radical alternative to the *Parzellenbauer* becomes not the "revolutionary peasant," much less the proletariat, but the "subaltern" as itself a species of *Parzellenbauer* that trumps

214

its oppressors by outflanking its would-be representation in the "imperialist social text," *viz.*, by its *"müssen sich nicht darstellen."* And so it is that Gramsci's nuanced, but precisely class-analytical concept comes to supply to a variant of secular poststructuralism a term able to solder within itself, medallion-like, the unalloyable metals of an historical agency and its textualist simulacrum, a term that, having once at least conveyed something of the uncanny subversiveness Spivak finds in Bhubaneswari Bhaduri's suicide one now hears used to qualify everything from hip-hop to middle class Franco-Ontarians.

Here too, in fact, a "desire" already readable in *The Eighteenth Brumaire* surfaces once more, and if "subaltern" serves the purpose of raising consciousness of the ethnic and gendered margins of the already superexploited (or perhaps already "unexploitable") then its textualist appropriation may have since become moot. Yet the fact remains that the real, genealogical order of determinations is turned upside down if we think of postcolonialism or the "subaltern" as the "theoretical" emissaries of the third world to the court of Western theory, whether poststructuralist or Marxist. Postcolonialism's origins are, at base, those of secular poststructuralism as a whole. The "colonial" is here a variation on a "post" theme, which travels from about as far East or South as a line traced by the lecture circuits and book distribution networks of French poststructuralist theory. Marxism, on the other hand, for all its history of Eurocentrist handicaps, has a better claim than postcolonialism to carry a non-European passport, having for generations rooted itself in colonial and neocolonial societies that never knew they were becoming postcolonial. But all told, the place where Marxism and postcolonialism might actually meet again isn't one that either theory needs to travel very far to get to.

V. Labor and the subaltern

To conclude, I want to propose that this is not the place of representation, nor even, at first, the place of politics, but that of labor – a theoretical category left implicit, for the most part, in *The Eighteenth Brumaire* and fundamentally excluded, except in immediate, empirical form, from postcolonial theory. The enormous interest of "political" works such as *The Eighteenth Brumaire* is that in them Marx sought to work out the concrete, even conjunctural implications of a critique of political economy already being formulated in works such as *The Poverty of Philosophy*. Labor in *The Eighteenth Brumaire* is mediated as politics through the category of class. It is the still primitive, under-socialized labor of the *Parzellenbauern* that ultimately determines its failure to become a class "for itself" and hence its reduction to a mere object of politics, of the class will of others. The labor of the proletariat, on the other hand (though here *The Eighteenth Brumaire* is curiously more parenthetical) is socialized labor in its highest form, and hence determines the historical potential of the proletariat to become a politically conscious class – not to "run" society but, come the revolution, to *become* (classless) society itself. Labor in *both* instances is in essence the abstract labor convertible to its value-form in commodities, money, and capital. But this fact is effectively occluded from consciousness in the case of the *Parzellenbauern* as a result of the illusion of private-property ownership created by the mortgaged "small holding" itself. Unlike the proletariat, the class of *Parzellenbauern* does not confront capital in its direct form as privatized means of production but indirectly in the form of its creditors. This same occlusion of class consciousness is expressed politically as support for Napoleon III.

In contrast to both, finally, the bourgeoisie, as owner or "bearer" of capital, owes its political efficacy as a class to its control of the labor of others. The irony – if not the "farce" – written into this form of "agency" is that, as such control assumes more and more automatic forms through the purely unconscious mechanism of exchange, "politics" itself is reduced to a question of guaranteeing the smooth functioning of this mechanism, making politics as a representational process – as a parliamentary or deliberative mechanism for the public play of competing interests – more and more superfluous. Only the periodic crises of capitalist accumulation and reproduction bring the political back into the foreground – but in ways that now may require the suppression of bourgeois parties and individuals in the "material" interest of the class as a whole.[3]

For *The Eighteenth Brumaire*, however, class mediates between politics and its ultimate basis in production not only on the level of the social totality but on that of the nation-state itself, of the "polis" of "political economy." Class relations are therefore political relations in another sense as well: as the variant relations to state power. "Class struggle" is rooted in labor as the prime, motion-giving factor of production itself, but its outcomes, its political history, take place within a state, or within a shifting, sometimes antagonistic constellation of states.

But what if conditions became such as to allow for, or even to force the politicization of labor – its acquisition of conscious social agency through its becoming-class – to take place simultaneously both inside and outside the state and inter-state arena? What if, to return to the terms of our earlier discussion of class consciousness in *The Eighteenth Brumaire* and "Can the Subaltern Speak?" it now becomes necessary to plot the immediately historical dialectic from the "in itself" to the "in and for itself" simultaneously on both sides of an "international division of labor"? The mediating role of class then becomes much more difficult to theorize, since the process through which class as structurally determined by labor and production *becomes* the class that possesses political, even revolutionary, agency can no longer simply presuppose a given state power or national polity as the *agendum*, the object to be acted upon.

Marx does not ask this question in *The Eighteenth Brumaire*, for the good reason that, in the mid-nineteenth century, the globalized market and its international division of labor remained "a secondary sphere subordinated to national economics and enclosed by the latter's military and political forms of self-affirmation" (Kurz 1997: 55). The transformation of the world market into the "immediate, functional space of economic subjects" and the dissolution of national economics by a "total system of commodity production" (56) is a possibility allowed for theoretically in the Marxism of *Capital* but only actualized – though this is obviously a controversial point for Marxists and non-Marxists alike – in the last two generations or so. From the perspective of "globalization," the need to rethink class and even labor itself in its political mediations and forms requires us to rethink as well the dialectical order of determinations in which labor's accession to self-consciousness, to the condition of a class-being for itself, grows negatively but *directly* out of its abstraction/commodification as "labor-power."

This dialectic too foregrounds the "political" criticism and theory of *The Eighteenth Brumaire*. The stripping away from the laboring subject of every last human attribute, leaving only an abstractly quantifiable object subordinated to the mass of dead labor that is capital is not only conceived as the impending, universal "negation of the negation" in which the now totalized object that is labor exercises its prerogative to become a total subject. For *The Eighteenth Brumaire* it is an impending *political* outcome as well, a "post"-bourgeois revolution. Not just the self-reproductive power of capital as a universal social relation but the class rule of the bourgeoisie, as embodied in a state or system of states, reads its historical epitaph in the social self-consciousness bound to grow out of labor's ever more total reification.

The contemporary history of "really existing globalization," however, presents us with a new reality in which the commodification of labor in much of the "postcolonial" world is nearly simultaneous with its becoming unemployable for capital. If Kurz and others are right, and the continued accumulation and valorization of capital now rests on levels of labor productivity (and an organic composition of capital) so elevated as to render superfluous – "unexploitable" – the labor-power of all but a dwindling number of individual laborers, then what comes into view is a dialectic in which labor bursts through its abstract form as labor-power only to become, so to speak, a subject *alongside* the commodity fetish, not (or not yet) in place of it. The commodification of labor continues to operate as, simultaneously, its socialization, but within the new terms set by a globalized society that also simultaneously desocializes a constantly increasing number of its members. This is the world inhabited, in Kurz's phrase, by "*Geldsubjekten ohne Geld*," of impending "*sekundär Barbarei*" (Kurz 1991: 223, 228), a world envisioned by the *Manifesto* as a scarcely thinkable "common ruin of the contending classes."

In this light, *The Eighteenth Brumaire*'s beckoning toward a social transformation "beyond" representation takes on a meaning as unsuspected, say, in Lenin's reading of it as in Spivak's. The "content" transcending the "phrase" would then read off not just as the class interest of labor but as *labor* itself – a labor that may now be ceasing to count as labor in its commodity form.

How, then, does a labor both "globalized" and, as part of the same movement, conscious of itself only as a "thing" but *without* value, as outside a society that was to have given way to labor's own social dialectic, mediate itself as a politics? This, I suggest, is the question that now defines a space in which Marxism and postcolonialism might discover a set of common, or even just commensurable, insights. One of these might, after all, be the insight into the "subaltern" as a social and political subject unrepresentable (or "ungovernable") within accepted notions of politics. But "representation" would have to be rethought here as governed not by the logic of "textuality" but by that of the labor theory of value itself in order for the idea of the subaltern to take on any real theoretical substance.[4] As *Geldsubjekt ohne Geld*, the subaltern points to a historical limit intrinsic to the commodification/valorization of labor, a limit that postcolonialism was perhaps intuitively poised to glimpse, but which it glimpsed only, and if at all, in the mystified form of a "deconstructive case." Postcolonialism will, in the end, have nothing to say to Marxism, nor Marxism to it, until the debt to the "French ideology," to the legacy of "secular poststructuralism" is canceled in full. No doubt Marxism has accounts to be settled as well, among these the loan of a secularized Protestant work ethic that, in Kurz's view, marked the ideological limits of a "Marxism of modernization" that the fall of Soviet socialism and the current global crisis of overaccumulation with its resulting devalorization of labor perhaps only now exposes fully. Whether the agency for revolutionary change under present conditions must still be sought at globalism's "weakest," now subalternized "links"; whether, in fact, the encroachments of "secondary barbarism" and the trend to pathological forms of rebellion such as religious fundamentalisms and ethnic particularisms (for these, too, are historical forms of the "subaltern") make all remaining hopes for emancipation from the margins baseless; whether, in the end, the very political form of revolution must now be entirely rethought: these are all questions neither camp can evade if society is "to create for itself the revolutionary point of departure."

NOTES

1 A longer version of this essay – chapter four of my work, *Determinations: Essays on Theory, Narrative and Nation in the Americas* (2001) – includes a critical analysis of Edward Said's citation of this same phrase (twice) in *Orientalism*. Suffice it to say here that, while the contexts for this citation suggest an interesting ambivalence in Said's – and postcolonial theory's – relation to Marx, *The Eighteenth Brumaire* itself has only an incidental role to play in *Orientalism*.

2 References here are to the version of the essay published in 1988. A somewhat revised version – with nothing in it to alter my critical assessment of it here – appears embedded in Spivak (1999): 247–70.

3 Bonaparte "sees himself as the representative of the middle class and issues decrees in this sense. However, he is only where he is because he has broken the political power of the middle class and breaks it again daily. He therefore sees himself as the opponent of the political and literary power of the middle class. But by protecting its *material power* he recreates its political power. The cause must be accordingly kept alive, but the effect must be done away with wherever it appears" (Marx 1972: 245; my emphasis).

4 The last place to look for any such logic is in Spivak's "Scattered Speculations on the Question of Value" (1987) – twin to "Can the Subaltern Speak?" in its here even more strained, Derridean confabulation of Marx. Basing her entire "reading" of *Capital* and the labor

theory of value, in true Althusserian fashion, on a single passage from volume I, chapter 1, in which the verb *"darstellen"* is used – and a passage which can in no conceivable way "bear the burden" of Spivak's reading of it – this essay repudiates the "continuist [i.e., non-textualist] urge" to treat that "common element" – value – that makes one commodity exchangeable with a certain quantity of others as the labor objectified in commodities" (158). Just what the "textualist" alternative to this "reading" of *Capital* might be is never made clear.

12

Postcolonialism and the problematic of uneven development

E. San Juan, Jr.

The paralysis and inconsequentiality of postcolonial theory in the face of globalized capitalism are so patently clear as to make it unnecessary to rehearse any further the criticisms of Aijaz Ahmad, Arif Dirlik, Neil Lazarus, and others (Ahmad 1995b; Dirlik 1994b; Lazarus 1999a; Schulze-Engler 1998; Stummer 1998). The objections to postcolonial theory leveled by these critics range from the charge that it fetishizes textuality and offers a sly if civil evasion of "contemporary imperialist practices" (Davies 1998: 23), to the charge that it exemplifies what Benita Parry calls an "elective disaffiliation from the variable articulations of an emancipatory politics" (1998: 48). This is not just because the genre is devoted to specialized studies of widow-burning or British colonization of the Indian subcontinent, Australia, Canada and South Africa (Ashcroft, Griffiths, and Tiffin 1989). The explanation is more than theoretical or discursive. Robert Young, the editor of the new magazine, *Interventions: The International Journal of Postcolonial Studies*, identifies its symptomatology: "The rise of postcolonial studies coincided with the end of Marxism as the defining political, cultural and economic objective of much of the third world" (1998: 8–9). This diagnosis is more wishful thinking than a factual statement.

Postcolonialism seems to require a post-Marxism as "supplement," a prophylactic clearing of the ground (Loomba 1998a; Moore-Gilbert 1997). What is meant by post-Marxism or the "end of Marxism" is really the reconfiguration of the international class struggle between the imperial metropoles and the masses of the periphery. It signifies the end of the bourgeois national project initiated by the Bandung Conference led by Nehru, Nasser, and Sukarno (Ahmad 1995b). This project of postcolonial states modernizing on the basis of anticommunism and pragmatic philosophy, reliance on Soviet military support and cynical playing of the "American card," collapsed with the bankruptcy of most neocolonial regimes that succumbed to World Bank/IMF "structural adjustment programs" and conditionalities.

Postcolonial normativity inheres in its claim to discover complexity and difference hitherto submerged by totalizing axioms. The principle of uneven and combined development, as adumbrated by Marx and Engels, Lenin, Trotsky, Gramsci, Ernst Bloch, and others in the socialist tradition, renders all the rhetoric of ambivalence, syncretism, and hybridity redundant. But this principle has been ignored or neglected because a linear teleological narrative of social evolution has been ascribed to Marxism, conflating it with ideas of unidirectional progress and developmentalism from Jean Bodin to W. W. Rostow and the gurus of modernization theory (Patterson 1997). I want to elaborate on this distortion of Marx's position because it functions as the crucial basis for arguing the alternative rationality of unpredictable social change offered by postcolonial theory. The metaphysical idealism underlying postcolonial dogma, its hostility to historical materialism, and its complicity with the "New World Order" managed by transnational capital can be made transparent by juxtaposing it with Marx's thesis of the uneven and unsynchronized process of development in specific social formations.

In essence, the most blatant flaw of postcolonial orthodoxy (establishment postcolonialism employing a poststructuralist organon) lies in its refusal to grasp the category of capitalist modernity in all its global ramifications, both the regulated and the disarticulated aspects. A mechanistic formula is substituted for a dialectical analytic of historical motion. Consequently, in the process of a wide-ranging critique of the Enlightenment ideals by postcolonial critics, the antithesis of capitalism – proletarian revolution and the socialist principles first expounded by Marx and Engels – is dissolved in the logic of the global system of capital without further discrimination. The obsession to do away with totality, foundations, universals, and systemic analysis leads to a mechanical reification of ideas and terminology, as well as the bracketing of the experiences they refer to, culminating in a general relativism, skepticism, and nominalism – even nihilism – that undercuts the postcolonial claim to truth, plausibility, or moral high ground (see Dews 1995; Callinicos 1989; Habermas 1987).

A typical exercise in repudiating a historical materialist approach can be seen in Dipesh Chakrabarty's objection to the institutional history in which Europe operates as "the sovereign theoretical subject." Modernity – "the metanarrative of the nation state" – is understood as European imperialism in collusion with third-world nationalisms. While Chakrabarty seeks to provincialize Europe by demonstrating the limits of Enlightenment rationalism (its coercive violence suppressed the heterogeneity of other cultures and civilizations), he also rejects cultural relativism and nativist histories. His obsession is to unmask, demystify, or deconstruct the themes of citizenship and the modern state as though they were permanent, transhistorical, and ubiquitous. In the end, he negotiates for a compromise which he labels a "politics of despair": "I ask for a history that deliberately makes visible, within the very structure of its narrative forms, its own repressive strategies and practices, the part it plays in collusion with the narratives of citizenships in assimilating to the projects of the modern state all other possibilities of human solidarity" (2000: 45). His intent is to unfold a radically heterogeneous world "where collectivities are defined neither by the rituals of citizenship nor by the nightmare of 'tradition' that 'modernity' creates" (46). Not to worry. The dreams of repressed subalternity in India and elsewhere await a Foucauldean genealogical excavation that the Subaltern Studies group has begun (see also Quayson 2000). On the other hand, the status quo of existing property relations and asymmetries of actual power relations (articulating class, gender, locality, religion) in India remain untouched.

I

Central to the postcolonial malaise is the belief that historical narratives of colonized peoples by Europeans have been permanently damaged, hence they are useless for recovering native or indigenous originality. Eurocentric knowledge (whether expressed by Cecil Rhodes or Joseph Conrad, by Black Elk or Bartolomé de las Casas) can never disclose the truth about the colonized. Following Lyotard, only local narratives can have validity from now on. Unless postcolonial historians naively believe they can return to a past where local narratives of tribal groups ran parallel and never intersected, the notions of locality and place are unintelligible outside of a wider global space from which they can be identified. What is missing in the critique of Eurocentric history is a dialectical comprehension of such relations – the relation between Europe and its Others – that precisely constitute the problems of one-sidedness, falsity, distortion, and all the evils that postcolonials discern in modernity (including Marxism alleged as a peculiarly European invention). Parallel or coeval modernities need to be theorized within a differentiated, not centralized, ontology of determinate and concrete social formations if we don't want to relapse into essentializing metaphysics.

In 1878, Marx wrote a letter to a Russian journal, complaining of a certain tendency that mistakenly elevated his hypothesis about capitalist development in Western Europe to a "suprahistorical theory." He wanted to correct the misapplication to Russia of his notion of the transition from feudalism to capitalism given in *Capital*: the emergence of capitalism premised on the expropriation of the agricultural producers can occur only when empirical preconditions exist. Russia will tend to become capitalist only if it has transformed the bulk of the peasantry into proletarians. Marx explains that this did not happen in Roman times when the means of production of the plebians or free peasants were expropriated; they became "not wage workers but an idle mob more abject than those who were called 'poor whites' in the southern United States"; after this appeared not a capitalist but a slave mode of production. Marx objects to his critic's attempt to generalize the hypothetical conclusion of his empirical inquiry:

> [My critic] absolutely insists on transforming my historical sketch of the genesis of capitalism in Western Europe into a historico-philosophical theory of the general course fatally imposed on all peoples, whatever the historical circumstances in which they find themselves placed, in order to arrive ultimately at this economic formation that ensures, together with the greatest expansion of the productive powers of social labor, the most complete development of man. . . . [However] events that are strikingly analogous, but taking place in different historical milieux, lead to totally disparate results. By studying each of these developments separately, and then comparing them, one can easily discover the key to this phenomenon, but one will never arrive there with the master key of a historico-philosophical theory whose supreme virtue consists in being suprahistorical. *(1982: 109–10)*

Now, it is clear that events can not be judged in themselves apart from the historical milieu, and that there is no "master key" to unlocking all phenomena – which is not to say that one doesn't need some schematic framework or methodological guidelines for gathering data, testing and evaluating them through some principle of falsifiability or verification, and finally formulating general albeit tentative observations. I think Marx was not disclaiming the validity of the notion of primitive accumulation he outlined, nor the scheme of historical development enunciated in the 1859 "Preface" to *A Contribution to the Critique of Political Economy*. The fundamental insight on the contradiction between the forces of production and the relations of production, manifest in class struggles and in the global phenomenon of uneven development, has served as a fertile framework of inquiry – an exploratory paradigm, if you like – in which to raise questions and clarify problems of social change.

There are at least two examples in Marx's theoretical practice that evince a sensitivity to the heterogeneous and disparate motions of diverse collectivities. The first deals with the subject of the Asiatic mode of production which departs from the teleological assumptions of Marx's theory of transition from the ancient and feudal to the capitalist mode of production. No necessary succession is implied in the unfolding of the transition sequence. Because the socioeconomic specificity of Asiatic society has led to a notion of despotic, stagnant and arbitrary societies quite inferior to the dynamic Western counterparts, the notion has become problematic and controversial.

Marx and Engels first became interested in investigating non-European societies when they engaged in journalistic criticisms of British foreign policy in 1853. They noted that despotism and stagnation characterized certain societies where the state management of public works predominated together with the self-sufficient isolated village community, as in ancient China. Later, in *Grundrisse*, Marx emphasized the fact of the communal ownership of land by autarchic communities, the stable basis for the social unity embodied by the state. In *Capital*, he presented the Asiatic mode as one way in which the social product is communally appropriated; this system is founded on the social relations of the self-sufficient village anchored to the unity of handicrafts and agriculture. The "secret of the unchangingness of Asiatic society" rested on the absence of private property (which precluded the rise of social classes as agents of change) and the simplicity of production methods. It is of course questionable how autonomous self-sufficient villages could coexist with the powerful interventions by centralized absolutist states whose origin also needs to be elucidated.

From a Weberian perspective, the stationary Asiatic mode displayed a lack of civil society and the dominance of a centralized state apparatus. Some scholars have claimed that Marx and Engels justified the "progressive" role of British imperialism in creating private property in land and thus destroying the stationary Asiatic mode. This modernizing effect, carried out through the railway system, free press, modern army, and means of communication (all technological determinants incorporated into social relations) has been used to apologize for if not legitimize imperial expansion as the only way of exploding an otherwise immutable and backward social formation. Here is Marx's own "apologia" for British rule in India written for the *New York Tribune* (25 June 1853) in Marx's original English:

> England, it is true, in causing a social revolution in Hindustan, was actuated only by the vilest interests, and was stupid in her manner of enforcing them. But that is not the question. The question is: Can mankind fulfill its destiny without a fundamental revolution in the social state of Asia? If not, whatever may have been the crimes of England, she was the unconscious tool of history in bringing about that revolution.
>
> *(Marx and Engels 1959: 480–81)*

Faced by the "cunning of Reason" (to use the Hegelian phrase), Marx counsels us to put aside "whatever bitterness the spectacle of the crumbling of an ancient world may have for our personal feelings" because we are also aware of the advances made possible by imperial cruelty: the destruction of barbarian egoism, the Oriental despotism which "restrained the human mind within the smallest possible compass, making it the unresisting tool of superstition, enslaving it beneath traditional rules, depriving it of all grandeur and historical energies" (480). Postcolonial skeptics condemn this narrative schema as reductive and positivistic. To my mind, however, it is the most graphic triangulation of opposites, a cognitive mapping of ruptures and contradictions that epitomizes the genuinely dialectical vicissitudes of history apprehended by Marx in his survey of historically specific milieus and concrete conjunctures.

The other example catalyzed by the discovery of the Asiatic mode of production is the possibility of a noncapitalist road to communism exemplified by Russia in the nineteenth century. In the midst of revolutionary struggles in Russia, Marx revised his early conception of Russia as "semi-Asiatic" and examined the nature of the Russian *mir* or commune. Could it provide the foundation for socialism or arrest its advent? Marx and Engels held that it could provide that capitalist relations of production did not strangle the whole countryside and that working-class revolutions in Europe coincided with any vast social change in Russia. Plekhanov disagreed with this, but it only proved that there is no deterministic and unilinear paradigm, nor evolutionary mechanistic formula, that would dictate how stages of development would unfold. It was Stalin who decreed in 1931 that Asian societies were subsumed under the categories of slavery or feudalism, thus pursuing the path of Western European development from primitive communism and then sequentially to slave, feudal, capitalist, and socialist stages. But, of course, that is not the end of the story.

It was the return of a serious concern with non-European routes to modernity in the 1960s that spurred discussions over dependency, uneven development and underdevelopment, world-systems theory, the specificity and complexity of "third world" societies, and African socialism. The theoretical liabilities of Orientalism incurred by the Asiatic mode have been spelled out by Bryan Turner: "its theoretical function was not to analyse Asiatic society but to explain the rise of capitalism in Europe within a comparative framework. Hence Asiatic society was defined as a series of gaps – the missing middle class, the absent city, the absence of private property, the lack of bourgeois institutions – which thereby accounted for the dynamism of Europe" (1983: 36). Nonetheless, the notion functioned as a heuristic tool that Marx deployed to eliminate any teleological determinism or evolutionary monism in his speculative instruments of historical investigation.

It is in the course of demarcating the precapitalist *Formen* – before full-fledged commodity production set in – that Marx revealed his commitment to an emancipatory if utopian vision. Whether in ancient Greek and Roman, Asiatic, or Germanic versions, these tribal communities contrasted favorably with the bourgeois epoch because "man always appears . . . as the aim of production, not production as the human goal." Marx continues: "In fact, however, when the narrow bourgeois form has been peeled away, what is wealth if not the universality of needs, capacities, enjoyments, productive powers, etc. of individuals, produced in universal exchange?" In effect, the totality of human development, "the absolute elaboration of his creative dispositions" and human powers signifies a "situation where man does not reproduce himself in any determined form, but produces his totality" (1965: 84–85). Informed by this synthesizing impulse in which de-alienation of labor becomes the aim of revolutionary praxis, Marx's method of historical specification does not degenerate into the disintegrating, anomic reflex that vitiates postcolonial discourse. His interpretation of the past in its uniqueness, which postcolonial hermeneutics inflates into an axiom of incommensurability, does not preclude a synoptic, all-encompassing apprehension; in fact, it presupposes that stagnant and paralyzing continuum that, as Walter Benjamin (1969: 262) puts it, must be blasted apart to release the forces of change.

It is in this context that Marx seized the moment of "the break-up of the old village communes" in India by British imperialism as a disastrous event pregnant with its contrary. It is progressive in the sense that it releases or unfolds human potential. On the other hand, Marx observed (in a letter to Vera Zasulich in 1881) that if the Russian village commune (*mir*) was left free to pursue its "spontaneous development," then it could be the point of departure for "social regeneration in Russia." This shows that Marx, far from being a unilinear determinist, posited the dialectical-materialist view that the peasantry can acquire a communist consciousness, depending on which aspects (the collectivist or privative) of the *mir* would be enhanced by a changing historical environment (Levine 1978: 175). This anticipates what Mao, Cabral, and others have recognized in appraising the conjuncture of forces in any contested situation, namely, "the sovereignty of the human factor in revolutionary warfare" (Ahmad 1971: 147).

George Lichtheim reflects that Marx's ideas on the various forms of social metabolism which are crystallized in different stages of society illustrate the modes in which humans individualize themselves through the historical process of "evolving various forms of communal and private property, i.e., various ways of organizing [their] social intercourse with nature and the – natural or artificial – preconditions of work ... The forcible disruption of the Indian or Chinese village community by European capital completes the process by rendering it truly global" (1967: 85). In any case, a revolutionary Marxist position does not prescribe a causal monism or a freewheeling causal pluralism. Gregor McLennan has summed up succinctly the dialectical imperative of the Marxist approach: "Structural principles must be complemented by, or even include, notions of individual action, natural causes, and 'accidental circumstances' ... Nevertheless, material and social relations can be long-term, effective real structures that set firm limits to the nature and degree of practical effect that accident and even agency have" (1981: 234). In other words, Marxism views the world not as a closed totality but an "open, structured whole, with irreducible differences" (Haug 1984: 16) comprehended dialectically, mindful of the play of contradictions.

I have dwelt at length on this topic because of postcolonial critics' insistence that the method of historical materialism is fatally compromised by its Enlightenment provenance. If Marx is a Eurocentric apologist for the "civilizing mission" of imperialism, then we should have nothing to do with his indictment of capitalism and advocacy of socialist revolution. It might be instructive to note that the charge of Eurocentrism leveled against Marx does not permit a nuanced and rigorous appraisal of his critique of bourgeois thought and practice, or distinguish the nature of capitalist modernity as a specific epochal form, one which is constituted by the complex, uneven relation between colonizer and colonized. Capitalism disappears when all of modernity, both positive and negative elements, become ascribed to a geopolitical region (the metropole vis-à-vis the periphery) that cannot be divorced from the world-system of which it is an integral part.

Samir Amin has perspicaciously described the historical genealogy of Eurocentrism in the drive of capital to subordinate everything to exchange value. But this drive to uniformity also precipitates its opposite, unequal accumulation or impoverishment of the masses. For Amin, the most explosive contradiction generated by transnational capital inheres in the center/periphery polarization and its corollary, the "imperialist dimension of capitalist expansion" (1989: 141). Postcolonial affirmation of cultural difference, or the interstitial and syncretic byproducts of the center/periphery dynamic, evades a critique of bourgeois economism and reproduces itself as an inverted Eurocentrism that cannot resolve the crisis of inequality. A genuine universalism cannot emerge from incommensurable and provincialized cultures, no matter how valorized as singular or cosmopolitan; the impasse can be broken only by a national popular-democratic breakthrough instanced by national liberation struggles.

II

It is not exorbitant to state that today all social relations and practices, as well as the process of social transformation, labor under the imperatives of accumulation, competition, commodification, and profit-maximization. Postcolonial paradigms of hybridity and ambivalence are unable to offer frames of intelligibility that can analyze and critique the internal contradictions embedded in the neoliberal reality and ideology of the "free market." Driven by a pragmatic empiricism, postcolonialism cannot offer a frame of intelligibility for a "cognitive mapping" of all those historical trends that marked the breakdown of developmentalism, modernization theory, and other theoretical solutions to the crisis of monopoly capital since the Bolshevik Revolution of 1917 up to the scrapping of the Bretton Woods agreement and a unitary monetary system. As many have noted, the logic and rhetoric of postcolonialism coincide suspiciously with the anarchic "free market" and the vicissitudes of finance capital on a global scale. Bound by its problematic, the postcolonial critic cannot even entertain the crucial question that Amin poses: "how can we develop the productive forces without letting commodity relations gain ground?" (1977: 101).

There have been many explanations for this inadequacy and limitation. Amin (1998) locates it in postcolonialism's rejection of Enlightenment narratives of emancipation and convivial democracy. The excesses of instrumental reason are ascribed to the teleology of progress instead of the logic of capitalism and its presuppositions (private property, entrepreneurship, wage labor, technological improvement, laws of the market). The conflation of the ideals of enlightenment with the telos of utilitarian capitalism and its encapsulation in the historiographic fortunes of modernity has led to a skeptical, nominalist conception of subjectivity and agency. Disavowing modernity and the principle of collective human agency – humans make their own history under determinate historical conditions – postcolonialism submits to the neoliberal bourgeois cosmos of fragmentation, individualist warfare, free-playing decentered monads, and a regime of indeterminacy and contingency. This ironic turn damages postcolonialism's claim to liberate humans from determinisms and essentialisms of all kinds.

I think the fundamental error may be traced to two sources. We have, first, the inability to conceptualize mediation or connections in a dialectical manner, substituting instead a seriality of differences whose equivalence or solidarity remains unpredictable; and second, entailed by the first premise, the incapacity to conceive of the conjunctural moment of society as inscribed in the uneven development of the world-system. Uneven development involves the inescapable polarization of the world into peripheral and central economies, tied with the intrinsic contradiction between labor and capital and the international division of labor whose boundaries were laid by the history of European colonialism and later by finance or monopoly capital. Uneven development implies a polyrhythmic configuration of history characterized by the *Ungleichmassigkeit der Zeit* (to use Ernst Bloch's category [1973]). Why theorize mediation and uneven development in a precise historicized fashion? Because our intent is to "master" and so escape the "nightmare of history and to win a measure of control over the supposedly blind and natural 'laws' of socioeconomic fatality." As Fredric Jameson suggests, historical reconstruction, "the positing of global characterizations and hypotheses, the abstraction from the 'blooming, buzzing' confusion of immediacy, was always a radical intervention in the here-and-now and the promise of resistance to its blind fatalities" (1998: 35).

From a historical-materialist perspective, the dynamic process of social reality cannot be grasped without comprehending the

connections and the concrete internal relations that constitute the totality of its objective determinations. Several levels of abstraction have to
be clarified among which is the relation between the knowing subject
and the surrounding world (both nature and the built environment).
Truth in this tradition comes from human practice, the intermediary
between consciousness and its object; and it is human labor (knowing
and making as a theorized synthesis) that unites theory and practice.
As Lenin puts it, everything is mediated and connected by transitions
that unite opposites, "transitions of every determination, quality, feature, side, property, into every other" so that "the individual exists
only in the connection that leads to the universal" (1963: 132). The reciprocal interaction of various levels of formal abstractions has been
elaborated by Bertell Ollman (1993) under the categories of "metamor-
phosis" and contradictions. These levels of abstract mediation, however, need to be transcoded into their concrete manifestation without
necessarily succumbing to the one-sided immediacy of empiricism
or pragmatism. Otherwise, what Fabian (1983) calls the allochronic
orientation of Eurocentric thought with its taxonomic, noncoeval representation of Others would continue to prevail.

What is required next is to confront the second-order mediations
which are historically specific and transcendable, namely, the market, money, private property, the transformation and subordination of
use-value to exchange value – in short, the sources of alienation and
perversion of what Meszaros calls "productive self-mediation" of individuals in social life. Alienation on the level of national struggle can
only be resolved in the colonized people's conquest of full sovereignty,
"the socialization of the principal means of production" (Meszaros
1983: 13) and reproduction in a socialist transformation. Indeed, it
is these historical phenomena of alienation and reification that poststructuralist thought hypostatizes into the nihilism of modernity,
converting mediation (transition) into serial negation and occlud-
ing its prefigurative, transformative phase or aspect (Lukács 2000).
Contradiction, sublation, and overdetermination do not figure as
meaningful concepts in postcolonial theorizing.

Without a concept of totality, however, the notion of mediation
remains vacuous and useless. All determination is mediation, Roy
Bhaskar reminds us in his magisterial study *Dialectic* (1993). Totality
in its historical concreteness becomes accessible to us in the concept
of uneven development, and its corollary ideas of overdetermination
(or, in Amin's thought, "underdetermination"), combined development in the coexistence of various modes of production in a specific

social formation, or in another framework, Wallerstein's world-system mapping of periphery and core societies. We have come to accept as a commonplace the differential rhythm of development of societies, the uneven pace due to presence or absence of cumulative growth in the use of production techniques, labor organization, and so on, as reflected in Marx's inquiry into Russia and Asia mentioned earlier.

Uneven development results from the peculiar combination of many factors which have marked societies as peripheral or central (Löwy 1981; Novack 1966). In many societies shaped by colonial conquest and imperial domination, uneven and combined development is discernible in the co-presence of a modern sector (usually foreign dominated or managed by the state) and a traditional sector characterized by precapitalist modes of production and ruled by merchant capitalist and feudal/tributary ruling classes. In these peripheral formations, we find a lack of cumulative growth, backward agriculture limited by the lack of an internal market, with the accumulated money capital diverted from whatever industrial enterprises there are into speculative activities in real estate, usury, and hoarding (Mandel 1983). This unsynchronized and asymmetrical formation, with variations throughout the postcolonial world, serves as the ideal habitat for "magic realism" and wild absurdist fantasies (Borges, Cortázar), as well as all those cultural expressions and practices described as hybrid, creolized, syncretic, ambivalent, multiplicitous, and so on, which postcolonial theory has fetishized and reified as permanent, ever-recurring, and ineluctable qualities (San Juan 1998).

In my view, this historical conjuncture of uneven and combined development can only be grasped by dialectical assessments of imperialism like those propounded by Gramsci, C. L. R. James, Walter Rodney, Amilcar Cabral, and others in the Marxist–Leninist tradition. It was Lenin who remedied the classical limitation of the Second International and the social democratic parties by integrating into his idea of world revolution the revolt of the industrial working class in Europe with the mass uprisings of small colonized nations, as well as peasant revolts against landowners. His post-1914 writings theorized how the "particular" of national liberation movements can, under certain conditions, become the road to the universal of socialism. In this discourse, mediation assumes the form of historically specific contradictions between oppressed peoples in the colonies and oppressor nations. As Kevin Anderson argues, "Lenin's theory of imperialism has become dialectical in the sense of pointing not only to the economic side of imperialism but also to a new revolutionary subject arising from within global imperialism: national liberation movements" (1995: 142). Unless we can improve on Lenin's theory of national liberation with its processual or dialectical materialist method, we will only be indulging in postcolonial verbal magic and vertiginous tropology that seems to be infinitely reproduced by a delirious "otherness machine" (Appiah 1991: 356).

III

As for the concrete translation of the Leninist tradition into situated historical praxis, I can only allude to the brilliant and enduring example of Amilcar Cabral. In what way does Cabral supersede the mechanical version of decolonization as a valorization of interstitiality, syncretism, and transculturation?

A few key features of Cabral's thought need to be underscored. His theory of national revolution is a creative application of Marxism as a dialectical theory of action in which history generates the unforeseen within the parameters of what objectively exists. Cabral understood the Marxist insight that "the process of history seeks itself and proves itself in praxis" (Lefebvre 1969: 162). He theorized national liberation in his concrete milieu (the Portuguese colonies of Guinea Bissau and Cape Verde islands) through the paradigm of interacting modes of production in history. He insisted on the centrality of the level of productive forces as the "true and permanent driving power of history" (Cabral 1973: 42). Imperialist rule deprived the colonized peoples of agency, the vocation of shaping their own history. Since imperialist domination negated "the historical development of the dominated people" (42–43) by means of violently usurping the free operation of the process of development of the productive forces, the goal of decolonization is "the liberation of the process of development of national productive forces" (43). The struggle for national liberation is not simply a cultural fact, but also a cultural factor generating new forms and content in the process (Cabral 1979: 211).

For Cabral, culture is the salient or key constituent of the productive forces. Culture becomes the decisive element in grasping the dialectic of subjective and objective forces, the level of productive forces and the production relations, as well as the uneven terrain of class struggles: "Culture is simultaneously the fruit of a people's history and a determinant of history, by the positive or negative influence which it exerts on the evolution of relationships between man and his environment, among men or groups of men within a society, as well as among different societies" (1979: 41). But Cabral urges a concrete differentiation of tendencies and possibilities: "Nor must we forget that culture, both as a cause and an effect of history, includes essential and secondary elements, strengths and weaknesses, merits and defects, positive and negative aspects, factors both for progress and stagnation or regression, contradictions, conflicts... Culture develops unevenly at the level of a continent, a 'race,' even a community" (210, 212). If liberation is an act of culture, it is also a struggle to shape a richer culture that is simultaneously "popular, national, scientific and universal" (212).

Framed within the problematic of a non-linear narrative, Cabral conceives of national liberation as a wide-ranging transformation of the combined political, economic, and cultural institutions and practices of the colonized society. It is not narrowly culturalist or merely superstructural because culture refers to the "dynamic synthesis of the material and spiritual historical reality of a society." In a broad sense, it is the recovery of specific African forms of subjectivity, a "regaining of the historical personality of the people, its return to history through the destruction of imperialist domination." This recovery is staged as a popular cultural renaissance with the party as the chief pedagogical agency wielding the "weapon of theory," the organized political expression of a mass, national-popular culture in the making. This renaissance occurred in the praxis of the liberated zones controlled by the PAIGC (African Party for the Independence of Guinea and Cape Verde) where the culture-changing processes of criticism and self-criticism, democratic discussion, teaching and learning from the participants, and so on were encouraged and institutionalized. This will recall Marx's dialectical thesis of an alternative to unilinear evolutionism of the Russian village commune: if the subjective force of the peasantry acquires consciousness and organized identity, the objective situation can be transformed in a liberatory direction (Marx 1971b).

Cabral was called by his people *Fundador da Nacionalidade,* Founder of the Nationality, not Founder of the Nation. According to Basil Davidson, this is because "the nation was and is a collectivity and necessarily founds itself, but [Cabral was the] founder of the process whereby this collectivity could (and does) identify itself and continue to build its post-colonial culture" (1986: 39). Cabral also believed that "the dialectical nature of identity lies in the fact that it both *identifies* and *distinguishes*" (1979: 208). Seizing the strategic initiative, Cabral exhorted his comrades and fighters to engage in a double and totalizing task cognizant of the uneven cultural and ideological strata of the geopolitical terrain:

> every element of the population in our land in Guinea and Cape Verde, should be aware that our struggle is not only waged on the political level and on the military level. Our struggle – our resistance – must be waged on all levels of the life of our people. We must destroy everything the enemy can use to continue their domination over our people, but at the same time we must be able to construct everything that is needed to create a new life in our land. *(qtd. in Cohen 1998: 44).*

Cabral combined national and social elements into an insurrectionary movement in which the partisan unit, no longer a local entity but a "body of permanent and mobile cadres around whom the local force is formed" (Hobsbawm 1973: 166), became the germ of the "new life," the embryonic nationality becoming the nation.

Developing certain themes in Fanon, Cabral's Marxism is unique in concentrating on the potential nation as "a form of revolutionary collective subjectivity" mediating actual classes, sectors, and groups into a "nation-for-itself" that can reclaim the "inalienable right of every people to have their own history" based on their right to control "the process of development of national productive forces." Cabral located the roots of this subjectivity in the cultural resistance of the masses which was "protracted and multiple," "only possible because by preserving their culture and their identity the masses retain consciousness of their individual and collective dignity despite the vexations, humiliations and cruelties they are exposed to" (1979: 209). As Timothy Luke acutely remarks, Cabral valued the "emancipatory forms of collective subjectivity" in the colonized subjects and so promoted "the politically organized and scientifically rationalized *reconstitution* of the traditional African peoples' history-making and culture-building capacities" (1990: 191). Cabral urged his activists: "I am asking you to accomplish things on your own initiative because everybody must participate in the struggle" (qtd. in Chaliand 1969: 68). Cabral's originality thus lies in his recognizing that the nation-in-itself immanent in the daily lives of African peoples can be transformed into a nation-for-itself, this latter concept denoting the peoples' exercise of their historical right of self-determination through the mediation of the national liberation movement, with the PAIGC as an educational organizing force that seeks to articulate the national-popular will.

Contrary to postcolonial speculation, Cabral's project is the making of a nation in the course of the anti-imperialist struggle. Comprised of numerous ethnic groups living apart, highly fragmented with over a dozen languages, Guinea-Bissau and Cape Verde did not fulfill the orthodox qualifications of a nation laid down by Stalin: "a stable community of people formed on the basis of a common language, territory, economic life and psychological make-up manifested in the common culture" (Stalin 1970: 68). Cabral's exceptional contribution consists in articulating the nation-in-process (of transition from potentiality to actuality) in the struggle against Portuguese colonialism. The project of the party he founded, the PAIGC, aimed to generate national awareness by mass mobilization of the peasants in conjunction with the petty bourgeoisie, the embryonic proletariat, and the declassed youth. Through skillful organization and painstaking ideological education, the PAIGC converted the cultural resistance of the tribal villages into a dynamic and formidable force capable of defeating a technologically sophisticated enemy.

Cabral began from the paradoxical phenomenon of the indigenous petty bourgeoisie beginning to acquire a consciousness of the totality by comparison of the various parts of colonized society. He exhorted the petty bourgeoisie to commit class suicide in order to coalesce with the peasantry (the workers constituted a tiny minority; a national bourgeoisie did not exist); but Cabral had no illusions that such alliances would spontaneously firm up in a postcolonial environment. He stated before his assassination on 20 January 1973: "You know who is capable of taking control of the state apparatus after independence . . . The African petty bourgeoisie has to be the inheritor of state power, although I wish I could be wrong. The moment national liberation comes and the petty bourgeoisie takes power we enter, or rather return, to history and the internal contradictions break out again" (qtd. in Davidson 1969: 134). Cabral's insight warns us of the dangers of reifying postcolonial culture as an interstitial, ambiguous space of contestation devoid of any outside from which critique can be formulated. Contradictions persist even in transitory class alliances (the famous unity of opposites in Lenin's discourse), hence the need to calculate the stages of the struggle which demand strategic mutations and tactical alterations, while keeping in mind a constant theme: "the masses keep intact the sense of their individual and collective dignity"

(Cabral 1973: 69). The axiom of uneven and combined development rules out postcolonial assumptions of contingent heterogeneity and incommensurable disparities of individuals that ignore mass native cultural resistance. Cabral upheld an anti-postcolonial belief in the "supremacy of social life over individual life," of "society as a higher form of life" (1979: 208), which in effect contradicts the neo-Kantian attribution of moral and rational agency to bourgeois individuals, a criterion that "postpositivist realists" (Mohanty 1995) and assorted deconstructionists espouse.

Notwithstanding the resurgence of armed anti-imperialist insurgency in "third world" neocolonies like Colombia, the Philippines, Mexico (Chiapas), the moment of Cabral might be deemed irretrievably remote now from our present disputes. However, the formerly subjugated peoples of color grudgingly acknowledged by Western humanism cannot be simply pacified by reforming capitalism's international division of labor. The postcolonial cult of the Leibnizian conceit (Harvey 1996), in which alterity and marginality automatically acquire subversive entitlement, has carried out the containment of Marxist ideas and ideals of national liberation by an aestheticizing maneuver analogous to what Neil Larsen discerned in cultural studies: "a subtle transfer of emancipatory aims from the process of objective social transformation to the properly 'cultural' task of intervention in the 'subject'-forming play of discourse(s)" (1995: 201). But as long as capitalism produces uneven and polarizing trends in all social formations, there will always exist residual and emergent agencies challenging the reign of "the law of value" and postmodern barbarism (Amin 1998).

We cannot of course return wholesale to the classic period of national liberation struggles indexed by the names of Nkrumah, Cabral, Ho Chi Minh, Guevara, Fanon, and others. My purpose in bringing up Cabral is simply to refute the argument that historical materialist thinking is useless in grasping the complexity of colonialism and its aftermath. Would shifting our emphasis then on studying the subaltern mind remedy the inadequacies and limitations of postcolonial theory? I might insert here the view of Jon Stratton and Ien Ang, who believe that the limits of the postcolonial/diasporic trajectory can be made up by the voices of the indigenous and the subaltern within the context of the "relativization of all discursive self/other positionings within the Anglophone cultural studies community" (1996: 386). This intervention in the site of textual-discursive representation is salutary, but the problem of articulating a counter-hegemonic strategy focusing on the "weak links" (where the IMF/World Bank's "structural conditionalities" continue to wreak havoc) remains on the agenda. For it cannot be denied that within the hybridizing, syncretic, borderless milieu of the postcolonial episteme one encounters, without much uncanny afterthought, "the still globally culturally hegemonic realm of the USA" (King 1995: 117).

Finally, I want to situate postcolonialism as a symptomatic recuperation of finance capital, at best the imaginary resolution of contradictions between exploited South and exploiting North, within the altered geopolitical alignments of the world-system (Wallerstein 1995). The world-wide protest against the World Trade Organization, the International Monetary Fund, and the World Bank, instanced by the popular demonstrations in Seattle, Washington, in November 1999 augurs the sharpening of contradictions at the heart of globalizing capital, revitalizing traditional "left" coalitions and generating new agencies of revolutionary transformation in the peripheries and within the metropolitan heartlands. The "third world" has now migrated into the centers whose "weak links" offer opportunities for a variety of interventions that seem to elude postcolonial intellects.

The "third world" was a viable conceptualization of the nationalist bourgeois struggles that led to the independence of India, Ghana, the Philippines, Egypt, Indonesia, and other nation-states after World War II. The classic postcolonial states created the Bandung coalition of non-aligned states which gave a semblance of unity to the "third world." However, United States hegemony during the Cold War continued until the challenge in Vietnam, Cuba, and elsewhere. The last expression of "third world" solidarity, the demand for a "New International Economic Order" staged in the United Nations, came in the wake of the oil crisis of 1973; but the OPEC nations, with their political liabilities, could not lead the "third world" of poor, dependent nations against US hegemony. Notwithstanding the debacle in Vietnam and the series of armed interventions in the Caribbean and elsewhere, US world supremacy was maintained throughout the late 1970s and 1980s by economic force. This mode of winning consent from the "third world" used monetarist policies that caused lower export earnings and high interest rates, reducing these polities to dependencies of the IMF/WB and foreign financial consortia. The defeat of the "third world" bloc in 1982 allowed the US-led Western bloc to exploit "international civil society" into a campaign against global Keynesianism. From 1984 to the 1990s, however, global Reaganomics, the instability of the financial markets, the fall of the dollar, worsening

US deficit, etc. posed serious problems to the US maintenance of hegemony over the Western bloc. Despite the success, and somewhat precipitous collapse, of the Asian Newly Industrializing Countries, the "third world" as an independent actor, with its own singular interests and aspirations, has virtually disappeared from the world scene. Postcolonial theory, whose provenance owes more to finance capital than has heretofore been understood, serves to compensate for this disappearance. But wherever neocolonialism (Woddis 1972) prevails, the ideal and practice of national liberation will continue to thrive.

13

Adorno, authenticity, critique

Keya Ganguly

> For the mind (*Geist*) is indeed not capable of producing or
> grasping the totality of the real, but it may be possible to
> penetrate the detail, to explode in miniature the mass of merely
> existing reality.   (*Theodor Adorno, "The Actuality of Philosophy"*)

Among the many quandaries facing postcolonial studies today is the
question of how to reckon with the problem of saying something substantial about colonial and imperial history, experience, and effects,
while remaining true to the linguistic turn and its decapitation of the
body of foundationalist ideas about reality, truth, and indeed history
itself. Poststructuralist theory is supposed to have performed the kind
of correction on cultural and historical analysis that disallows claims
about the real on the grounds that operations of language thoroughly
muddy the waters of all determination and experience. Not that linguistic mindfulness has prevented anybody from making elaborate
pronouncements about the postcolonial "predicament" – by referring
such a predicament to the terms of culture, identity, nationhood, discourse, subjectivity, and so on. But, qualified as *readings*, they enable
the rhetorical flourish we have come to expect from the discourse of
postcolonialism at the same time as they keep the vexations of truth at
bay. What results from much hand-wringing about postcoloniality –
and the ambiguities, aporia, and ambivalences therein – closely re-
sembles the genres of criticism taken to task nearly two decades ago
by Edward Said in *The World, the Text, and the Critic*:

Orphaned by the radical Freudian, Saussurean, and Nietzschean critique
of origins, traditions, and knowledge itself, contemporary criticism has
achieved its methodological independence by forfeiting an active situation in the world. It has no faith in traditional continuities (nation, family,
biography, period); rather it improvises, in acts of an often inspired

bricolage, order out of extreme discontinuity. Its culture is a negative one of absence, antirepresentation, and . . . ignorance.   *(1983a: 146)*

In this essay I should like to explore some possibilities that emerge from a road less taken than the more commonly trodden path of theory targeted early on by Said as orphaned and impoverished. If the time has come to move postcolonial scholarship beyond its now two-decade-old preoccupation with poststructuralist and deconstructive derivations of Freudian, Saussurean, and Nietzschean ideas, it may be worth casting another analytic look at the concepts and objects that were swept to the wayside on the march to "self-reflexivity." It may, in other words, be time to question the purportedly anti-metaphysical superiority of relying on the constructionism of "discourse" over the essentialism of "reality." But since such a wholesale questioning of the epistemological and methodological claims of poststructuralism *tout court* is entirely beyond my capacity (and, moreover, has been undertaken admirably by others, most notably Dews [1987, 1995] and Jameson [1990a]), I shall restrict myself to a small part in the broader project of considering how to rescue postcolonial critique from being locked in an endless embrace of ideals of difference, deferral, and constitutive paraphrasis that inform myriad readings in the literature about hybridity, liminality, mimicry, and so on.

My objective here is to revisit the conceptual utility of the old-fashioned problem of authenticity. As an objective, it is very much in the mode of keeping an appointment for which one knows one is already too late. But it is an effort to regain some purchase on a conceptual as well as experiential problematic that resists the demand that one must choose between keeping a naive though ideological faith in the authenticity of origins, being, and experience, or conversely, avowing a more self-consciously "anti-essentialist" and "decentered" view of the world in which everything and everybody is remitted to the ineffabilities of signification and textuality. Posed in this manner, there can of course be no contest between choosing to be naive and ideological on the one hand, or reflexive and theoretically sophisticated on the other. What remains out of sight are the possibilities for alternate, materialist conceptions of knowledge and experience that have a long history and explanatory force but which these days have fallen out of favor on account of their unmetaphoric – or, in the preferred idiolect, "non-discursive" – view of the world and its truths. Lurking behind current moves toward the decentered, the textual, and the anti-essentialist, is the specter of Marxist thought with its reliance on the hoary concepts of class, determination, exploitation, and utopia. The burden of vulgarity and outdatedness weighs heavily in comparison to the gestures of performativity, semiotic play, and indeterminacy that are supposed to give us our preferred coordinates for all criticism, but certainly those pertaining to colonial and post-colonial realities in which, according to one South Asian historian, for example, "the effect of colonial power [can be seen as] the production of hybridization rather than the noisy command of colonial authority or the silent repression of native traditions" (Prakash 1992: 112).

In contrast to the theoretical vocabularies in vogue within postcolonial criticism today, my points of reference in what follows will be the ideas and arguments of Theodor Adorno as he elaborated a version of the social philosophy associated with the critical theory of the Frankfurt Institute. Constraints of time and space do not allow me to provide a sustained consideration of the differences between and similarities among the various figures and positions developed in the work of the Frankfurt critics. So I can do no more than acknowledge that there are several points of departure and convergence that, in an overall sense, define Adorno's own preoccupations relative to the rest of his institutional colleagues (not to mention the Institute's more critical interlocutors, such as Siegfried Kracauer).[1] Frankfurt School social philosophy, while making a comeback in cultural-theory circles, has yet to find its way into postcolonial analysis – except for some all-too-metaphoric and allusive references to the "ruins" of history, the "catastrophe" of the nation, the "dialectic of enlightenment" governing modernity, and the like. To be sure there are important exceptions to this characterization (not least in the writings of Jameson and Said themselves), but for the most part the frameworks and modes of thinking about issues of postcoloniality have taken their lead from the dominance within contemporary theoretical discourse in general of the Derridean, Freudian, and Foucauldian orthodoxies that were the object of Said's early critique of the prevailing currents of thought in the humanities.[2] Indeed with regard to the problem of authenticity, these orthodoxies might be seen to have something in common with Adorno's ideas given the "elaborate translation schemes," as Jameson has argued, by means of which the critical theory of the Frankfurt School has been made to seem reconcilable with poststructuralism.[3]

Moreover, any thought of repatriating the concept of authenticity by referring to Adorno may, at first glance, appear doubly difficult given his commitment to a critique of the existentialist idealization of being, most elaborately laid out in his well-known polemic (adapted from themes first taken up by Walter Benjamin) against Heidegger and his followers in *The Jargon of Authenticity* (Adorno 1973a). If, however, we take a closer look at the dialectical logic underwriting Adorno's propositions about truth, authenticity, and related conceptual matters, a very different picture emerges of his fundamental interests – which were always in the "actualities" of thought and experience, rather than in their textualization. Far from resigning himself to an exclusively linguistic conception of meaning in which the real is only regarded as a signifying trace or subject to discursive ambiguity, Adorno (like other members of the Frankfurt Institute) continued in the tradition of a historical materialism whose constitutive political and epistemological commitments to adequating concept and object, truth and knowledge are not at all similar to theoretical frameworks in which questions of truth, objectivity, and meaning are taken to be the effects of various discursive productions. It is by this light that Adorno's struggles to reckon with the concreteness of experience or the necessity of determination have much to teach us as we attempt to wrest the problems of history, pastness, memory, tradition, and so on, away from their dissipation in idealist versions of theory. In addition, it is precisely this light that illuminates the necessity and value of authenticity as a concept and an experiential force so that the attempt to think concretely about the lived realities of colonial and postcolonial existence can no longer be waved off as naïveté about the real or nostalgia for an irrecuperable past.

Take, for instance, the section entitled "Bequest" in *Minima Moralia* (Adorno 1974: 150–52). It demonstrates that conceptualizing the quiddity of existence does not have to follow the dead-end of positivism. In other words, if the rock-kicking realism of positivistic thought is untenable, the consequence does not have to be a pendulum swing to the opposite extreme of epistemological uncertainty and theoretical relativism. Here, as elsewhere, Adorno takes his cue from Benjamin to propose the following:

If Benjamin said that history had hitherto been written from the standpoint of the victor, and needed to be written from that of the vanquished, we might add that knowledge must indeed present the fatally rectilinear succession of victory and defeat, but should address itself to those things which were not embraced by this dynamic, which fell by the wayside – what might be called the waste products and blind spots that have escaped the dialectic. It is in the nature of the defeated to appear, in their impotence, irrelevant, eccentric, derisory . . . Theory must needs deal with cross-grained, opaque, unassimilated material, which as such admittedly has from the start an anachronistic quality, but is not wholly obsolete since it has outwitted the historical dynamic. *(151)*

Even a cursory glance at this passage reveals that, for Adorno, the lesson of history is not about the undecidability of winners and losers. History clearly belongs to the ruling classes. Likewise, there is no temporizing about the "binarism" of victory and defeat (which, when it comes to the colonizer–colonized dyad, has been so exaggeratedly deconstructed in postcolonial notions about ambivalence and the otherness of the self). Unburdened from any self-consciousness about the alleged naïveté of a binaristic conception of victor and vanquished, Adorno is able to focus on more important considerations facing a rigorous conception of history: first, he proposes that the mode of materialist history needs to pursue the fundamentally dissimilar standpoints of the victorious and the defeated. As alluded to in the title of this section, the only "bequest" one can make to future generations is that they not be confused about the stakes. Second, and relatedly, this task is enabled by the logic of history itself wherein there are "things" that have "escaped the dialectic." Adorno emphasizes the *force* of ruling ideology which tendentiously rides over not just subordinated histories and points of view but denies the validity of their existence at all. Positivism is such a ruling ideology, although in our own time we need to consider other ideologies – such as that of a totalizing textualism – which have risen to dominate in the humanities. At any rate, positivism is the form of bourgeois thought *par excellence* in that it consigns the unverifiable to non-existence or, at best, to the kind of irrelevance Adorno contends is the lot of the defeated in history.

If Adorno criticizes positivism's reliance on transcendental and verifiable notions of Truth, his position is equally far from merely discursivist renditions of truth as "phrase regimens" (à la Jean-François Lyotard) or, in the more current vocabulary of postcolonial studies (given the Derridean strains in the work of critics such as Homi Bhabha or Gayatri Chakravorty Spivak), as the "play of the trace." Precisely because there are determinations and points of view that, as Adorno puts it, "fell by the wayside," they are not subject to assimilation under an exclusively linguistic order. In that sense, they signal their resistance to being appropriated by a conceptual system that seeks to render them as eccentric, impotent, and we might add, inauthentic. The passage above also reveals Adorno at pains to say that the responsibility of dialectical thought to rescue the apparently irrelevant detail of the past from the surface placidity of the present has less to do with the abstract inclusion of the eccentric or marginal than it does with the substantiality of material that has "outwitted" the dynamic of history. That such material has *outwitted* history, gives it an agency that is its own, not simply one that relegates it to the status of a supplement in the dominant historical narrative. Also, insofar as such material is "opaque" or "unassimilated," it is more than an effect or a trace of the subaltern's inability to speak in any deconstructive sense. It is material that stands *in opposition to* ruling modes of understanding and, by that token, signifies meanings that actively belong to a distinct – not merely semanticized or translated – reality.

This is to say that the terms and conditions governing the intelligibility of "anachronistic" elements from the past respond to a very different epistemological protocol than the one familiarly given to us in the form of a hermeneutic suspicion. Had Adorno been thinking in the manner of Derrida or Foucault – with the former touting the logic of the supplement, the latter that of the episteme, both suspending the question of truth per se as inherently metaphysical and deterministic – he would not have insisted, in the middle of the passage quoted above, that "[w]hat transcends the ruling society is not only the potentiality it develops but also all that which did not fit properly into the laws of historical movement" (1974: 151). Nor would he have ended his "bequest" by recalling Benjamin's warning that, "[t]he very grandeur of logical deductions may inadvertently take on a provincial quality." Dialectical thinking does not proceed from a methodological imperative alone – the ruse of reason; rather its parameters are given by "the existing" itself. What this shows is that, for Adorno, writing history from the "standpoint of the vanquished" requires a materialist conviction about a fundamentally untranscendable horizon of truth. To give oneself over to the idea that any such truth is, as the phrase goes, "always already" subject to the constitutive errors of intention and meaning is to dissimulate a dialectical difficulty into something that amounts to a methodological tic.

We need, then, a protocol of understanding that is different from the garden variety suspicion of the claims of truth and authenticity evident in recent critical trends. At the very least, we are obliged not to authorize ourselves by citing Adorno as a ready-to-hand theoretical resource on the matter, because his skepticism about the meaning of authenticity had to do with questioning the uses and motivations prompting its idealization in Nietzschean and Heideggerian thought and not with deriding the possibility of authenticity itself. The irony that laces Adorno's pronouncements such as, "If nothing else can be bindingly required of man, then at the least he should be wholly and entirely what he is" (also in *Minima Moralia* in a fragment entitled "Gold Assay"), can only be missed if we misread as well his deliberate linking of the likes of Nietzsche with Fascist philosophy. To wit: "In Nietzsche's analysis the word genuine stands unquestioned, exempt from conceptual development. To the converted and unconverted philosophers of Fascism, finally, values like authenticity, heroic endurance of the 'being-in-the-world' of individual existence, frontier-situations, become a means of usurping religious-authoritarian pathos without the least religious content" (1974: 152). We ignore at our own peril the kind of distinction, important to Adorno, that formed the basis of his critique of the "enemy's" thinking – long before the Fascist affiliations of Heidegger or proto-fascist leanings of Nietzsche were unveiled: it is only by appropriating the language of suffering from the sufferers that the untruths of history's victors can be passed off as genuine. However, such appropriation says nothing about that which, trodden upon, remains hidden and waiting to be recovered not as some indestructible principle of truth about oneself – which remains a preoccupation with subjectivity, the *telos* of existentialism and bourgeois philosophy in general – but rather as a turning away from what Adorno calls the absolutism of psychology and individuality to the reality of social relations.

The point about Adorno's continuing reliance on a non-discursive conception of truth can be reinforced if we look at the way that the idea of truth-content (*Wahrheitsgehalt*) surfaces in his writing and spans the entirety of his work. In his inaugural lecture to the philosophy faculty of the University of Frankfurt where he taught until 1933, entitled "The Actuality of Philosophy," Adorno unhesitatingly broached the problem of the "totality of the real," stating that "[w]hile our images of perceived reality may very well be *Gestalten*, the world in which we live is not; it is constituted differently than out of mere images of perception" (1977: 126). The distance between images of perception, i.e., language, and the world itself was, for Adorno, a challenge to be met through a program of thinking through and with irreducible reality (the non-deducible given or *unableitbaren Gegebenheit*). In fact, the responsibility of philosophy to be authentic is exactly what Adorno charges Heidegger as having abrogated. So there is no contradiction in Adorno's demand that philosophy level with "the power of freshly disclosed reality" and his critique of Heidegger's idealization of being. Adorno's is a call for a philosophy rescued from its fate in the hands of both the positivist sciences (which would deny all unverifiable philosophic judgments) and Kierkegaardian or Heideggerian traditions of philosophy (which would render all questions of experience and truth into suppositions about man's subjective being).

What I want to underscore are the particulars of Adorno's rejection of Heideggerian thinking, the form and content of which were as visible in 1933 as they were three decades later in *The Jargon of Authenticity* (originally published in 1964). Throughout, the issue is not that Adorno rejected the idea of authenticity and that this was at the heart of his stringent criticisms of Heideggerian "jargon." On the contrary, he averred, it is the authentic content of history and experience that had disappeared from view in purely conceptual systems of thought. According to him, these systems have tried to close the gap between "the eternal ideas and reality" by moving from the error of transcendental idealism to the error of existential categories that "are in fact not able to banish the fullness of what is living" (1973a: 124). The smugness with which literary theory today pretends to have taken over the mantle of philosophy (at least in the restricted sense of the disciplinary location in which Adorno or, for that matter, Hegel is often taught) sometimes leads to a forgetting of the fact that Adorno's commitments were to sociology and, more particularly, to a sociology of music. The sociological imperative in Adorno has sometimes been represented as a departure, even an aberration in his career as a philosopher, most prominently by adducing his years in exile in the US; a period that bears witness to some undistinguished social scientific research. But this periodization of his interests would have to ignore his early writings on the sociology of music (during the 1930s) as well as his late work on Beethoven, Mahler, and Alban Berg, not to mention the important critiques of the culture industry he produced in collaboration with Max Horkheimer. In all the venues of Adorno's writing, a preoccupation with "liquidating" idealist philosophy informs his desire to rejoin philosophy with social criticism. Critical theory, in the view of its various authors, had to challenge bourgeois or traditional philosophy on all fronts and Adorno took it to mean, among other things, that a "logic of disintegration," the negation of philosophy's own inherent investments and historically developed logic, was the way to break out of bourgeois idealism and into revolutionary materialism. So if philosophy provided a corrective to the narrowness that had taken over sociological inquiry, it is no less the case that Adorno thought sociology could provide some of the terms for rescuing philosophy. Significantly as well, Adorno emphasized the objective aspects of social existence – in his words, "the fullness of what is living" – in order to promote a conception of truth that was neither about the illusory transcendence of fiction nor about the propadeutics of philosophy.

The aim to interject sociological concerns into philosophy was shared by all the critics associated with the *Institut für Sozialforschung*.[4] We see this aim made daringly evident in Adorno's inaugural lecture to his colleagues in the philosophy faculty at the University of Frankfurt. Against the very backdrop of Heidegger's preeminence, Adorno proposed that philosophy can only be "actualized" by forsaking philosophical systems themselves. What is required, instead, is "grouping and trial arrangement, . . . constellation and construction" – clearly the vocabulary of experimental sociological investigation (1977: 131). But such constructions are also not self-evidently given as facts of history; they must be resolved, dialectically, out of the tension between historical reality and interpretive forms. That is, knowledge is not merely interpretation but an attempt at validating the truth. Accordingly, Adorno went on to say,

The historical images, which do not constitute the meaning of being (*Dasein*) but dissolve and resolve its questions are not simply self-given. They do not lie organically ready in history; not showing (*Schau*) or intuition is required to become aware of them. They are not magically sent by the gods to be taken in and venerated. Rather, they must be produced by human beings and are *legitimated in the last analysis alone by the fact that reality crystallizes about them in striking conclusiveness* (*Evidenz*). Here they divorce themselves centrally from the archaic, the mythic archetypes (*Urbilder*) which psychoanalysis lights upon, and which [Ludwig] Klages hopes to preserve as categories of our knowledge. Should they be equivalent to them in a hundred characteristics, they separate themselves at the point where those [archetypes] describe their fatalistic orbit in the heads of human beings.[5]   (*131, emphasis added*)

A critique of purely conceptual thinking, Adorno's words indict idealist philosophy but they also hardly represent a ringing endorsement of psychoanalysis and its claims. His criticism of the latter may come as a bit of a surprise given the commonplace in circulation about Adorno's faith in psychoanalysis. If today readings of the unconscious are seen to provide the most complete picture of the mechanisms of culture, history, and subjectivity, it is all the more reason to scrutinize the extent to which Adorno both did and did not assent to the explanations of reality provided by psychoanalysis. He sought to triangulate the archetypal constructions of psychoanalysis by conceptualizing an approach which drew its interpretive schema from the observable world unhypostatized. Representing such an approach he said:

One may see here an attempt to re-establish that old concept of philosophy which was formulated by Bacon and passionately contended around the time of Leibniz, a conception which idealism derided as a fad: that of the *ars inveniendi* [art of invention]. Every other conception of models would be gnostic and indefensible. But the *organon* of this *ars inveniendi* is fantasy. An exact fantasy; fantasy which abides strictly within the material which the sciences present to it, and reaches beyond them only in the smallest aspects of their arrangement: aspects, granted, which fantasy itself must originally generate.   *(1977: 131)*

It is of course possible to read the idea of an *"ars inveniendi"* as akin to the contemporary buzzword of a "social construction." But this could only happen by means of a presentism that anachronistically recasts the problem of knowledge from Adorno's terms to something else. Within Bacon's own framework, the term *"ars inveniendi"* bespoke technological innovation rather than anything resembling what we today might call a discursive or social construct and only the most ahistorical or presentist distortion could render the former into the latter. This point should not need any belaboring (and Adorno certainly understood it) but the uncritical importation of early philosophers such as Bacon, Leibniz, or Spinoza into gurus of contemporary thought – as if their ideas easily travel across the centuries to be applied without historical qualification to our own circumstances – makes the reinforcement necessary. Adorno, in any case, was highly attuned to the specificity of Baconian and Leibnizian terminology and rigorously distinguished methodological valences from a corresponding worldview in which mastery over nature was the objective of philosophy as well as the goal of future society (Bacon's "New Atlantis"). Proposing that an art of invention is a form that "abides strictly within the material which the sciences present to it," he argued for a model of knowledge that would re-establish the relationship between philosophical or cultural constructs and empirical experimental investigation. Although it may sound quite contrary to our ears, accustomed as we are to assertions about the impossibility of validating the truth, Adorno's emphasis was on "exactness," on the struggle to find a fit between truth-content and conceptual form; neither to take the fit for granted nor to disavow it, but to reach for it as the "organon," as he called it, of a philosophical project recouped from idealist fads.

In the context of giving us a new protocol for "actualizing" philosophy through empirical investigation, Adorno's simultaneous deployment of exactness and fantasy can only strike us, his latter-day readers, as odd if not downright contradictory. But this simultaneity is at the crux of Adorno's rethinking of the problem of knowledge, a simultaneity he evokes with the expression "exact fantasy" (*exakte Phantasie*). Part of the problem in encountering this phrase has to do with the literal and philosophical difficulties of translation involved in his use of the term "fantasy," given its psychoanalytic connotations. Nonetheless, as Shierry Weber Nicholsen has argued in her insightful elaboration of Adorno's aesthetics, Adorno meant to evoke Kant rather than Freud by recruiting fantasy as a criterion of precise thought (Nicholsen 1997: 229).

In fact, Nicholsen herself uses "exact imagination" as a translation of *exakte Phantasie* to avoid confusion about Adorno's philosophical emphasis on the imaginative aspects of any empirical investigation which must take truth as its object but must also find a way to construe that truth. As she puts it, Adorno "invokes the exact – as opposed to the creative – imagination as the organon of this art or technique." She goes on: "In emphasizing the imagination's capacity to discover, or produce, truth by reconfiguring the material at hand, Adorno makes knowledge inseparable from the configurational form imagination gives it ... The primacy of the object – the material at hand – produces, as it were, the need for configurational form" (4–5). It needs to be acknowledged that there is some ambiguity in Adorno's conceptualization of an "exact imagination" with respect to whether truth is "discovered" or "produced." Nicholsen glosses over this ambiguity without comment but we may want to add that Adorno never settles it in one direction or the other – in favor of mere discovery or wholesale invention. If fantasy or the imagination provide the terms of philosophical inquiry, they are subject to the obligation to abide strictly, he says, to "material which the sciences present"; likewise, the configurational form he advocates can reach beyond such materials "only in the smallest aspects of their arrangement." Indeed, what Adorno called "the demand to answer the questions of a pre-given reality each time, through a fantasy [imagination] which rearranges the elements of the question without going beyond the circumference of the elements," represented his earliest concerns as well as the terminus of his philosophical project of negative dialectics (1977: 131).[6]

An exact fantasy or an exact imagination. With this conception, Adorno proposes a way to think about the conjunction of knowledge, experience, and aesthetic form. In either formulation, the term designates a non-discursive form of truth; that is to say, the primacy of the object over language. The concern with retaining a conception of the object that remains untouched by its capture within a formal system – a concern, in other words, with the potential of the object to be authentic despite the inauthenticity of language – finds expression throughout Adorno's writings. And although it is important to recognize that most of his meditations on the problem take place in the context of discussing aesthetic experience, discussions whose modernist rarefaction put them at a great distance from a focus on quotidian forms of cultural and social experience, it is too simple to say that in Adorno's vision only the aesthetic remains capable of authentic communication. As Nicholsen shows in her historicization of Adorno's thought, "the aesthetic dimension of Adorno's work holds out, and is indeed premised on, the possibility of a valid, that is 'adequate' or 'authentic' subjective experience" (1997: 4). The ideal of genuine subjective experience, not the "jargon" of *Eigentlichkeit* (the "essence-mythology" of Being expressed in German existentialism, most grandly by Heidegger), refers to the truth-content of material, sensuous reality and the task of a philosophy premised on historical materialism is to decipher this re-authenticated truth understood in terms of the social contradictions governing its production.

Going back to Adorno's critique of Heideggerian essentialism, then, we can see why, when Adorno derided the idealism of an "in-itself" (the reformulation of a Kantian notion into ontological quiddity), he did not eliminate the idea of authenticity. Rather, his purpose was consistent with the method of immanent critique and, as Trent Schroyer points out in the foreword to the English translation of *Jargon der Eigentlichkeit*, Adorno's intent was to "include in the perspective of critical reason the *truth of the existentialist concern for the fundamentalness of human subjectivity*" (Adorno 1973a: viii, emphasis added). Thus Adorno saw the rescue of truth to be residing in the negation of the "pathos of archaic primalness" hidden in the "philosophy of As-If" (the "as-if" of existential subjectivism, the "as-if" of ideology as language, and so on). We ought to be able to draw some salutary lessons from Adorno's thinking that the authentic does not disappear merely because language is incapable of grasping it. In this, as in much else, his thinking follows very differently from that of the French Heideggerians, a point of intellectual history that many critics would prefer to ignore as they appropriate Adorno into an eclectic and idealist amalgam of theory. Significantly, he referred to the overburdened readings of the power of meaning alone as "linguistic mendacity" (Adorno 1973a: 163). However much one wants to indict Adorno for the inconsistencies and limitations of his perspective, the range of his works reveals a conviction about the content of truth pressuring what exists (as art or nature) through its preponderance, without itself becoming identical with truth.

If a certain conception of truth and authenticity is inextricable within Adorno's oeuvre, it is not out of some residual and unworked-out impulse about what Derrida grandiosely calls the "ontico-ontological." Rather, Adorno proceeded from less exorbitant assumptions about the nature of truth and this in turn allowed him to make less sweeping claims about its demise or, at a minimum, its complete deferral. More importantly, as I have suggested all along, Adorno's epistemology is materialist; one that takes its cue not from the problematic of language but from historical truth-content.[7] Consequently, Adorno was not as susceptible to the seductions of a radically decentered view of the world in which everything is subject to the "openness" of history. On the contrary, he was convinced of the necessity of overthrowing bourgeois philosophies that placed their faith in the capacity of thought to defy its mystification by the determining forces of capitalism. In this as in much else, Adorno followed in the tracks of Marx who, we may recall, castigated the Left Hegelians' presumption about the autonomy of thought in history as "The German Ideology." Likewise, Adorno considered it important to refute the terms of a political epistemology grounded in simple reversals of the subject–object paradigm. Such an epistemology may well critique the Husserlian or Heideggerian idealization of objective "Being," but its own solutions represent only the reverse: a preoccupation with the subjective as expressed, for example, in various calls within contemporary criticism to declare one's "positionality" (among the few things left to declare in an exclusively signifying regime). In complete contrast to such fine-tunings of the vicissitudes of "subject position," as Snow points out in his translator's introduction to Adorno's inaugural address, Adorno took "judgments of true or false [to be] the necessary ground for the validation of theory. In an era when metaphysics had lost all legitimacy, Adorno kept asking the metaphysical question . . ." (Snow 1977: 117).

This leaves us with having to reckon with the paradox of Adorno who, as Snow puts it, was a "metaphysician with no faith in metaphysics." Just as paradoxically, Adorno conjoined a non-discursive rationality and the aesthetic dimension. Important critiques of Adorno's contrary enterprise have emerged from members of later generations of the Frankfurt School, such as Jürgen Habermas and Albrecht Wellmer, both of whom see Adorno indefensibly blurring the boundaries between art and reason, and argue that his configurational texts can claim the status neither of knowledge nor of art (Nicholsen 1997: 5–6). But as Nicholsen also suggests in her reevaluation of Adorno's writings on aesthetics, even when Adorno speaks of aesthetic experience, the dimension of form and the dimension of experience are equally crucial for understanding "the 'negative dialectical' structure of his thought" (3). Moreover, his concern for the concreteness of experience should exempt Adorno, at least partially, from the charge of an unalloyed aestheticism. Ultimately, what all of this has to do with our own reckoning of aesthetic and experiential matters in their relation to Adorno's thought is that he did not take for granted the polarity between aesthetic and practical or even revolutionary consciousness, but regarded it as something to overcome through aesthetic, philosophical, and political praxis. That he failed in his own efforts at realizing such a project might very well provide the spur to our own critical enterprise; again, not through any simplistic ascription of what he called a "positive vision of Utopia" but from within the experience of history itself and as its critical cancellation (Adorno 1973a: 207).

A few last words may be in order so that this discussion of Adorno's work can be squared in terms of its usefulness and importance for our times and, more specifically, for postcolonial analysis. One is forced to admit that even those who would grant the value of Adorno's theories for the future of Anglo-American philosophy, might be less inclined to see in it any particular potential for forms of postcolonial critique. The objection, as I imagine it, may come from those who charge the Frankfurt School with a disregard for the history and dynamics of imperialism and colonialism. Or it may emerge from quarters in which the consideration of authenticity needs no defense from the theoretical discourses of an Adorno or anyone else, given the ampleness and sophistication of its treatment by postcolonial authors such as Derek Walcott or Satyajit Ray, and social critics such as C. L. R. James or Eduardo Galeano. Let me just say that my purpose in attempting a theoretical reflection on the problem of authenticity and truth has less to do with evading or justifying the Eurocentrism of Adorno (or any of the other Frankfurt School critics) than it does with finding a vocabulary and lineage within philosophical thinking which would admit that some conception of authenticity is essential to critique rather than a banalization of it.[8] As long as postcolonial studies takes some of its leads from European theoretical sources, I would submit that Adorno has as much if not more utility for us than do the standard-issue references to Foucault, Derrida, or Lacan. But neither has it been my goal to represent Adorno as an oracle from whom we derive the right answer to the question of how to transvalue authenticity from an epistemological problem to a category of materialist knowledge. Instead, I should like this essay to serve as part of an ongoing conversation in the history of Marxist and dialectical criticism that speaks to the inattention of Marxism or the Frankfurt School to the dynamics of imperialism and colonialism in the terms of a dialectical incompletion.

Accordingly, a provisional conclusion: the recognition that historical materialist criticism has been inadequate or one-sided is reason enough to reclaim it for ourselves in ways that would provide a riposte to those who would say that the complexities of postcoloniality require the complicated rhetorical maneuvers of poststructuralist theory. If nothing else, let us remember that poststructuralism's apotheosis of otherness often proceeds by rendering otherness as an aporetic predicament of linguistic difference rather than as the outcome of the brute realities of domination.[9] And, finally, if it is our lot as modern subjects (as surely it must be) to rethink our inheritance from modernist forms of thinking – as a defining feature of our own historicity – then some of what remained shadowed in Adorno's own struggle to rescue hope from hopelessness may well be illuminated through its parallels in postcolonial experience.

NOTES

1 Kracauer's criticisms of the Frankfurt Institute, along with a history of the development of the concerns and interests of its members have been very usefully elaborated by Rolf Wiggershaus in his intellectual history of the Frankfurt School (1994).

2 Such a critique of the dominance of poststructuralist theory in the body of postcolonial criticism is also the premise underwriting the present collection of essays. The editors, along with other critics writing in this volume, regard it as the imperative for reintegrating Marxism and post-colonial thinking.

3 Jameson argues in his magisterial retrospections on the fate of the dialectic: "The seventies – the age, in this country at least, of Theory and theoretical discourse, of *jouissances* that ranged from structuralism to poststructuralism, from Maoism to narrative analysis, and from libidinal investments to Ideological State Apparatuses – were essentially French; Adorno (along with Lukács and so many other Central European thinkers, with the signal exceptions of Benjamin and Brecht) seemed an encumbrance, not to say an embarrassment, during the struggles of that time, and prompting those still committed to him into

elaborate translation schemes, to 'reconcile' Adorno with Derridean orthodoxy. While all this was going on over here, the French intelligentsia was in the meantime in the process of full de-Marxification; so that the next decade drew the curtain open on a wealthy and complacent, depoliticized Europe, whose great theoreticians were dead and whose indigenous philosophical traditions were buried" (Jameson 1990a: 5).

4 This is worth noting because of the highly abstract and rarefied ways in which particularly the work of Adorno and Benjamin (less so that of Horkheimer, Herbert Marcuse, or Leo Lowenthal) finds its way into contemporary theoretical discourse. Benjamin Snow suggests, in his translator's introduction to Adorno's "The Actuality of Philosophy," that the only distinction worth making with regard to the differing sociological interests of Adorno and Horkheimer (the long-standing director of the Frankfurt Institute) is the following: "[W]hereas the Institute was more interested in a (philosophical) *sociology* of art, Adorno's primary concern was in a (sociological) *philosophy* – of aesthetics as well as of epistemology" (1977: 114, n. 4; emphasis in the translation).

5 We may speculate, in passing, as to whether such trends as the recent growth in "trauma studies" emblematize a contemporary variant of the move Adorno identifies in Klages: a faith in the capacity of an archetypal, psychoanalytic category (in this case, "trauma") to explain the fullness of human historical experience. (See, for instance, Caruth 1996.)

6 The continuity in Adorno's thinking has been remarked by many critics. Benjamin Snow points out that Adorno's early essay on "The Actuality of Philosophy" looked forward to themes later elaborated in *Negative Dialectics*. I draw attention to this continuity between the early and late Adorno to reinforce the argument that there are no clear shifts of emphasis in his thinking; throughout he remains committed to the goal of transcending idealism by returning philosophy to social criticism (Snow 1977: 119, n. 32).

7 Jameson has brilliantly expanded on this in his *Late Marxism*. He reminds us that "Adorno's materialism . . . wishes above all to elude the representational; in it fulfillment and the somatic realization of the object world must somehow exclude the intermediation of the image" (1990a: 119). This position is immediately supported with a quote from Adorno's *Negative Dialectics*: "The materialist longing to grasp the thing wills precisely the opposite of that; the full object can be conceived only in the absence of images..." (Jameson 1990a: L. 119; Adorno 1973b: 207).

8 For instance, see the reduction of the problem of authenticity to the social-scientism of "primordialism" in Appadurai (1997, esp. 139–49). Alternatively, see the transposition of the claim to authenticity into the trope of "homecoming" – rendered as "a seduction of the already seduced" – in Chow (1998: 9).

9 See, for instance, Derrida (1998) for the wholly unsupportable claim that he, as a *pied noir*, is the most alienated of all the victims of French colonialism on account of the fact that the Algerians at least had their own language. Even were we to take this in the spirit of a language

game whose hyperbolic excess is intended as a provocation, its self-servingness can hardly be overlooked. This proposition is forwarded by Derrida in sentiments such as the following: "My hypothesis is, therefore, that I am perhaps the *only* one here who can call himself at once a Maghrebian (which is not a citizenship) and a French citizen" (13). And further: "My language, the only one I hear myself speak and agree to speak, is the language of the other" (25).

References

Adorno, Theodor W. 1973a, *The Jargon of Authenticity*, trans. Knut Tarnowski and Frederic Will, Evanston: Northwestern University Press.

1973b, *Negative Dialectics*, trans. E. B. Ashton, New York: Continuum.

1974, *Minima Moralia: Reflections from Damaged Life*, trans. E. F. N. Jephcott, London: Verso.

1977, "The Actuality of Philosophy," trans. Benjamin Snow, *Telos* 31: 120–33.

Ahmad, Aijaz 1992, *In Theory: Classes, Nations, Literatures*, London: Verso.

1995a, "The Politics of Literary Post-Coloniality," *Race and Class* 36.3: 1–20.

1995b, "Postcolonialism: What's in a Name?" in Roman de la Campa, E. Ann Kaplan, and Michael Sprinker, eds., *Late Imperial Culture*, London: Verso: 11–32.

1996, "Imperialism and Progress," *Lineages of the Present: Political Essays*, New Delhi: Tulika, 1–43.

Ahmad, Eqbal 1971, "Revolutionary Warfare and Counterinsurgency," in Norman Miller and Roderick Aya, eds., *National Liberation: Revolution in the Third World*, New York: Free Press: 137–213.

Alexander, Neville (No Sizwe) 1979, *One Azania, One Nation: the National Question in South Africa*, London: Zed.

Allen, Theodore 1994, *The Invention of the White Race*, vol. I: *Racial Oppression and Social Control*, London: Verso.

Althusser, Louis 1977a, "Letter from Louis Althusser," Appendix 2 to Régis Debray, *A Critique of Arms* vol. 1, Harmondsworth: Penguin.

1977b, *For Marx*, trans. Ben Brewster, London: Verso.

1995, "Lam," *Écrits philosophiques et politique*, vol. 2, Paris: IMEC: 597–99.

Amin, Samir 1977, *Imperialism and Unequal Development*, New York: Monthly Review.

1989, *Eurocentrism*, trans. Russell Moore, New York: Monthly Review.

1990, *Delinking: Towards a Polycentric World*, trans. Michael Wolfers, London: Zed.

1997, *Capitalism in the Age of Globalization*, London: Zed.

References

1998, *Spectres of Capitalism: a Critique of Current Intellectual Fashions*, trans. Shane Henry Mage, New York: Monthly Review.

Amsden, Alice 1989, *Asia's Next Giant: South Korea and Late Industrialization*, New York: Oxford University Press.

Anderson, Benedict 1991, *Imagined Communities: Reflections on the Origins and Spread of Nationalism*, London: Verso.

Anderson, Kevin 1995, *Lenin, Hegel and Western Marxism*, Urbana: University of Illinois Press.

Anderson, Perry 1974, *Lineages of the Absolutist State*, London: New Left Books.

1976, *Considerations on Western Marxism*, London: New Left Books.

1983, *In the Tracks of Historical Materialism*, London: Verso.

Andrews, K. R., N. P. Canny and P. E. H. Hair, eds. 1978, *The Westward Enterprise: English Activities in Ireland, the Atlantic, and America 1480–1650*, Detroit: Wayne State University Press.

Appadurai, Arjun 1997, *Modernity at Large: Cultural Dimensions of Globalization*, Minneapolis: University of Minnesota Press.

Appiah, Kwame Anthony 1991, "Is the Post- in Postmodernism the Post- in Postcolonial?" *Critical Inquiry*: 336–57.

Armitage, David 1999, "Greater Britain: a Useful Category of Historical Analysis?" *American Historical Review* 104: 427–45.

Arnold, David 1983, *Colonizing the Body: State Medicine and Epidemic Disease in Nineteenth-Century India*, Berkeley: University of California Press.

Arrighi, Giovanni 1982, "A Crisis of Hegemony," in Samir Amin, Giovanni Arrighi, Andre Gunder Frank, and Immanuel Wallerstein, *Dynamics of Global Crisis*, New York: Monthly Review: 55–108.

1994, *The Long Twentieth Century: Money, Power, and the Origins of Our Times*, London: Verso.

1996, "The Rise of East Asia: World-Systemic and Regional Aspects," *International Journal of Sociology and Social Policy* 16.7/8: 6–44.

Arrighi, Giovanni, Beverly Silver, and Iftikhar Ahmad 1999, *Chaos and Governance in the Modern World System*, Minneapolis: University of Minnesota Press.

Arrighi, Giovanni, Satoshi Ikeda, and Alex Irwan 1993, "The Rise of East Asia: One Miracle or Many?" in R. A. Palat, ed., *Pacific-Asia and the Future of the World-System*, Westport: Greenwood: 41–65.

Ashcroft, Bill, Gareth Griffiths, and Helen Tiffin 1989, *The Empire Writes Back*, London: Routledge.

Association des écrivains progressifs 1935, "Manifesto of Indian Writers in London," *Commune* 28: 462.

Avineri, Shlomo 1968, Introduction to *Karl Marx on Colonialism and Modernization*, ed. Shlomo Avineri, New York: Doubleday: 1–28.

Barnard, T. C. 1990, "Crisis of Identity among Irish Protestants, 1641–1845," *Past and Present* 127: 39–83.

Barnet, Richard J. and Ronald E. Müller 1974, *Global Reach: the Power of the Multinational Corporations*, New York: Simon and Schuster.

Bartels, Emily 1997, "Othello and Africa: Postcolonialism Reconsidered," *William and Mary Quarterly* 54.1–2: 45–64.

Barthelemy, Anthony 1987, *Black Face Maligned Race: the Representation of Blacks in English Drama from Shakespeare to Southerne*, Louisiana State University Press.

Bartlett, Thomas 1988, " 'What Ish My Nation?' Themes in Irish History: 1550–1850," in Thomas Bartlett, Chris Curtin, Riana O'Dwyer, and Gearoid O'Tuathaigh, eds., *Irish Studies: a General Introduction*, Dublin: Gill and Macmillan: 44–59.

Bataille, Georges 1991, 1993, *The Accursed Share*, 3 vols., New York: Zone.

Bauman, Zygmunt 1991, *Modernity and the Holocaust*, Cambridge: Cambridge University Press.

1994, "Morality without Ethics," *Theory, Culture and Society* 11: 1–34.

1995, "Searching for a Centre that Holds," in Mike Featherstone, Scott Lash and Roland Robertson, eds., *Global Modernities*, London: Sage: 140–54.

Bayly, C. A. 1988, *Indian History and the Making of the British Empire*, Cambridge: Cambridge University Press.

Benjamin, Walter 1969, *Illuminations*, trans. Harry Zohn, New York: Schocken.

1999, *The Arcades Project*, trans. Howard Eiland and Kevin McLaughlin, Cambridge: Belknap.

Bennett, Lerone Jr. 1975, *The Shaping of Black America*, Chicago: Johnson.

Bernard, Mitchell and John Ravenhill 1995, "Beyond Product Cycles and Flying Geese: Regionalization, Hierarchy, and the Industrialization of East Asia," *World Politics* 47.2: 171–209.

Bernasconi, Robert 1997, "African Philosophy's Challenge to Continental Philosophy," in Emmanuel Chukwudi Eze, ed., *Postcolonial African Philosophy*, Oxford: Blackwell: 183–96.

1998 "Philosophy's Paradoxical Parochialism," in Keith Ansell-Pearson, Benita Parry, and Judith Squires, eds., *Cultural Readings of Imperialism: Edward Said and the Gravity of History*, London: Lawrence and Wishart: 212–26.

Bhabha, Homi 1994, *The Location of Culture*, London: Routledge.

Bhaskar, Roy 1993, *Dialectic: the Pulse of Freedom*, London: Verso.

Blackburn, Robin 1970, Introduction to Régis Debray, *Strategy for Revolution*, London: Cape: 1–23.

1997, *The Making of New World Slavery*. London: Verso.

Bloch, Ernst 1973, *Erbschaft dieser Zeit*, Frankfurt-am-Main: Bibliothek Suhrkamp.

Boehmer, Elleke 1995, *Colonial and Postcolonial Literature: Migrant Metaphors*, Oxford: Oxford University Press.

Bogues, Anthony 1997, *Caliban's Freedom: the Early Political Thought of C. L. R. James*, London: Pluto.

Boli, John 1993, "Sovereignty from a World Polity Perspective," paper presented at the Annual Meeting of the American Sociological Association, Miami.

References

Bongie, Chris 1991, *Exotic Memories: Literature, Colonialism, and the Fin de Siècle*, Stanford: Stanford University Press.

Boose, Lynda E. 1994, " 'The Getting of a Lawful Race': Racial discourse in early modern England and the unrepresentable black woman," in Margo Hendricks and Patricia Parker, eds., *Women, 'Race,' and Writing in the Early Modern Period*, London: Routledge: 35–54.

Bose, Sugata, and Ayesha Jalal 1998, "Eighteen Fifty-Seven: Rebellion, Collaboration, and the Transition to Crown Raj," *Modern South Asia: History, Culture, Political Economy*, London: Routledge: 88–96.

Bottigheimer, Karl 1978, "Kingdom and Colony: Ireland in the Westward Enterprise 1536–1660," in K. R. Andrews, N. P. Canny, and P. E. H. Hair, eds., *The Westward Enterprise: English Activities in Ireland, the Atlantic, and America 1480–1650*, Liverpool: Liverpool University Press: 45–56.

Bourdieu, Pierre 1990, *The Logic of Practice*, trans. Richard Nice, Stanford: Stanford University Press.

Bourke, Angela 1999, *The Burning of Bridget Cleary: a True Story*, London: Pimlico.

Boylan, Thomas A. and Timothy P. Foley 1992, *Political Economy and Colonial Ireland*, London: Routledge.

Brady, Ciarán 1989, "The Road to the *View*: On the Decline of Reform Thought in Tudor Ireland," in Patricia Coughlan, ed., *Spenser and Ireland: an Interdisciplinary Perspective*, Cork: Cork University Press: 25–45.

Brasted, H. V. 1980, "Indian Nationalist Development and the Influence of Irish Home Rule, 1870–1886," *South Asia* 8.1–2: 24–45.

Braude, Benjamin 1997, "The Sons of Noah and the Construction of Ethnic and Geographical Identities in the Medieval and Early Modern Periods," *William and Mary Quarterly* 54.1–2: 103–42.

Braudel, Fernand 1984, *The Perspective of the World*, New York: Harper and Row.

Brennan, Timothy 1997, *At Home in the World: Cosmopolitanism Now*, Cambridge, MA: Harvard University Press.

Brenner, Robert 1977, "The Origins of Capitalist Development: a Critique of Neo-Smithian Marxism," *New Left Review* 104: 63–118.

Brewer, Anthony 1984, *Marxist Theories of Imperialism: a Critical Survey*, London: Routledge.

Brown, Paul 1985, " 'This thing of darkness I acknowledge mine': *The Tempest* and the Discourse of Colonialism," in Jonathan Dollimore and Alan Sinfield, eds., *Political Shakespeare: New Essays in Cultural Materialism*, Manchester: Manchester University Press: 48–71.

Buck-Morss, Susan 1986, "The Flâneur, the Sandwichman and the Whore: the Politics of Loitering," *New German Critique* 39: 99–139.

Buhle, Paul, ed. 1986 *C. L. R. James: his Life and Work*, London: Allison and Busby.

Bukharin, Nikolai 1972, *Imperialism and World Economy*, New York: Monthly Review.

Bürger, Peter 1984, *Theory of the Avant-Garde*, Minneapolis: University of Minnesota Press.

Burkholder, Mark A. and Lyman L. Johnson 1994, *Colonial Latin America*, Oxford: Oxford University Press.

Burton, Jonathan 1998, "'A most wily bird': Leo Africanus, *Othello* and the trafficking in difference," in Ania Loomba and Martin Orkin, eds., *Post-Colonial Shakespeares*, London: Routledge: 43–63.

Cabral, Amilcar 1972, "The Weapon of Theory," *Revolution in Guinea: Selected Texts*, trans. Richard Handyside, New York: Monthly Review: 90–111.

1973, *Return to the Source: Selected Speeches of Amilcar Cabral*, New York: Monthly Review.

1974, *Toward Final Victory: Selected Speeches and Documents*, Canada: LSM Information Center Press.

1979, "The Role of Culture in the Liberation Struggle," in Armand and Michele Mattelart, eds., *Communication and Class Struggle*, vol. 1: *Capitalism, Imperialism*, New York: International General: 205–11.

1980, *Unity and Struggle: Speeches and Writings*, London: Heinemann.

n.d., *The Struggle in Guinea*, Cambridge, MA: Africa Research Group.

Cairns, David and Shaun Richards 1988, *Writing Ireland: Colonialism, Nationalism and Culture*, Manchester: Manchester University Press.

Cairns, Stephen, Sanjay Seth, Michael Dutton, and Leela Gandhi 2000, Editorial, *Postcolonial Studies* 3.3: 247–62.

Callaghan, John 1997–98, "Colonies, Racism, the CPGB and the Comintern in the Inter-War Years," *Science & Society* 61.4: 513–25.

Callinicos, Alex 1989, *Against Postmodernism: a Marxist Critique*, New York: St. Martin's.

Canny, Nicholas 1973, "The Ideology of English Colonization: From Ireland to America," *William and Mary Quarterly* 30.4: 575–98.

1976, *The Elizabethan Conquest of Ireland: a Pattern Established*, New York: Barnes and Noble.

1979, "The Permissive Frontier: the Problem of Social Control in English Settlements in Ireland and Virginia, 1550–1650," in K. R. Andrews, N. P. Canny and P. E. H. Hair, eds., *The Westward Enterprise: English Activities in Ireland, the Atlantic, and America, 1480–1650*, Detroit: Wayne State University Press: 17–44.

1987, *Colonial Identity in the Atlantic World 1500–1800*, Princeton: Princeton University Press.

1988, *Kingdom and Colony: Ireland and the Atlantic World, 1560–1800*, Baltimore: Johns Hopkins University Press.

Canny, Nicholas ed. 1998, *The Oxford History of British Empire*, vol. 1: *The Origins of Empire*, Oxford: Oxford University Press.

Canny, Nicholas and Anthony Pagden, eds. 1987, *Colonial Identity in the Atlantic World 1500–1800*, Princeton: Princeton University Press.

Carpentier, Alejo 1985, *Obras completas*, México: Siglo Veintiuno.

Caruth, Cathy 1996, *Unclaimed Experience: Trauma, Narrative, and History*, Baltimore: Johns Hopkins University Press.

Cassou, Jean 1935, "Nous autres negroides," *Commune* 27: 257–71.

References

Césaire, Aimé 1972, *Discourse on Colonialism*, trans. Joan Pinkham, New York: Monthly Review.

Chakrabarty, Dipesh 2000, *Provincializing Europe: Postcolonial Thought and Historical Difference*, Princeton: Princeton University Press.

Chaliand, Gerard 1969, *Armed Struggle in Africa*, New York: Monthly Review.

Chandler, Alfred 1990, *Scale and Scope. The Dynamics of Industrial Capitalism*, Cambridge: Belknap.

Chase-Dunn, Christopher 1996, "World Systems: Similarities and Differences," in S. C. Chew and R. Denemark, eds., *The Underdevelopment of Development*, Thousand Oaks: Sage: 246–58.

Chase-Dunn, Christopher and Thomas D. Hall 1993, "The Historical Evolution of World-Systems," paper presented at the Annual Meeting of the American Sociological Association, Miami.

1997, *Rise and Demise: Comparing World-Systems*, Boulder: Westview.

Chatterjee, Kumkum 1996, *Merchants, Politics, and Society in Early Modern India: Bihar 1733–1820*, Leiden: E. J. Brill.

Chatterjee, Partha 1989, *Nationalist Thought and the Colonial World: a Derivative Discourse?* Minneapolis: University of Minnesota Press.

1993, *The Nation and its Fragments: Colonial and Postcolonial Histories*, Princeton: Princeton University Press.

Childs, Peter and Patrick Williams 1997, *An Introduction to Post-Colonial Theory*, New York: Prentice Hall.

Chinweizu, 1975, *The West and the Rest of Us: White Predators, Black Slavers and the African Elite*, New York: Vintage.

Chow, Rey 1998, "The Seductions of Homecoming: Place, Authenticity, and Chen Kaige's *Temptress Moon*," *Narrative* 6.1: 3–17.

Chrisman, Laura 1995, "Inventing Post-Colonial Theory: Polemical Observations," *Pretexts* 5.1–2: 205–12.

Clark, Katerina 1995, *Petersburg, Crucible of Cultural Revolution*, Cambridge, MA: Harvard University Press.

Clifford, James 1988, "On Ethnographic Surrealism," *The Predicament of Culture*. Cambridge, MA: Harvard University Press: 117–51.

Cohen, Sylvester 1998, "Amilcar Cabral: an Extraction from the Literature," *Monthly Review*: 39–47.

Collins, Henry and Chimen Abramsky 1965, *Karl Marx and the British Labour Movement: Years of the First International*, London: Macmillan.

Cook, S. B. 1993, *Imperial Affinities: Nineteenth Century Analogies and Exchanges between Ireland and India*, London: Sage.

Coronil, Fernando 1996, "Beyond Occidentalism: Toward Nonimperial Geohistorical Categories," *Cultural Anthropology* 11.1: 77.

Coundouriotis, Eleni 1999, *Claiming History: Colonialism, Ethnography, and the Novel*, New York: Columbia University Press.

Cox, Oliver 1959, *Foundations of Capitalism*, New York: Philosophical Library.

Crane, Diana 1987, *Transformations of the Avant-Garde: the New York Art World 1940–1985*, Chicago: University of Chicago Press.

Critchley, Simon 1995, "Black Socrates? Questioning the Philosophical Tradition," *Radical Philosophy* 69: 17–26.

Crotty, Raymond 1986, *Ireland in Crisis: a Study in Capitalist Colonial Undevelopment*, Dingle: Brandon.

Cumings, Bruce 1997, "Japan and Northeast Asia into the Twenty-first Century," in Peter Katzenstein and T. Shiraishi, eds., *Network Power: Japan and Asia*, Ithaca: Cornell University Press: 136–68.

2000, "The American Ascendancy: Imposing a New World Order," *The Nation* 270.18: 13–20.

Cunard, Nancy 1970, *Negro: an Anthology*, New York: Frederick Ungar.

Curtin, Philip D. 1990, *The Rise and Fall of the Plantation Complex: Essays in Atlantic History*, Cambridge: Cambridge University Press.

Curtis, L. Perry Jr. 1997, *Apes and Angels: the Irishman in Victorian Caricature*, Washington: Smithsonian.

Datta Gupta, Sobhanlal 1980, *Comintern, India and the Colonial Question, 1920–1937*, Calcutta: K. P. Bagchi.

David, Richard ed. 1981, *Hakluyt's Voyages*, Boston: Chatto and Windus.

Davidson, Basil 1969, *The Liberation of Guiné*, New York: Penguin.

1978, *Let Freedom Come: Africa in Modern History*, Boston: Little, Brown.

1986, "On Revolutionary Nationalism: the Legacy of Cabral," *Race and Class* 28.3: 21–45.

1992, *The Black Man's Burden*, London: James Currey.

Davies, Carol Boyce 1998, "The Trap of Postcoloniality," *Interventions* 1.1: 22–23.

Davis, David Brion 1997, "Constructing Race: A Reflection," *William and Mary Quarterly*, third series, 54.1–2: 7–18.

Deane, Seamus 1991, "The Famine and Young Ireland," in *The Field Day Anthology of Irish Writing*, vol. II, Derry: Field Day: 115–21.

1997, *Strange Country: Modernity and Nationhood in Irish Writing since 1790*, Oxford: Clarendon.

Debray, Régis 1970, *Strategy for Revolution*, London: Cape.

1977, *Revolution in the Revolution?* Harmondsworth: Penguin.

Derrida, Jacques 1998, *Monolingualism of the Other; or, The Prosthesis of Origin*, trans. Patrick Mensah, Stanford: Stanford University Press.

Deutscher, Isaac 1977, "Maoism: its Origin and Outlook," in Robin Blackburn, ed., *Revolution and Class Struggle: a Reader in Marxist Politics*, London: Fontana/Collins: 191–223.

Dews, Peter 1987, *Logics of Disintegration: Post-Structuralist Thought and the Claims of Critical Theory*, London: Verso.

1995, *The Limits of Disenchantment: Essays on Contemporary European Philosophy*, London: Verso.

Dirlik, Arif 1993, "Post-Socialism/Flexible Production: Marxism in Contemporary Radicalism," *Polygraph* 6/7: 133–69.

1994a, *After the Revolution: Waking to Global Capitalism*, Hanover: Wesleyan University Press.

1994b, "The Postcolonial Aura: Third World Criticism in the Age of Global Capitalism," *Critical Inquiry* 20: 328–56.

References

1997a, "Mao Zedong and 'Chinese Marxism,'" in Brian Carr and Indira Mahalingam, eds., *Companion Encyclopaedia of Asian Philosophy*, New York: Routledge: 593–619.

1997b, "Modernism and Antimodernism in Mao Zedong's Marxism," in Arif Dirlik, Paul Healy, and Nick Knight, eds., *Critical Perspectives on Mao Zedong's Thought*, New York: Humanities: 59–83.

1999, "Is There History after Eurocentrism? Globalism, Postcolonialism, and the Disavowal of History," *Cultural Critique* 42: 1–34.

Documents of the First International: The Hague Congress of the First International, 2–7 September, 1872, Minutes and Documents 1978, Moscow: Progress, 1978.

Draper, Hal 1984, *The Annotated Communist Manifesto*, Berkeley: Center for Socialist History.

Drucker, Peter F. 1993, *Post-Capitalist Society*, New York: Harper and Row.

During, Simon 1998, "Postcolonialism and Globalisation: a Dialectical Relation after all?" *Postcolonial Studies* 1.1: 31–47.

Dussel, Enrique 1997, "The Architectonic of the Ethics of Liberation," *Philosophy and Social Criticism* 23.3: 1–35.

1998, "Beyond Eurocentrism: the World-System and the Limits of Modernity," in Fredric Jameson and Masao Miyoshi, eds., *The Cultures of Globalization*, Durham: Duke University Press: 3–31.

Eagleton, Terry 1990, "Nationalism: Irony and Commitment," in Terry Eagleton, Fredric Jameson, and Edward W. Said, *Nationalism, Colonialism and Literature*, Minneapolis: University of Minnesota Press: 23–39.

Edwards, Brent Hayes 1998, "The Ethnics of Surrealism," *Transition* 78: 84–135.

El Saadawi, Nawal 1997, *The Nawal El Saadawi Reader*, London: Zed.

Elliott, Gregory 1987, *Althusser: the Detour of Theory*, London: Verso.

Elliott, Gregory, ed. 1994, *Althusser: a Critical Reader*, Oxford: Blackwell.

Ellis, Steven G. 1994, "Writing Irish History: Revisionism, Colonialism, and the British Isles," *The Irish Review* 27.2: 1–21.

Emmanuel, Arghiri 1972, "White-Settler Colonialism and the Myth of Investment Imperialism," *New Left Review* 73: 35–57.

Eribon, Didier 1991, *Michel Foucault*, Cambridge: Harvard University Press.

Eudin, Xenia Joukoff and Robert C. North 1957, *Soviet Russia and the East, 1920–1927: A Documentary Survey*, Stanford: Stanford University Press.

Evans, Peter 1995, *Embedded Autonomy: States and Industrial Transformation*, Princeton: Princeton University Press.

Fabian, Johannes 1983, *Time and the Other*, New York: Columbia University Press.

Fanon, Frantz 1967a, *Black Skin, White Masks*, trans. Charles Lam Markmann, New York: Grove.

1967b, *Toward the African Revolution*, trans. Haakon Chevalier, New York: Grove.

1967c, *A Dying Colonialism*, trans. Haakon Chevalier, New York: Grove.

1968, *The Wretched of the Earth*, trans. Constance Farrington, New York: Grove.

Fieldhouse, D. K. 1965, *The Colonial Empires: a Comparative Survey from the Eighteenth Century*, London: Weidenfeld and Nicholson.

Fields, Barbara 1990, "Slavery, Race and Ideology in the United States of America," *New Left Review* 181: 95–118.

Foster, Hal 1996, *Return of the Real: the Avant-Garde at the End of the Century*, Cambridge: MIT.

Foucault, Michel 1973, *The Order of Things: an Archaeology of the Human Sciences*, trans. Alan Sheridan-Smith, New York: Vintage.

1984, "What is an Author?", trans. Josué V. Harari, in *The Foucault Reader*, ed. Paul Rabinow, New York: Pantheon: 101–20.

Franco, Jean 1988, "Beyond Ethnocentrism: Gender, Power and the Third-World Intelligentsia," in Cary Nelson and Lawrence Grossberg, eds., *Marxism and the Interpretation of Culture*, Urbana: University of Illinois Press: 503–15.

Frank, Andre Gunder 1994, "The World Economic System in Asia Before European Hegemony," *The Historian* 56.2: 259–76.

1998, *ReOrient. The Global Economy in the Asian Age*, Berkeley: University of California Press.

Fredrickson, George 1985, *The Arrogance of Race: Historical Perspectives on Slavery, Racism and Social Inequality*, Middletown: Wesleyan University Press.

FRELIMO 1974, *Mozambique Revolution*, Dar es Salaam; reprinted and distributed by Liberation Support Movement Information Center, Richmond, Canada.

1976, *Establishing People's Power to Serve the Masses*, Toronto: Toronto Committee for the Liberation of Southern Africa.

Freud, Sigmund 1952, *An Autobiographical Study*, trans. James Strachey, New York: Norton.

1961, *Beyond the Pleasure Principle*, trans. James Strachey, New York: Norton.

Frieden, Jeffrey A. 1987, *Banking on the World: the Politics of American International Finance*, New York: Harper and Row.

Galeano, Eduardo 1991, "A Child Lost in the Storm," trans. Asa Katz, in Robin Blackburn, ed., *After the Fall: the Failure of Communism and the Future of Socialism*, London: Verso: 250–54.

Gandhi, Leela 1998, *Postcolonial Theory: a Critical Introduction*, New York: Columbia University Press.

General Council of the First International, *1864–1871: Minutes* 1962–1974, 5 vols., Moscow: Progress.

Georges, Michael 1923, "Où en est la France? Le Colonialisme Intercapitaliste," *Clarté* 38: 469–70.

Gibbons, Luke 1991, "Race Against Time: Racial Discourse and Irish History," *The Oxford Literary Review* 13.1–2: 95–113.

1996, *Transformations in Irish Culture*, Cork: Cork University Press.

Gills, Barry and Andre Gunder Frank 1994, "The Modern World System under Asian Hegemony: the Silver Standard World Economy 1450–1750," unpublished paper.

References

Gilpin, Robert 1975, *US Power and the Multinational Corporation*, New York: Basic.

Gilroy, Paul 1993, *The Black Atlantic: Modernity and Double Consciousness*, Cambridge, MA: Harvard University Press.

Glissant, Edouard 1989, *Caribbean Discourse: Selected Essays*, trans. J. Michael Dash, Charlottesville: University of Virginia Press.

Gramsci, Antonio 1971, *Selections from the Prison Notebooks of Antonio Gramsci*, trans. Quintin Hoare and Geoffrey Nowell Smith, London: Lawrence and Wishart.

1990, *Selections from Political Writings 1910–1920*, Minneapolis: University of Minnesota Press.

Griffiths, Trevor R. 1983," 'This Island's Mine': Caliban and Colonialism," *Yearbook of English Studies* 13: 159–80.

Guha, Ranajit 1983, *Elementary Aspects of Peasant Insurgency in Colonial India*. Delhi: Oxford University Press.

Guinnane, Timothy W. 1997, *The Vanishing Irish: Households, Migration, and the Rural Economy in Ireland, 1850–1914*, Princeton: Princeton University Press.

Habermas, Jürgen 1987, *The Philosophical Discourse of Modernity: Twelve Lectures*, trans. Frederick Lawrence, Cambridge, MA: MIT.

Habib, Irfan 1995, *Essays in Indian History: Towards a Marxist Perspective*, New Delhi: Tulika.

Hadfield, Andrew 1998, *Literature, Travel, and Colonial Writing in the English Renaissance 1545–1625*, Oxford: Clarendon.

Hakluyt, Richard 1903–05, *The Principal Navigations Voyages, Traffiques and Discoveries of the English Nation*. 12 vols., Glasgow: James Maclehose.

Hall, Kim F. 1995, *Things of Darkness: Economies of Race and Gender in Early Modern England*, Ithaca: Cornell University Press.

1998, " 'These bastard signs of fair': Literary whiteness in Shakespeare's sonnets," in Ania Loomba and Martin Orkin, eds., *Post-Colonial Shakespeares*, London: Routledge: 64–83.

Hall, Stuart 1986, "Gramsci's Relevance for the Study of Race and Ethnicity," *Journal of Communication Inquiry* 10.2: 5–27.

1996a, "When was the 'post-colonial'? Thinking at the Limit," in Iain Chambers and Lidia Curtis, eds., *The Post-Colonial Question: Common Skies, Divided Horizons*, London: Routledge: 242–60.

1996b, "The West and the Rest: Discourse and Power," in Stuart Hall, David Held, Don Hubert, and Kenneth Thompson, eds., *Modernity: an Introduction to Modern Societies*, Oxford: Blackwell: 184–227.

Hamashita, Takeshi 1994, "The Tribute Trade System and Modern Asia," in A. J. H. Latham and H. Kawakatsu, eds., *Japanese Industrialization and the Asian Economy*, London: Routledge: 91–107.

1997, "The Intra-Regional System in East Asia in Modern Times," in Peter Katzenstein and T. Shiraishi, eds., *Network Power: Japan and Asia*, Ithaca: Cornell University Press: 113–35.

Hannaford, Ivan 1996, *Race: The History of an Idea in the West*, Baltimore: Johns Hopkins University Press.

References

Harootunian, Harry 2000, *History's Disquiet: Modernity, Cultural Practice, and the Question of Everyday Life*, New York, Columbia University Press.

Harris, R. Cole 1977, "The Simplification of Europe Overseas," *Annals of the Association of American Geographers* 67.4: 469–83.

Harris, R. Cole and Leonard Guelke 1977, "Land and Society in Early Canada and South Africa," *Journal of Historical Geography* 3.2: 135–53.

Harrison, Royden 1965, *Before the Socialists: Studies in Labour and Politics, 1861–1881*, London: RKP.

Harrod, Roy 1969, *Money*, London: Macmillan.

Harvey, David 1989, *The Condition of Postmodernity: an Enquiry into the Origins of Cultural Change*, Oxford: Blackwell.

1996, *Justice, Nature and the Geography of Difference*, London: Blackwell.

Haug, Wolfgang Fritz 1984, "Learning the Dialectics of Marxism," in Sakari Hanninen and Leena Paldan, eds., *Rethinking Marx*, New York: International General: 15–20.

Hendricks, Margo 1998, " 'Tis not the fashion to confess': Shakespeare–Post-coloniality–Johannesburg, 1996," in Ania Loomba and Martin Orkin, eds., *Post-Colonial Shakespeares*, London: Routledge: 84–97.

Hiller, Susan, ed. 1991, *The Myth of Primitivism: Perspectives on Art*, London: Routledge.

Hind, Robert J. 1984, " 'We Have No Colonies': Similarities within the British Imperial Experience," *Comparative Studies in Society and History* 26: 3–35.

Hobsbawm, E. J. 1973, *Revolutions*, New York: New American Library.

1994, *The Age of Extremes: a History of the World, 1914–1991*, New York: Pantheon.

Hodgkin, Thomas 1973, "Nkrumah's Radicalism," *Présence Africaine* 85: 62–72.

Huberman, Leo and Paul M. Sweezy, eds. 1968, *Régis Debray and the Latin American Revolution*, New York: Monthly Review.

Hui, Po-keung 1995, "Overseas Chinese Business Networks: East Asian Economic Development in Historical Perspective," Ph.D. diss., Sociology, SUNY Binghamton.

Hulme, Peter 1981, "Hurricanes in the Caribbees: the Constitution of the Discourse of English Colonialism," in Francis Barker, Jay Bernstein, John Coombes, Peter Hulme, Jennifer Stone, and Jon Stratton, eds., *1642: Literature and Power in the Seventeenth Century*, University of Essex Press: 55–83.

1989, "Subversive Archipelagoes: Colonial Discourse and the Break-Up of Continental Theory," *Dispositio* 14.36–38: 1–23.

Huntington, Samuel 1998. *The Clash of Civilizations and the Remaking of World Order*, London: Touchstone.

Hymer, Stephen and Robert Rowthorn 1970, "Multinational Corporations and International Oligopoly: the Non-American Challenge," in C. P. Kindelberger, ed., *The International Corporation: A Symposium*, Cambridge, MA: MIT: 57–91.

References

Irwan, Alex 1995, "Business Networks and the Regional Economy of East and Southeast Asia in the Late Twentieth Century," Ph. D. diss., Sociology, SUNY Binghamton.

Jackson, Robert 1990, *Quasi-States: Sovereignty, International Relations and the Third World*, Cambridge: Cambridge University Press.

Jacobson, John Kurt 1994, *Chasing Progress in the Irish Republic: Ideology, Democracy and Dependent Development*, Cambridge: Cambridge University Press.

James, C. L. R. 1960, *Modern Politics*, Detroit: Bewick.

  1977, *Nkrumah and the Ghana Revolution*, Westport: Lawrence Hill.

  1992, *The C. L. R. James Reader*, ed. Anna Grimshaw, Oxford: Blackwell.

Jameson, Fredric 1971, *Marxism and Form*, Princeton: Princeton University Press.

  1990a, *Late Marxism: Adorno, or the Persistence of the Dialectic*, London: Verso.

  1990b, "Modernism and Imperialism," in Terry Eagleton, Fredric Jameson and Edward W. Said, *Nationalism, Colonialism, and Literature*, Minneapolis: University of Minnesota Press: 43–68.

  1991, *Postmodernism, or The Cultural Logic of Late Capitalism*, London: Verso.

  1998, *The Cultural Turn: Selected Writings on the Postmodern, 1983–1998*, London: Verso.

Johnson, Chalmers 1987, "Political Institutions and Economic Performance: the Government–Business Relationship in Japan, South Korea, and Taiwan," in F. C. Deyo, ed., *The Political Economy of the New Asian Industrialization*, Ithaca: Cornell University Press: 136–64.

  1988, "The Japanese Political Economy: a Crisis in Theory," *Ethics and International Affairs* 2: 79–97.

Jordan, Winthrop 1969, *White Over Black: American Attitudes toward the Negro: 1550–1812*. Baltimore: Penguin.

Joshi, P. C. 1957, "1857 in Our History," in P. C. Joshi, ed., *Rebellion 1857: a Symposium*, New Delhi: People's Publishing House.

Katzenstein, Peter 1987, *Policy and Politics in West Germany: the Growth of a Semisovereign State*, Philadelphia: Temple University Press.

Kawakatsu, Heita, 1994, "Historical Background," in A. J. H. Latham and H. Kawakatsu, eds., *Japanese Industrialization and the Asian Economy*, London and New York: Routledge: 4–8.

Kennedy, Paul 1987, *The Rise and Fall of the Great Powers: Economic Change and Military Conflict from 1500 to 2000*, New York: Random House.

  1993, *Preparing for the Twenty-First Century*, New York: Random House.

Kermode, Frank 1974, "Othello, the Moor of Venice," in G. Blakemore Evans, ed., *The Riverside Shakespeare*, Boston: Houghton Mifflin: 1198–202.

Kesteloot, Lilyan 1991, *Black Writers in French: A Literary History of Negritude*, Washington, DC: Howard University Press.

Kiberd, Declan 1995, *Inventing Ireland: the Literature of the Modern Nation*, London: Cape.

Kindleberger, Charles 1969, *American Business Abroad*, New Haven: Yale University Press.

King, Anthony D. 1995, "The Times and Spaces of Modernity (Or Who Needs Postmodernism?" in Mike Featherstone, ed., *Global Modernities*, London: Sage: 108–23.

Kraar, Louis 1993, "The New Power in Asia," *Fortune*, October 31: 38–44.

Krader, Lawrence 1972, *The Ethnological Notebooks of Karl Marx*, Assen: Van Gorcum.

Krasner, Stephen 1988, "A Trade Strategy for the United States," *Ethics and International Affairs* 2: 17–35.

Krauss, Rosalind 1994, *The Originality of the Avant-Garde and Other Modernist Myths*, Cambridge, MA: MIT.

Kuper, Adam 1988, *The Invention of Primitive Society: Transformations of an Illusion*, London: Routledge.

Kurz, Robert 1991, *Der Kollaps der Modernisierung*, Frankfurt-am-Main: Eichborn.

1997, "*One World* e nacionalismo terciário," in *Os ultimos combates*, Petropolis, Brazil: Editora Vozes. Originally published as "*One World* und jüngster Nationalismus," *Frankfurter Rundschau*, 4 January 1992.

Lane, Frederic 1966, *Venice and History*, Baltimore: Johns Hopkins University Press.

1979, *Profits from Power. Readings in Protection Rent and Violence-Controlling Enterprises*, Albany: SUNY.

Larrain, Jorge 1989, *Theories of Development, Capitalism, Colonialism and Dependency*, Oxford: Polity.

Larsen, Neil 1995, *Reading North by South: On Latin American Literature, Culture, and Politics*, Minneapolis: University of Minnesota Press.

2001, *Determinations: Essays on Theory, Narrative and Nation in the Americas*, London: Verso.

Laue, Theodore von 1987, *The World Revolution of Westernization: the Twentieth Century in Global Perspective*, Oxford: Oxford University Press.

Lazarus, Neil 1990, *Resistance in Postcolonial African Fiction*, New Haven: Yale University Press.

1993, "Disavowing Decolonization: Fanon, Nationalism, and the Problematic of Representation in Current Theories of Colonial Discourse," *Research in African Literatures* 24.2: 69–97.

1997, "Transnationalism and the Alleged Death of the Nation State," in Keith Ansell-Pearson, Benita Parry, and Judith Squires, eds., *Cultural Readings of Imperialism: Edward Said and the Gravity of History*, London: Lawrence and Wishart: 28–48.

1999a, *Nationalism and Cultural Practice in the Postcolonial World*, Cambridge: Cambridge University Press.

1999b, "Hating Tradition Properly," *New Formations* 38: 9–30.

Lazitch, Branko and Milorad M. Drachkovitch 1972, *Lenin and the Comintern*, vol. 1., Stanford: Stanford University Press.

Lebow, R. N. 1979, *White Britain and Black Ireland: the Influence of Stereotypes on Colonial Policy*, Philadelphia: Institute for the Study of Human Issues.

Leerssen, Joseph Th. 1996, *Mere Irish and Fíor-Ghael: Studies in the Idea of Irish Nationality, its Development and Literary Expression prior to the Nineteenth Century*, Cork: Cork University Press.

Lefebvre, Henri 1969, *The Sociology of Marx*, trans. Norbert Guterman, New York: Vintage.

1992, *Critique of Everyday Life*, trans. John Moore, London: Verso.

Leininger, Lorrie Jerrell 1980, "The Miranda Trap: Sexism and Racism in Shakespeare's Tempest," in Carolyn Lenz, Gayle Greene, and Carol Neely, eds., *The Woman's Part: Feminist Criticism of Shakespeare*, Urbana: University of Illinois Press: 285–94.

Lenin, V. I. 1939, *Imperialism: the Highest Stage of Capitalism*, New York: International Publishers.

1943, *State and Revolution*, New York: International Publishers.

1963, "The Unity and Conflict of Opposites," in Howard Selsam and Harry Martel, eds., *Reader in Marxist Philosophy*, New York: International Publishers: 130–32.

1969, "The Discussion on Self Determination Summed Up," *The National Liberation Movement in the East*, Moscow: Progress: 184–93.

1975a, "The Right of Nations to Self-Determination," *The Lenin Anthology*, New York: Norton: 153–180.

1975b, "Socialism and War," *The Lenin Anthology*, New York: Norton: 183–95.

Leon, Abram 1970, *The Jewish Question: a Marxist Interpretation*, New York: Pathfinder.

Levine, Norman 1978, "Dialectical Materialism and the Mir," in Donald McQuarie, ed., *Marx: Sociology/Social Change/Capitalism*, New York: Quartet: 162–78.

Lichtheim, George 1967, *The Concept of Ideology and Other Essays*, New York: Vintage.

Ling, Trevor 1980, *Karl Marx and Religion*, New York: Barnes and Noble.

Lloyd, David 1991, "Race under Representation," *The Oxford Literary Review* 13.1–2: 62–94.

1993, *Anomalous States: Irish Writing and the Post-Colonial Moment*, Durham, Duke University Press.

1999, *Ireland after History*, Cork: Cork University Press.

Lloyd, Jill 1991, "Emil Nolde's Ethnographic Still Lifes: Primitivism, Tradition, and Modernity," in Susan Hiller, ed., *The Myth of Primitivism: Perspectives on Art*, London: Routledge: 90–112.

Lockhart, James and Stuart B. Schwarz 1983, *Early Latin America: a History of Colonial Latin America and Brazil*, Cambridge: Cambridge University Press.

Loomba, Ania 1998a, *Colonialism/Postcolonialism*, London: Routledge.

1998b, "Local Manufacture Made-in-India Othello Fellows: Issues of Race, Hybridity and Location in Post-Colonial Shakespeares," in Ania Loomba and Martin Orkin, eds., *Post-Colonial Shakespeares*, London: Routledge: 143–63.

Loomba, Ania and Martin Orkin, eds. 1998, *Post-Colonial Shakespeares*, London: Routledge.

Lowe, Lisa and David Lloyd, eds. 1997, *The Politics of Culture in the Shadow of Capital*, Durham: Duke University Press.

Löwy, Michael 1981, *The Politics of Combined and Uneven Development*, London: New Left Books.

1993, "The First Revolution of the Twentieth Century," in *On Changing the World: Essays in Political Philosophy from Karl Marx to Walter Benjamin*, Atlantic Highlands: Humanities.

Lu, Aiguo 2000, *China and the Global Economy since 1840*, New York: St. Martin's Press; and London: Macmillan.

Lukács, Georg 1997, *History and Class Consciousness*, trans. Rodney Livingstone, Cambridge, MA: MIT.

2000, *In Defence of History and Class Consciousness*, London: Verso.

Luke, Timothy W. 1990, *Social Theory and Modernity*, Newbury Park: Sage.

Lustick, Ian 1993, *Unsettled States, Disputed Lands: Britain and Ireland, France and Algeria, Israel and the West Bank-Gaza*, Ithaca: Cornell University Press.

Luxemburg, Rosa 1976, *The National Question*, New York: Monthly Review.

MacDonagh, Oliver 1991, *O'Connell: the Life of Daniel O'Connell 1775–1847*, London: Weidenfeld and Nicholson.

MacLaughlin, Jim 1994, "Emigration and the Peripheralization of Ireland in the Global Economy," *Review* 17.2: 243–73.

Majumdar, R. C. 1963, *The Sepoy Mutiny and the Revolt of 1857*, Calcutta: Firma K. L. Mukhopadhyay.

Mandel, Ernest 1983, "Uneven Development," in Tom Bottomore, ed., *A Dictionary of Marxist Thought*, Cambridge: Harvard University Press: 502–03.

1995, *Trotsky as Alternative*, trans. Gus Fagan, London: Verso.

Marrouchi, Mustapha 1997, "Decolonizing the Terrain of Western Theoretical Productions," *College Literature* 24: 1–34.

Marx, Karl 1965, *Pre-Capitalist Economic Formations*, New York: International Publishers.

1968, *Karl Marx on Colonialism and Modernization*, ed. Shlomo Avineri, New York: Doubleday.

1971a, *A Contribution to the Critique of Political Economy*, trans. S. W. Ryazanskaya, London: Lawrence and Wishart.

1971b, "Peasantry as a Class," in Teodor Shanin, ed., *Peasants and Peasant Societies*, New York: Penguin: 229–37.

1972, *The Eighteenth Brumaire of Louis Bonaparte*, in *Surveys from Exile: Political Writings*, vol. 2, David Fernbach, ed. and trans. Harmondsworth: Penguin.

1982, "Pathways of Social Development: a Brief Against Suprahistorical Theory," in Hamza Alavi and Teodor Shanin, eds., *Introduction to the Sociology of "Developing Societies"*, New York: Monthly Review: 109–11.

1984, *Der achtzehnte Brumaire des Louis Bonaparte*, Berlin: Dietz.

1990, *Capital: a Critique of Political Economy*, vol. I, trans. Ben Fowkes, London, Penguin.

1993, *Grundrisse: Foundations of the Critique of Political Economy*, trans. Martin Nicolaus, London: Penguin.

Marx, Karl and Friedrich Engels 1959, *Basic Writings on Politics and Philosophy*, New York: Doubleday.

1959b, *The First Indian War of Independence, 1857–1859*, Moscow: Progress.

1971, *On Ireland*, London: Lawrence and Wishart.

1975a [in progress], *Collected Works*, New York: International Publishers.

1975b [in progress], *Gesamtausgabe (MEGA)*, Berlin: Dietz.

1988, *Manifesto of the Communist Party*, Beijing: Foreign Languages.

Mattingly, Garrett 1988, *Renaissance Diplomacy*, New York: Dover.

McCarney, Joseph 1989, "For and Against Althusser," *New Left Review* 176: 115–28.

McLennan, Gregor 1981, *Marxism and the Methodologies of History*, London: Verso.

McNally, David 1993, *Against the Market: Political Economy, Market Socialism and the Marxist Critique*, London: Verso.

McNeill, William 1984, *The Pursuit of Power: Technology, Armed Force, and Society since A.D. 1000*, Chicago: University of Chicago Press.

Meszaros, Istvan 1983, "Mediation," in Tom Bottomore, ed., *A Dictionary of Marxist Thought*, Cambridge: Harvard University Press: 329–30.

Metcalf, Thomas 1964, *The Aftermath of Revolt: India, 1857–1870*, Princeton: Princeton University Press.

Miller, Christopher 1990, *Theories of Africans: Francophone Literature and Anthropology in Africa*, Chicago: University of Chicago Press.

Miller, Daniel 1991, "Primitive Art and the Necessity of Primitivism to Art," in Susan Hiller, ed., *The Myth of Primitivism: Perspectives on Art*, London: Routledge: 50–71.

Miller, Norman and Roderick Aya, eds. 1971, *National Liberation: Revolution in the Third World*, New York: The Free Press.

Mohanty, Chandra Talpade 1994, "Under Western Eyes: Feminist Scholarship and Colonial Discourses," in Patrick Williams and Laura Chrisman, eds., *Colonial Discourse and Postcolonial Theory: a Reader*, New York: Harvester: 196–220.

Mohanty, Satya 1995, "Colonial Legacies, Multicultural Futures: Relativism, Objectivity, and the Challenge of Otherness," *PMLA* 110.1: 108–18.

Mondlane, Eduardo 1983, *The Struggle for Mozambique*, London: Zed.

Moore, David Chioni 1998, proposal to publish Langston Hughes, *A Negro Looks at Soviet Central Asia* (orig. publ. Moscow: Cooperative Publishing Society of Foreign Workers in the USSR, 1934).

Moore-Gilbert, Bart 1997, *Postcolonial Theory: Contexts, Practices, Politics*, London: Verso.

Morgan, Hiram 1991–92, "Mid-Atlantic Blues," *Irish Review* 11: 50–55.

MPLA 1972, *Revolution in Angola*, London: Merlin, 1972.

Mugabe, Robert 1983, *Our War of Liberation: Speeches, Articles, Interviews 1976–1979*, Zimbabwe: Mambo.

Mulhern, Francis 1998, *The Present Lasts a Long Time: Essays in Cultural Politics*, Cork: Cork University Press.

Nandy, Ashis 1995, *The Savage Freud and Other Essays on Possible and Retrievable Selves*, Princeton: Princeton University Press.

Nehru, Jawaharlal 1965, *The First Sixty Years*, vols. I and II, ed. Dorothy Norman, London: Bodley Head.

1989, *The Discovery of India*, Delhi: Oxford University Press.

References

Neill, Michael 1998, "'Mulattos,' 'Blacks,' and 'Indian Moors': *Othello* and Early Modern Constructions of Human Difference," *Shakespeare Quarterly* 49.4: 361–74.

Neto, Agostinho 1974, *Sacred Hope*, Dar es Salaam: Tanzanian Publishing House.

Newman, Karen 1987, "'And wash the Ethiop white': femininity and the monstrous in *Othello*," in Jean Howard and Marion O'Connor, eds., *Shakespeare Reproduced: the Text in History and Ideology*, London: Methuen: 140–62.

Ngugi wa Thiong'o 1987, *Decolonising the Mind: the Politics of Language in African Literature*, London: James Currey.

2000, "Europhonism, Universities, and the Magic Fountain: the Future of African Literature and Scholarship," *Research in African Literatures* 31.1: 1–11.

Nicholsen, Shierry Weber 1997, *Exact Imagination, Late Work: On Adorno's Aesthetics*, Cambridge, MA: MIT.

Nimtz, August 1993, "Marxism," *The Oxford Companion to Politics of the World*, New York: Oxford University Press.

2000, *Marx and Engels: Their Contribution to the Democratic Breakthrough*, Albany: SUNY.

Nixon, Rob 1987, "Caribbean and African Appropriations of *The Tempest*," *Critical Inquiry* 13.3: 557–78.

Nkrumah, Kwame 1964, *Consciencism: Philosophy and Ideology for Decolonization and Development with Particular Reference to the African Revolution*, London: Heinemann.

1973, *Revolutionary Path*, London: Panaf.

1980, *Neo-Colonialism: the Last Stage of Imperialism*, New York: International Publishers.

Novack, George 1966, *Uneven and Combined Development in History*, New York: Merit.

Nyerere, Julius 1968, *Ujamaa: Essays on Socialism*, Dar es Salaam: Oxford University Press.

Ó Buachalla, Breandán 1996, *Aisling Gheár: Na Stíobhartaigh agus an t-Aos Léinn, 1703–1788*, Baile Átha Cliath: An Clóchomhar.

Ollman, Bertell 1993, *Dialectical Investigations*, New York: Routledge.

Osterhammel, Jürgen 1997, *Colonialism: a Theoretical Overview*, trans. Shelley L. Frisch, Princeton: Markus Wiener.

Outlaw, Lucius 1996, *On Race and Philosophy*, London: Routledge.

Panikkar, K. M. 1959, *Asia and Western Dominance*, London: Allen and Unwin.

1989, "The First Major Challenge: the Revolt of 1857," in B. Chandra, M. Mukherjee, A. Mukherjee, S. Mahajan, and K. Panikkar, eds., *India's Struggle for Independence, 1857–1947*, New Delhi: Penguin: 31–40.

Parry, Benita 1998, "Liberation Movements: Memories of the Future," *Interventions* 1.1: 45–51.

Patterson, Thomas C. 1997, *Inventing Western Civilization*, New York: Monthly Review.

References

Paz, Octavio 1974, *Children of the Mire: Modern Poetry from Romanticism to the Avant-Garde*, Cambridge, MA: Harvard University Press.

Petri, Peter A. 1993, "The East Asian Trading Bloc: an Analytical History," in J. A. Frankel and M. Kahler, eds., *Regionalism and Rivalry. Japan and the United States in Pacific Asia*, Chicago: University of Chicago Press: 21–52.

Poggioli, Renato 1968, *The Theory of the Avant-Garde*, trans. Gerald Fitzgerald, Cambridge: Belknap.

Porter, Bernard 1968, *Critics of Empire: British Radical Attitudes to Colonialism in Africa 1895–1914*, London: Macmillan.

Poster, Mark 1975, *Existential Marxism in Postwar France: from Sartre to Althusser*, Princeton: Princeton University Press.

1979, *Sartre's Marxism*, London: Pluto.

Prakash, Gyan 1990, "Writing Post-Orientalist Histories of the Third World: Perspectives from Indian Historiography," *Comparative Studies in Society and History*: 383–408.

1992, "Postcolonial Criticism and Indian Historiography," *Social Text* 31/32: 8–19.

Pratt, Mary Louise 1992, *Imperial Eyes: Travel Writing and Transculturation*, London: Routledge.

Quayson, Ato 2000, *Postcolonialism: Theory, Practice or Process?* Cambridge: Polity.

Quinn, David Beers 1966, *The Elizabethans and the Irish*, Ithaca: Cornell University Press.

1991, *Ireland and America: their Early Associations, 1500–1640*, Liverpool: Liverpool University Press.

Rabinowitz, Paula 1991, *Labor and Desire: Women's Revolutionary Fiction in Depression America*, Chapel Hill: University of North Carolina Press.

Racine, Nicole and Louis Bodin 1982, *Le Parti communiste français pendant l'entre-deux-guerres*, Paris: Presses de la fondation nationale des sciences politiques.

Ram, Kalpana 1996. "Rationalism, Cultural Nationalism and the Reform of Body Politics," in Patricia Uberoi, ed., *Social Reform, Sexuality and the State*, London: Sage.

Rashid Jahan 1988, "Mera ek Safar" [One of My Journeys], *Vah* [That One], New Delhi: Shabdakar: 75–86.

1993, "That One," trans. M. T. Khan, in Susie Tharu and K. Lalita, eds., *Women Writing in India*, volume II: *The Twentieth Century*, New York: Feminist Press: 119–22.

Reich, Robert 1992, *The Work of Nations: Preparing Ourselves for Twenty-first-Century Capitalism*, New York: Random House.

Richardson, Thomas, ed. 1996, *Refusal of the Shadow: Surrealism and the Caribbean*, London: Verso.

Riddell, John, ed. 1993, *To See the Dawn: Baku, 1920 – First Congress of the Peoples of the East*, New York: Pathfinder.

Rodney, Walter 1982, *How Europe Underdeveloped Africa*, Washington, DC: Howard University Press.

1990, *Walter Rodney Speaks: the Making of an African Intellectual*, Trenton: Africa World Press.

Roediger, David 1991, *The Wages of Whiteness: Race and the Making of the American Working Class*, London: Verso.

Roy, M. N. 1943, *The Communist International*, Bombay: The Popular Printing Press.

1964, *Memoirs*, Bombay: Allied Publishers.

Rubel, Maximilien 1975, *Marx without Myth*, New York: Harper and Row.

Rubin, William 1984, "Modernist Primitivism: an Introduction," in *Primitivism in Twentieth-Century Art*, exhibition catalogue, New York: Museum of Modern Art.

Said, Edward W. 1979, *Orientalism*, New York: Vintage.

1980, *The Question of Palestine*, New York: Vintage.

1983, *The World, the Text and the Critic*, Cambridge, MA: Harvard University Press.

1990, "Yeats and Decolonization," in Terry Eagleton, Fredric Jameson, and Edward W. Said, *Nationalism, Colonialism and Literature*, Minneapolis: University of Minnesota Press: 69–95.

1993, *Culture and Imperialism*, New York: Knopf.

1995, "East Isn't East," *Times Literary Supplement* 4792: 3–5.

2000, "My Encounter with Sartre," *London Review of Books*, 22.11: 42–43.

San Juan, E. 1998, *Beyond Postcolonial Theory*, New York: St. Martin's.

Sankara, Thomas 1988, *Thomas Sankara Speaks: the Burkina Faso Revolution 1983–1987*, trans. Samantha Anderson, New York: Pathfinder.

Sarkar, Sumit 1989, *Modern India 1885–1947*, London: Macmillan.

2000, "The Decline of the Subaltern in *Subaltern Studies*," in Vinayak Chaturvedi, ed., *Mapping Subaltern Studies and the Postcolonial*, London and New York: Verso: 300–23.

Sartre, Jean-Paul 1968a, Preface to Frantz Fanon, *The Wretched of the Earth*, trans. Constance Farrington, New York: Grove: 7–31.

1968b, *Search for a Method*, trans. Hazel Barnes, New York: Vintage.

1972, Introduction to *Lumumba Speaks: the Speeches and Writings of Patrice Lumumba 1958–1961*, trans. Helen R. Lane, Boston and Toronto: Little, Brown and Co.: 3–52.

1974, *Sartre on Cuba*, Westport: Greenwood.

1976a, "Black Orpheus," Introduction to *An Anthology of New Negro and Malagasy Poetry*, trans. S. W. Allen, Paris: Présence africaine: 7–65.

1976b, *Critique of Dialectical Reason*, trans. Alan Sheridan-Smith, London: New Left Books.

Schram, Stuart and Hélène Carrère D'Encausse 1965, trans. and eds., *Le Marxisme et l'Asie, 1853–1964*, Paris: Armand Colin.

Schulze-Engler, Frank 1998, "The Politics of Postcolonial Theory," in Gordon Collier, Dieter Riemenschneider, and Frank Schulze-Engler, eds., *Postcolonial Theory and the Emergence of a Global Society*, Frankfurt-am-Main: ACOLIT 31–34.

Schurmann, Franz 1974, *The Logic of World Power: an Inquiry into the Origins, Currents, and Contradictions of World Politics*, New York: Pantheon.

Schwarz, Roberto 1992, "Misplaced Ideas," in *Misplaced Ideas: Essays on Brazilian Culture*, London: Verso: 19–32.

Serequeberhan, Tsenay 1996, "Fanon and the Contemporary Discourse of African Philosophy," in Lewis R. Gordon, T. Denean

Sharpley-Whiting, and Renée T. White, eds., *Fanon: A Critical Reader*, Oxford: Blackwell: 244–54.

1997, "The Critique of Eurocentrism and the Practice of African Philosophy," in Emmanuel Chukwudi Eze, ed., *Postcolonial African Philosophy*, Oxford: Blackwell: 141–61.

Shohat, Ella and Robert Stam 1994, *Unthinking Eurocentrism: Multiculturalism and the Media*, London: Routledge.

Slater, Eammon and Terence McDonough 1994, "Bulwark of Landlordism and Capitalism: the Dynamics of Feudalism in Nineteenth Century Ireland," *Research in Political Economy* 14: 63–118.

Smedley, Audrey 1993, *Race in North America: Origin and Evolution of a Worldview*, Boulder: Westview.

Smith, Neil 1984, *Uneven Development: Nature, Capital, and the Production of Space*, Oxford: Blackwell.

Smyth, William J. 2000, "Ireland a Colony: Settlement Implications of the Revolution in Military-Administrative, Urban and Ecclesiastical Structures, c. 1550 to c.1730," in Terry Barry, ed., *A History of Settlement in Ireland*, London: Routledge: 158–86.

Snow, Benjamin 1977, "Introduction to Adorno's 'The Actuality of Philosophy,'" *Telos* 31: 113–19.

So, Alvin Y. and Stephen W. K. Chiu 1995, *East Asia and the World-Economy*, Newbury Park: Sage.

Spivak, Gayatri Chakravorty 1987, "Scattered Speculations on the Question of Value," in *In Other Worlds: Essays in Cultural Politics*, London: Methuen: 154–75.

1988, "Can the Subaltern Speak?" in Cary Nelson and Lawrence Grossberg, eds., *Marxism and the Interpretation of Culture*, Urbana: University of Illinois Press: 271–313.

1993, "The Politics of Translation," *Outside in the Teaching Machine*, New York: Routledge: 179–200.

1994, "How to Read a 'Culturally Different' Book," in Francis Barker, Peter Hulme, and Margaret Iverson, eds., *Colonial Discourse/Postcolonial Theory*, Manchester: Manchester University Press: 126–50.

1995, "Academic Freedom," *Pretexts* 5.1–2: 117–56.

1999, *A Critique of Postcolonial Reason: Toward a History of the Vanishing Present*, Cambridge, MA: Harvard University Press.

Sprinker, Michael 1987, *Imaginary Relations: Aesthetics and Ideology in the Theory of Historical Materialism*, London: Verso.

1999, "The Grand Hotel Abyss," *New Left Review* 237: 115–36.

Stalin, Joseph 1936, *Marxism and the National and Colonial Question*, London: Lawrence and Wishart.

1970, "Marxism and the National Question," in *Selections from Lenin and J. V. Stalin on National Colonial Question*, Calcutta: Calcutta Book House.

Stokes, Eric 1978, *The Peasant and the Raj*, Cambridge: Cambridge University Press: 65–103.

Stoler, Ann Laura 1995, *Race and the Education of Desire: Foucault's History of Sexuality and the Colonial Order of Things*, Durham: Duke University Press.

Stratton, Jon and Ien Ang 1996, "On the Impossibility of a Global Cultural Studies: 'British' Cultural Studies in an 'International' Frame," in David Morley and Kuan-Hsing Chen, eds. *Stuart Hall: Critical Dialogues in Cultural Studies*, London: Routledge: 361–91.

Stummer, Peter 1998, "Some Pragma-Theoretical Considerations," in Gordon Collier, Dieter Riemenschneider, and Frank Schulze-Engler, eds., *Postcolonial Theory and the Emergence of a Global Society*, Frankfurt-am-Main: ACOLIT: 43–44.

Subramaniam, Lakshmi 1996, *Indigenous Capital and Imperial Expansion: Bombay, Surat, and the West Coast*, Delhi: Oxford University Press.

Sweet, James 1997, "The Iberian Roots of American Racist Thought," *William and Mary Quarterly*, third series, 54.1–2: 143–66.

Tabata, I. B. 1974, *The Awakening of a People*, Nottingham: Russell.

Terry, Les 1995, " 'Not A Postmodern Nomad': a Conversation with Stuart Hall on Race, Ethnicity and Identity," *Arena Journal* 5: 51–70.

Tharu, Susie and K. Lalita 1993, *Women Writing in India*, volume II: *The Twentieth Century*, New York: Feminist Press.

Therborn, Göran 1996, "Dialectics of Modernity: on Critical Theory and the Legacy of Twentieth-Century Marxism," *New Left Review* 215: 59–82.

Torgovnick, Marianna 1990, *Gone Primitive: Savage Intellects, Modern Lives*, Chicago: University of Chicago Press.

Trotsky, Leon 1969, *The Permanent Revolution and Results and Prospects*, New York: Pathfinder. (The individual booklets are also available separately.)

1974, *The Third International After Lenin*, New York: Labor Publications.

1997, *The History of the Russian Revolution*, London: Pluto.

Turner, Bryan S. 1983, "Asiatic Society," in Tom Bottomore, ed., *A Dictionary of Marxist Thought*, Cambridge, MA: Harvard University Press: 32–36.

Tzara, Tristan 1977, *Seven Dada Manifestoes* and *Lampisteries*, trans. Barbara Wright, London: John Calder.

Unruh, Vicky 1994, *Latin American Vanguards: the Art of Contentious Encounters*, Pittsburgh: Pittsburgh University Press.

Vaughan, Alden T. and Virginia Mason Vaughan 1997, "Before Othello: Elizabethan Representations of Sub-Saharan Africans," *William and Mary Quarterly*, third series, 54.1–2: 24–44.

Vogel, Jeffrey 1996, "The Tragedy of History," *New Left Review* 220: 36–61.

Wade, Robert 1990, *Governing the Market: Economic Theory and the Role of Government in East Asian Industrialization*, Princeton: Princeton University Press.

1996, "Globalization and its Limits: Reports of the Death of the National Economy are Greatly Exaggerated," in S. Berger and R. Dore, eds., *National Diversity and Global Capitalism*, Ithaca: Cornell University Press.

Wallerstein, Immanuel 1980, *The Modern World System*, II: *Mercantilism and the Consolidation of the European World-Economy, 1600–1750*, New York: Academic Press.

1995, "Revolution as Strategy and Tactics of Transformation," in Antonio Callari, Stephen Cullenberg, and Carole Biewener, eds., *Marxism in the Postmodern Age*, New York: Guilford: 225–34.

Warehime, Marja 1986, " 'Vision sauvage' and Images of Culture: Georges Bataille, Editor of *Documents*," *The French Review* 60.1: 39–45.

Warren, Bill 1980, *Imperialism: Pioneer of Capitalism*, London: New Left Books.

Washbrook, D. A. 1988, "Progress and Problems: South Asian Economic and Social History, c. 1720–1860," *Modern South Asia Studies* 22.1: 57–96.

Watts, David 1987, *The West Indies: Patterns of Development, Culture and Environmental Change since 1492*, Cambridge: Cambridge University Press.

Whelan, Kevin 1993, "Ireland in the World-System 1600–1800," in Hans-Jürgen Nitz, ed., *The Early-Modern World-System in Geographical Perspective*, Stuttgart: Franz Steiner: 204–18.

White, Stephen 1974, "Communism and the East: The Baku Congress, 1920," *Slavic Review* 33.3: 492–514.

Wiggershaus, Rolf 1994, *The Frankfurt School: Its History, Theories, and Political Significance*, trans. Michael Robertson, Cambridge, MA: MIT.

Williams, Eric 1996, *Capitalism and Slavery*, New York: G. P. Putnam's Sons.

Williams, Raymond 1983, *The Year 2000*, New York: Pantheon.

1989, *The Politics of Modernism: Against the New Conformists*, London: Verso.

Williams, Robert A. Jr., 1990, *The American Indian in Western Legal Thought: the Discourse of Conquest*, New York: Oxford University Press.

Wills, Clair 1991, "Language Politics, Narrative, Political Violence," *The Oxford Literary Review* 13.1–2: 20–60.

Wilson, Elizabeth 1992, "The Invisible Flâneur," *New Left Review* 191: 90–110.

Woddis, Jack 1972, *Introduction to Neo-Colonialism*, New York: International Publishers.

Young, Robert 1990, *White Mythologies: Writing History and the West*, London: Routledge.

1995, "Foucault on Race and Colonialism," *New Formations* 25: 57–65.

1998, "Ideologies of the Postcolonial," *Interventions* 1.1: 1–9.

Zizek, Slavoj 1997, "Multiculturalism, Or the Cultural Logic of Multinational Capitalism," *New Left Review* 225: 28–51.

Index

(The editors wish to acknowledge the assistance of Katheryn Giglio in the preparation of the index)

Index

Index

Derain, Paul, 192
Derrida, Jacques, 186–87, 187–88,
192, 201n.1, 207, 211, 245, 252, 254,
255–56n.9; *Specters of Marx*, 204,
211; Derridean thought, 242, 244;
254–55n.3
Deutscher, Isaac, 148n.5
development, 12, 146, 229; combined
and uneven, 10, 77, 96n.3, 121, 128,
136, 191, 193, 198, 222, 224–25,
227–29, 230–33, 237–39; dependent,
102; and underdevelopment, 50, 51,
114, 120, 227
Devi, Mahasweta, 195
Dews, Peter, 222, 241
Diaspora (journal), 2
Dirks, Nicholas, 60
Dirlik, Arif, 3, 10, 13, 49, 61, 63n.1,
64n.5, 126, 145–46, 147, 221
Disraeli, Benjamin, 93
Djebar, Assia, 14
Douglas, Mary, 8
Drachkovitch, Milorad M., 194
Draper, Hal, 80n.5
Drucker, Peter, 26
DuBois, W. E. B., 204
During, Simon, 144
Dussel, Enrique, 12, 64n.5

Eagleton, Terry, 101
East Asia, 8, 24, 25, 26, 31, 34, 123;
peculiarities of nation-state form in,
27– 28, 33, 35; post-1945 US-centric
dispensation in, 29–31, 34; rise to
epicenter of capitalist world system,
21, 22, 26 41, 42
Eden, Richard, 178
Edo period (1603–1867, Japan), 23
Edwards, Brent Hayes, 191, 193
Egerö, Bertil, 145
Egypt, 80n.6, 115, 238
Elizabeth I (Queen of England), 170
Elliott, Gregory, 127–28
Ellis, Steven G., 123n.2
Emmanuel, Arghiri, 108, 115
Engels, Friedrich, 6, 10, 65–80, 83, 85,
222, 225; on Algeria, 68, 78; on China,
67, 225; on colonialism, 225–26; on
India, 68–69, 78, 93, 97n.11; on
Ireland, 73–74, 78, 120; on Mexico,
68, 69; on the peasant question,
67–68, 75–76, 80n.5; on revolutionary
potential of English working class,
71–74, 78; on Russia, 74–79; *Condition*

of the English Working Class, 74;
Communist Manifesto (Marx and
Engels), 6–7, 8, 37, 47–48, 66, 76, 79,
80n.5, 85, 91, 147, 198, 218; *Demands
of the Communist Party of Germany*
(Marx and Engels), 67; *The First
Indian War of Independence* (Marx and
Engels), 92–93; *The German Ideology*
(Marx and Engels), 66; *The Peasant
Question in France and Germany*, 68
England, consolidation of capitalism
in, 172; Revolution (1642), 172;
see also Britain
English working class, Marx and
Engels on, 71–74
Eribon, Didier, 199
Ethiopia, 195, 197
Eudin, Xenia Joukoff, 203n.11
"Eurocentrism," 10, 16, 44, 186, 223–24,
228–29; in academic history, 61–63;
attempts to "unthink" it, 54, 55–58;
defined, 94; as social vision, 49–50,
231; and modernity, 59, 221–22; *see
also* Marxism, postcolonial studies
Europe 8, 10, 22, 35, 52, 105, 171–72,
174, 175; conquest of the Americas,
25, 35, 112, 122; expansion into Asia,
22, 23; revolutions of 1848–49, 65,
66– 67, 79; Eastern, 6, 45; Western,
28, 42, 45, 67, 88, 106, 114, 122; *see also*
"West"
European system of nation-states,
24–26, 34, 35, 37
Evans, Peter, 26
existentialism, 246, 251
expressionism, 189

Fabian, Johannes, 231
Faiz, Faiz Ahmad, 151
Fanon, Frantz, 6, 58, 64n.3, 125, 132,
142, 144, 149n.12, 162, 165, 190, 195,
202n.7, 204, 235, 237; "Medicine and
Colonialism," 150, 152, 159–60; and
Sartre, 130–31, 134
Farrar, Straus and Giroux
(US publishers), 17n.4
Fascism, 246
feminism, and Marxism, 151–52
Feuerbach, Ludwig, 200
Field Day Theatre Company, 101
Fieldhouse, D. K., 110
Fields, Barbara, 170–71, 172, 181n.4
First, Ruth, 149n.13
Flerovsky, N., 74

Index

Index

Index